11-6-2004

Alaska's Daughter

Elizabeth Bernhardt Pinson

Alaska's Daughter

*An Eskimo Memoir of the Early
Twentieth Century*

Elizabeth Bernhardt Pinson

Utah State University Press
Logan, Utah

Utah State University Press
Logan, Utah 84322-7800

Cover design by Bret Corrington and Curt Gullan
Map by Tom Child
Photos from the collection of the author

Manufactured in the United States of America
Printed on acid-free paper

Library of Congress Cataloging-in-Publication Data

Pinson, Elizabeth Bernhardt, 1912-
    Alaska's daughter : an Eskimo memoir of the early twentieth century / by Elizabeth
Bernhardt Pinson.
        p. cm.
    ISBN 0-87421-596-X (alk. paper) -- ISBN 0-87421-591-9 (pbk. : alk. paper)
    1. Pinson, Elizabeth Bernhardt, 1912- 2. Iñupiaq women--Alaska--Teller--Biography.
3. Iñupiaq women--Alaska--Teller--Social conditions. 4. Iñupiaq--Alaska--Teller--Social
life and customs. 5. Teller (Alaska)--History. 6. Teller (Alaska)--Social life and customs. I. Title.
    E99.E7P517 2004
    979.8004'9712'0092--dc22
                                    2004016131

To my father and my teenaged brother Tommy,
who risked their lives traveling through a cold cruel world
of ice and snow to save my life

Thank you to my nephew John Reimer, who, along with his wife Catherine and her sister Coleen Engle, retyped the original manuscript in a word processing program.

Foreword

Bret Corrington

Once in a while, maybe only a few times in a lifetime, we stumble upon something truly unique and undeniably beautiful. I met Elizabeth B. Pinson, "Betty," on a park bench in Seattle the summer of 2002. This was clearly one of those moments. Never before had I encountered a stronger embodiment of the human spirit, courage, and grace. At ninety years old, this half German, half Iñupiaq Eskimo from Teller, Alaska, held more life in her eyes than many a quarter her years. Though our encounter was brief, it would mark an important point in both our lives, and the beginning of a very special relationship. Because of it her manuscript fell into my hands.

Every year in August, a time in the Northwest when dark clouds seem most reluctant to blanket the skies, a reunion is held. This reunion is not centered on a family or graduating class; rather, it is centered on a town, the small but infamous town of Nome, Alaska. Since 1972, past and present residents of Nome have flocked to Woodland Park in Seattle's Greenwood district for what has come to be known as the Nome Picnic. Nomeites, as we like to be called, mill from table to table filling paper plates from

Tupperware containers and brandishing nametags which include our years of residency. My nametag read: Bret, 73–75.

I was born in Nome though until that summer had not attended the picnic. As luck would have it my mother, a Nomeite from 1967 to 1975, was visiting the same weekend the picnic was being held. We decided to go with nostalgic hopes of uncovering lost memories from what seemed like a different lifetime. More than anything, I imagine, I was hoping to hear stories about my parents when they were my age—maybe even hit the jack-pot with something vaguely incriminating that would make for interesting conversation over Christmas dinner. What I would hear instead would be a bit more profound.

I loaded a fresh roll of film into my camera as my mother and I coasted along slowly down the park drive looking for picnic site twelve where the reunion was being held. Large-leafed maple trees filtered the sunlight in broken patches across the green of the park and the blacktop, leaving some patches slightly cooler in the wake of the shade. That summer began my senior year in college, and I was enrolled in a black and white photography class. I imagined this gathering of displaced Alaskans to be an ideal opportunity to get some interesting photographs. As we pulled into the parking lot of site twelve, a group of mingling picnickers standing under the shade of a large shelter came into focus through the lens of my camera.

We were greeted by the Gallehers, dear friends of my parents who once ran a small airline out of Nome and now live in the Norwegian community of Poulsbo, Washington. After several introductions, I sank into the milling of the crowd, in search of photographs and stories of my own. Making my way around the grounds, snapping off candid shots here and there, I eventually came upon a kind elderly woman whose name tag read: Ruth, 32–37. Not wanting to be intrusive with my camera, we spoke for quite a while before I asked permission to take her photograph. A moment later, a younger woman approached and slightly out of breath announced that Betty had just arrived and was about to tell her story.

I helped Ruth to the area where I was told Betty was sitting. As we came upon a picnic table nestled in the shade, others were arriving and eager to listen. Some, I am sure, had heard Betty's story many times before, but for others including me, this would be a first. Ruth sat down and was met with a warm smile. There, delicate and kind with soft blue eyes contrasting her Eskimo features, sat Betty, poised and elegant. She reached over and gave

Ruth's hand a gentle squeeze of recognition. Ruth smiled. Betty pulled her hands back and folded them in her lap and began to speak.

Her voice, soft yet halting, carried an air of wisdom that was easily sensed. You could feel the mood of the small crowd that gathered around Betty change with her expressions. Her face told the story of her life almost as much as her words. When she spoke of the death of her grandparents during the influenza epidemic of 1918 and the tragedy that followed, which forever changed her life, her face was carved in stone. When she spoke of her father's love and devotion, teaching her to once again walk after the loss of her legs, and the great outpouring of support she received from her village and from across the country, her face was soft as fresh snow. Her story took many twists and turns as she recalled witnessing Alaska's history unfold before her, much of it centered on the small village of Teller, located seventy-five miles west of Nome. The sincerity and enthusiasm in her voice was infectious.

It's hard to say how long Betty was telling her story; time seems to become a bit mischievous in the presence of a good storyteller. I was, by far, not the only person deeply moved and more than a little enchanted by her words, but I was the last person sitting with her long after her story had been told. We spoke for what must have been several hours, sharing one another's experiences and finding many similarities outside of any generational barriers. When Betty mentioned that she had a completed manuscript that she had worked on for over twenty years and was at a loss to know what to do with, I nearly dropped my camera. I told her at that moment I would do everything in my power to help get her manuscript published. I kept my word.

The annals of history are rich with stories reflecting moments in time as perceived by individuals, heroic and otherwise. Many stories, however, are never told and pass quietly by, fading with the memories of the individual and those they have touched. Betty's story is one that must not fade and needs to be told. The reflections of Alaska's past seen through her eyes offer unique glimpses into an Alaska on the cusp of change, as well as of the difficulties and triumphs of growing up in a family of crossed cultures. Her incredible story of tragedy and survival offers a glimpse deeper still into the depths of human courage, strength, and compassion.

Betty made quite an impression on me that August afternoon at the park. It is rare to come across an individual as passionate and enthusiastic about life at any age, let alone at ninety. Betty embraces the best qualities of

Eskimo and western cultures with a tenderness and wisdom that is ageless. I gained a great deal of understanding from our encounter that day, both of history and of life. I was reminded that it is never too late to see a dream through to the end, and with just the right amounts of love, hope, and grace, anything is possible.

East is East and West is West
and never the twain shall meet.

—Rudyard Kipling,
"Ballad of East and West"

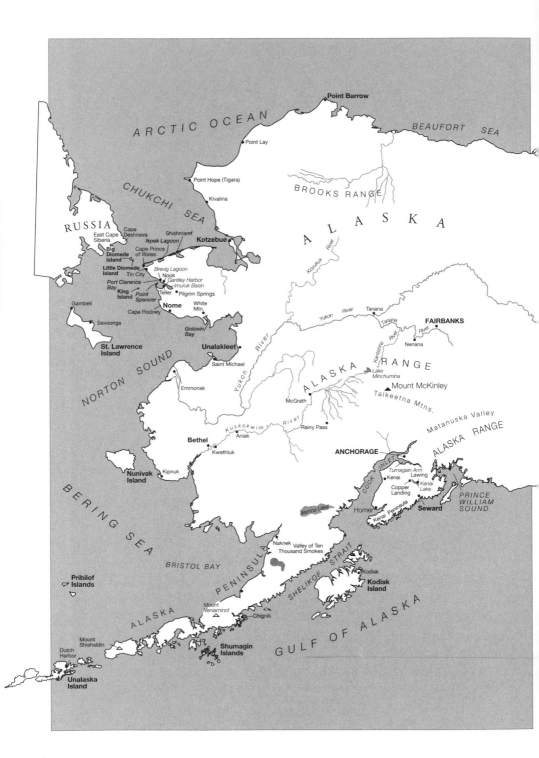

1

On my mother's side of the family I am Eskimo. My father was a German sailor shipwrecked in the Arctic Ocean off Alaska's northernmost coast. Oui-yaghasiak (pronounced ow-ee-yag-has-ee-ak), my mama, was born about 1889, daughter of Ootenna (pronounced oo-ten-nah) and Kinaviak (pronounced kin-ah-vee-ak), at the village of Shishmaref, Alaska, just below the Arctic Circle, facing on the Chukchi Sea about sixty miles from the eastern-most point of Siberia across the Bering Strait. By the time of Mama's birth, whalers, sealers, explorers, and traders from the outside world had already brought alcohol and diseases into the North, which began to decimate our people. With repeating rifles, iron-pointed lances, and harpoon guns—the modern methods of those days—the foreign seafarers had thinned out the once great population of ocean mammals that had provided my ancestors with clothing, food, fuel, and shelter.

While sailing ships and steamers were returning from Arctic voyages with their holds loaded to capacity with casks of whale oil, baleen, walrus hides and ivory tusks, sheaves of seal skins, and otter and fox skins, the Na-tives on the shore were starving. With their age-old weapons and tactics, they could no longer obtain sustenance from the dwindling animals and fish of the land, sea, and ice pack. Until the late 1800s it was unlawful for an Alaska Eskimo, Indian, or Aleut to own a breech-loading firearm because the reasoning went in Washington, D.C., that the Natives would wipe out their food supply by improvident hunting practices. There were no such restrictions against white outsiders, who could simply sail away from a region when they had depleted the waters or the land of animals and their operations were no longer profitable.

At the same time, the Indians of the interior of Alaska and Canada were being forced by hunger and destitution to leave their traditional hunting grounds because of white trappers, miners, voyagers, and other adventurers who were depleting the inland herds of caribou, moose, and other animals of the tundra and the mountains. Migrating toward the sea in search of food, the Indians, forced to leave their interior habitats, met and warred with the coastal Eskimos. My grandparents, Ootenna and Kinaviak, had vivid memories of battles their people fought with these strangers in defense of hunting lands and fishing waters.

Like a plague that swept the North, wherever the white man came in contact with the Native people, great numbers eventually died. Tuberculosis and communicable diseases, such as measles and chicken pox, wiped out whole tribes and villages. One of the most tragic aspects for the Natives was a quickly acquired taste for liquor, to which they had no more resistance than they had to the diseases of civilization. Intoxicated, the ordinarily peaceful, happy, family-loving Eskimo might murder his wife and children or best friend or lie in a drunken stupor while migrating game was all around.

In the summer of 1880, the United States revenue steamer *Corwin*, on a voyage to the Arctic Ocean in search of a fleet of overdue whalers, found mass suffering and death from starvation among the Eskimos as a direct result of dealings with whiskey traders. Visiting St. Lawrence Island in the northern Bering Sea, the *Corwin*'s crew examined several villages where everyone lay dead as a result of murder and starvation. Captain C. L. Hooper, the master of the vessel, wrote: "These people lived directly in the track of vessels bound to the Arctic Ocean for trading or whaling; they subsisted upon whales, walrus and seals, taking only as much as they actually needed for their immediate use, never providing for the future. They make houses, boats, clothing, etc., from the skins of walrus and seals, and sell the bone and ivory to traders for rum and breech-loading arms. So long as the rum lasts they do nothing but drink and fight. They had a few furs, some of which we tried to buy to make arctic clothing, but notwithstanding their terrible experience in the past refused to sell for anything but whiskey, breech-loading rifles, or cartridges."

Captain Hooper went on, "We saw thousands of walrus while passing the island, lying asleep on the ice, but not an Indian in sight. Having a few furs and a small amount of whalebone, they were waiting for the curse of Alaska, a whiskey-trader. As near as I can learn, over four hundred Natives had died of actual starvation on this island within the last two years. Unless some prompt action is taken by the Government to prevent them from obtaining whiskey, they will in a few years become extinct" (quoted in Bixby, 1965).

Hooper wrote further that the Natives of St. Lawrence Island were the best-looking men that he had seen in Alaska; tall, straight, and muscular, but perfect slaves to rum who would barter anything they had to procure it and remain drunk until it was gone. The problem had still not been solved when I was growing up in Alaska in the 1920s and the '30s.

My maternal grandparents were from Tigara, which is the Native name for Point Hope, a cape jutting into the Arctic Ocean north of the Arctic Circle and south of Point Barrow, which is the northernmost point on the North American continent. After an era of hunger and hardship directly related to the whalers and whiskey traders, nearly the whole village left Tigara in *oomiaks* (which are big, broad-beamed, walrus-skin boats, framed with whalebone and driftwood) and traveled southward in search of a place where food was more plentiful. Some traveled south about 150 miles and settled at Shishmaref, where my mother was born, along with three brothers and one sister.

The hunting was much better, not because there were more animals in the sea but because pods of whales and herds of seal and walrus, migrating from southern waters to feeding ranges around and under the polar ice, came close to the shore on their path north. In addition, offshore shoals kept sailing ships well away from the coast where they were not competitive with the Natives who hunted from shallow-draft, open boats and on the ice pack. Hunting was as hazardous for the Eskimos at Shishmaref as it had been at Point Hope, and there was seldom a year when men, afoot on the ice or following open leads in *oomiaks* and kayaks, were not carried off by ocean currents and never seen again. But it was possible to supplement what the sea had to offer by hunting creatures of the land—caribou, arctic hare, squirrels, ptarmigan, geese, and such waterfowl as eider ducks, pintails, and mallards.

But in a few years hunger again drove the Ootennas (my grandparents) and others of their nomadic tribe and family to the south. They resettled at Ikpek Lagoon, fifty miles below Shishmaref and just sixty miles from East Cape, Siberia, which is on the west side of the Bering Strait. But, as steamships became more prevalent, hard times came to Ikpek as they had to Shishmaref and to Tigara. Not being dependent upon wind and current, the captains of the steam ships could thread through leads in the ice pack and hunt whales right up to the beaches and even into landlocked lagoons. When whaling was poor, the crews went out onto the ice and slaughtered walrus by the hundreds for blubber, hides, and ivory. It was soon obvious that the Ootennas would have to migrate again or starve.

While at Ikpek, they learned of the recent introduction of reindeer to Alaska. One herd was said to be at Teller Mission on Port Clarence Bay, eighty or so miles down the coast. Another was at Cape Prince of Wales, only about thirty miles down the coast. So with others of their family group, the Ootennas moved on to Wales, a village situated on the cape that is the westernmost tip of the North American continent. Asiatic Siberia was just over the horizon a few miles to the west. They could see the bluffs of Cape Dezhneva in Siberia on a clear day.

At the Eskimo village of Wales there was a mission school of the American Missionary Association operated by William T. Lopp and his wife. He was the first American missionary teacher in that part of Alaska. Devout but practical Christians, the Lopps were very fond of the Eskimos and were deeply loved by them. The missionary was acknowledged to be an expert in handling both animals and the Native herdsmen he trained.

The reindeer at Cape Prince of Wales and at Teller Reindeer Station were owned principally by the Missionary Association, with the remainder being the personal property of the Lopps and various Eskimos. The animals were used not only to provide food and clothing but also as beasts of burden. They carried packs and riders and pulled sleds in harness. My grandfather quickly learned from Mr. Lopp and fellow Eskimos how to care for reindeer and soon owned several of his own. To this day members of our family still hold an interest in some of the reindeer that descended from Ootenna's original animals.

Reindeer herd near Teller, Alaska, 1900.

Not all the white people who came to the North were blind to the problems of our people. Farsighted missionaries and teachers, like the Lopps, who lived with the Natives, ate their diet, wore their clothing, hunted with them, and shared their bounties and their hardships, could see the obvious. If something were not done, and soon, the Eskimos would become as scarce as the animals upon which they thrived. Though not so cold bloodedly deliberate, but just as effective, it was the same story as that of the Plains Indians and the buffalo—destroy the food supply and you eliminate those who depend upon it, which was official U.S. government policy in the 1870s and '80s.

Allowing the Alaska Natives to have modern guns so they could compete with the white men was not the answer. This would only hasten the extinction of the wildlife. The methods of the earliest hunters with their spears, bows and arrows, snares, and slings required great skill and patience. Even when game was plentiful, it was hard to take more than the immediate needs of a village or family. But the inborn instinct of the hunter was to kill all he could when it was available because tomorrow there might be nothing. Those who knew this Eskimo trait feared that if given a rapid-firing rifle, the Native was apt to go out and bang away as long as there was something to shoot at and his bullets lasted. That was why firearms had been outlawed to begin with.

By the nature of their environment, my ancestors were meat eaters. Except for berries, leaves, and roots that were eaten during the brief Arctic summer and put up for winter use, their diet was almost entirely meat, fish, and animal oil. The Natives put into seal pokes all the edible leaves they could find in the summer and early fall. The women and the children would walk for miles around where they camped to hunt and gather these edibles to supplement their diet. They picked several kinds of berries, which they also put up for winter use in wooden kegs or seal pokes. By the middle of winter the greens, which had been mixed with a small amount of seal oil, would be quite tart to the taste buds and, perhaps to the novice, a little strong to the nostrils. To those in authority who sought an answer to the problem of the Eskimo's dwindling food supply, agriculture was hardly considered. Even if fruits and vegetables could have been grown, they would not supply the rich nourishments required to fuel the body in the frigid climate. The Eskimos had to have the fats, proteins, and vitamins inherent in fresh meat and fish.

The only solution seemed to be the introduction of domestic animals that could flourish in northern regions. Sheep and cattle would quickly starve on the sparse tundra vegetation or be killed by the harshness of the climate. Inland vast herds of caribou ranged a land similar to that adjacent to the northwest coast of Alaska and Canada. Occasionally seen along the coast, they were wild and migratory. One day there might be 10,000 of the animals in sight, and a week later not one could be found within a hundred miles.

As an experiment in 1892 sixteen gentle reindeer, the tame European cousin of the caribou, were brought from Siberia to Teller Mission. The deer certainly would furnish meat and skins, but could Eskimos be changed from hunters to herdsmen? Over the next ten years another thousand or so reindeer were imported, and herders were brought from Lapland to teach the Natives how to care for these animals. The plan was highly successful. The Eskimo and the reindeer seemed to have been made for each other. Our people ceased to be nomads, moving from region to region in search of food, and adapted easily to the life of the deer herder.

For the 300 American whalers and the 500 Eskimo residents of Point Barrow at the top of the continent, the introduction of reindeer to Alaska was a timely godsend. Were it not for the reindeer, one of the great sagas of the Arctic would never have occurred, and the lives of 800 humans might have ended tragically.

In the fall of 1897 a ship returning to the United States reported that eight whaling vessels had been caught in the ice off Point Barrow. Some ships were crushed, and their crews and the Eskimos whose food they had to share faced starvation. When the Coast Guard revenue cutter *Bear* returned to Seattle from her six-month-long patrol of the Bering Sea, she was directed by President Grover Cleveland to return immediately to the Arctic. Her orders were to sail north until stopped by ice, then put a rescue party ashore with dog teams, hire Eskimo guides, and proceed overland to Cape Prince of Wales. Here they were to arrange with Mr. Lopp to drive a herd of reindeer to Point Barrow to be used to feed the destitute whalers and the local villagers. Quickly refitted and supplied, the three-masted, barkentine-rigged steamer departed Seattle for the Arctic on the twenty-seventh of November, 1897. She met the southward creeping ice pack in a storm off Cape Vancouver, 150 miles below the delta of the Yukon River. In a straight line the *Bear* was only 800 miles from Point Barrow, but to get there the rescuers would have to travel a circuitous route of nearly 2,000 miles.

The party consisted of three revenue cutter service officers, lieutenants D. H. Jarvis and E. P. Bertholf, and surgeon S. J. Call. They landed at Cape Vancouver with dogs and sleds, camping equipment and supplies. The *Bear* then returned to Unalaska at Dutch Harbor in the Aleutians to wait out the winter. When the ice went out the following summer, she was to proceed to Barrow and pick up her officers and the surviving whalers—if there were any. Being long before the days of wireless, it would be at least June or August of 1898 before it could be learned whether the mission had succeeded or failed.

At the village of Tanunak, the expedition officers hired Eskimo guides with sleds, dogs, and feed, and on the seventeenth of December departed for St. Michael, 250 miles north on Norton Sound. The route took them over ice-locked inlets of the Bering Sea, across frozen ponds and lakes and streams, and finally to the Yukon. Reaching the coast again, they raced on to St. Michael. From there they mushed their dogsleds over the Norton Sound ice pack to Golovin Bay, where they saw their first reindeer. Sending the Tanunak men and dogs back to Cape Vancouver, they hired local Eskimos with harness deer and sleds for the next leg of the journey, a jaunt of 120 miles westward along the coast to Cape Rodney. Being near mid-January they were well into the northern winter, with deep-freeze temperatures and violent blizzards. The sun along the sixty-fifth parallel, when not obscured by clouds or driving snow, was above the southern horizon for less than four hours each day. At Cape Rodney a small herd of reindeer was purchased from a herder, Artisarlook, who was hired to care for the deer during the long drive to Barrow. After a nearly disastrous experience, the party learned to avoid Native villages where vicious, half-wild dogs would attack the reindeer. There were few such villages on the Seward Peninsula, but one place even Artisarlook, though himself an Eskimo, refused to remain.

They reached Wales on the twenty-fourth of January. Mr. Lopp was astounded that government officers would be in the region at that time of year. When the circumstances were explained, he readily agreed to furnish the needed reindeer and accompany them to Barrow, insisting that six of his best "boys" go along to care for the deer. They were Sokweena; Keuk; Ituk; Netaxite; Kivyearzruk, a cousin of my mother; and my grandfather, Ootenna. The revenue cutter service officers were somewhat concerned about Mr. Lopp leaving his wife and small children alone with the Eskimos during his absence, which would be several months. "There is not a thing to worry about," he said. "They are all fine people." And Mrs. Lopp herself encouraged him to go.

On the third of February, the party left for Point Barrow, 700 miles north, with 438 reindeer and 18 deer-drawn sleds loaded with equipment and supplies. My mother, who was eight years old at the time, watched with my grandmother Kinaviak and the rest of the village while the rescue expedition left for Point Barrow with my grandfather in the lead.

The party was fortunate that the days were getting longer, and they did not have to travel during the total Arctic darkness. The further north they trekked, the less of the sun they saw each day. There could be no hurrying or forced march; the reindeer had to be allowed to plod along at the speed of the slowest animal in the herd, walking a few steps then stopping to paw down through the snow to forage the tundra moss and lichen. Each morning the deer-sled drivers would break camp and go on ahead and set up a new encampment and have tents and hot food ready when the herd arrived at dusk. Even though bad weather prevented them from traveling for days at a time, they averaged thirteen miles daily, reaching Point Barrow on the twenty-ninth of March. There were 382 reindeer remaining of the 438 they'd started with, the rest having been killed for food en route and by hungry wolves prowling at night.

They found the people at Barrow were not faced with starvation. The supplies from several of the frozen-in whalers had been sledded to shore and living quarters were built of timbers salvaged from vessels crushed by the ice pack. In addition, there was a local reindeer herd, and Charles Brower, the head man of Point Barrow and a trader known as the "King of the Arctic," had a warehouse full of frozen deer carcasses. The big problem was the maintaining of law and order among the 300 hard-boiled whalers. This the revenue service officers did until the *Bear* arrived in Barrow in late summer and returned the shipwrecked mariners to the United States. Mr. Lopp, my grandfather, and the rest of the "boys" returned to Wales soon after reaching Point Barrow the same way they had come, on foot. No human was lost or seriously injured during the entire trip.

My father, Albert Bernhardt, was one of the survivors of the ill-fated whaling ships crushed by the encroaching ice. His life in Alaska began in the year of 1897.

2

My mother, Ouiyaghasiak, attended the missionary school operated by William T. Lopp and his wife at Cape Prince of Wales, and during this time they gave her the Angelican name of Agnes. In her second year of school, at the age of ten or eleven, she learned rudimentary reading and writing. Mr. Lopp and his family soon moved to the Teller Reindeer Station, which later became Teller Mission. He took over management of the reindeer station there. It was during this period that my grandparents and their children also migrated to Teller Mission. For the remainder of their lives Ootenna and Kinaviak were never again out of sight of Port Clarence Bay. Nor was my mother. In all her life she was never more than eighty miles from her birthplace, Shishmaref.

Papa, however, was widely traveled, having begun his life in Germany, meandered through the seaport cities of five continents, and ended up in Alaska. He was born Albert Joseph Bernhardt in Danzig, Germany, in the year 1874, during the reign of Emperor Wilhelm I. He went off to sea as a cabin boy when he was fourteen years old in order to avoid military service in Bismarck's army. Generation after generation saw endless wars in Europe for which young men were constantly being conscripted. There also was much religious oppression. These conditions made my father eager to leave his country of birth if he was to live the life of a free man. His first sea voyage took him to the port of Riga, the capitol of Latvia, and after his ship sailed out of this seaport city for England, he was never to see or set foot on European soil again.

By the time he reached Alaska, he had sailed several times around the world, rounding the treacherous waters of Cape Horn, South America, and the Cape of Good Hope on the southern most tip of Africa, where storms and waves could be so powerful that often ships were swallowed up by the sea. The end of his sailing days came when he chose to live on the Seward Peninsula. For the next fifty-six consecutive years, other than crossing to Siberia, he never left Alaska. In early 1900 he went on a trading trip to Siberia with his friend Max Gottschalk on his schooner *New York*. Max Gottschalk, who mastered the schooner, was a colorful character. He was one of the toughest men who ever set foot in Alaska. He did things the way he wanted, legal or otherwise. Papa used to say, "Max will give you the shirt off his back, but don't trust him any further than you can throw a bull by the tail." A remark by others who knew him was that "he would steal from his own grandmother." He was known as a brigand in the Far North, and he didn't care who knew it. One summer after a trading spree to Siberia, he returned to Teller with a young white Russian bride. My father asked him if he wasn't "robbing the cradle."

His little schooner was always the first boat of the season in operation on the ice-clogged Bering Strait, plying between St. Michaels at the mouth of the Yukon River and north to Kotzebue around the first of June. Whenever we spotted that one mast appearing over the southern horizon, we knew that the freighters were not far behind, and that meant fresh vegetables and fruits soon would be available and a welcome addition to our meager winter diets. If we had any potatoes left at all by the middle of May, a whole month before the first steamer arrived, they would have sprouted eyes three or four inches long and would be pretty soft and not very palatable, but we ate them just the same for there was no such convenience as a grocery store. Sometimes we would be out of potatoes three or four weeks before the first shipment of the spring came in. By that time we would be so hungry for potatoes, we would have given anything for just one meal of them.

Papa didn't talk much about his early life in the old country, but there were many times when he would walk the beach at Nook in the evening, hands clasped behind his back, as if his thoughts were thousands of miles away in another era and another world. He spoke of his mother and two sisters now and then, and his two brothers. He said with pride though that his father was an officer in Napoleon's army during the Franco-Prussian War of 1870 and that his grandfather also fought in the Napoleonic wars. As these recollections came into his mind, it is no wonder that he wanted no part of the Kaiser's army when he sneaked on board a ship sailing out of Danzig Harbor.

After leaving Germany, my father shipped out of Liverpool, England, on British ships; he learned to speak English, but he never completely lost his heavy German accent. He went through the school of hard knocks. During his spare time, he taught himself to read and write English. He made his first voyage around Cape Horn before the age of fifteen in 1889 (incidentally, that was the year my mother was born). Sailing the oceans of the world in square riggers in the era of wooden ships and iron men, he soon became an able-bodied seaman and bosun. Following a particularly stormy and miserable trip around the Horn, he left his ship in San Pedro, California, and worked on tuna boats and, for a time, on the yacht of a wealthy Californian. He had a brief love affair with the rich man's blonde daughter, and about that time he decided to go to a fortune-teller to get a hint about what his future held for a wife. She told him he would marry a small dark-haired woman, so he gave up waiting around for the rich man's daughter and returned to deep-sea sailing.

In the spring of 1896, while ashore in San Francisco, he and eleven other sailors were shanghaied and put aboard a whaler bound for Point Barrow in the Arctic Ocean. They returned to San Francisco late that fall after a successful whaling season. My father came back from the Arctic with a love of Alaska and its ruggedness and shipped out voluntarily to return the next spring. In that fall of 1897 my father's ship and the other whalers were caught in a sudden Arctic storm—a sudden shift of tide and winds brought huge ice floes in from the Arctic Ocean and locked the ships in. The men left their ships with whatever they could pack into duffle bags and headed for Point Barrow over the ice. A few of the men never made it.

In the early spring there was a rumor that several prospectors had found gold in the hills of the Colville River area, which was about 150 miles southeast of Barrow. Some of the men died of scurvy and other diseases. My father was one who got "gold fever" and headed for the Colville. Having not the slightest knowledge where to look for the precious metal, and on top of it all, having contracted typhoid fever and nearly dying, he figured there must be another way to make a living or at least keep body and soul together. He headed back to Barrow where he caught a trading schooner going south. By this time there had been rumors again of gold strikes at Anvil Creek (what later became Nome). He joined up with a Finn by the name of Lindeberg and staked a claim in the hills back from the beach. The famous Alaska Gold Rush was just beginning to get into full swing. My father worked several claims, none of which turned out to be gold-bearing at the time, and since he was no miner, he staked on the hillsides rather than in the flats and creek beds which carried the gold, finally realizing that the heavy metal must have washed down to the beaches of Nome.

Word reached far and wide that gold had been discovered on the beaches and creeks, and by late summer thousands of people were arriving by the shiploads. Tents sprang up in every direction, and it was getting more difficult as the days passed to find even a place to sleep. About this same period, word of the major gold strike on the Klondike River, a tributary of the Yukon in northwestern Canada, brought a swarm of fortune seekers to Skagway in southeastern Alaska. They backpacked their supplies and gear over White Pass into Canada. Nearly everyone has heard or read of the hardships endured by the hordes of men who stampeded over White Pass into the Klondike. Reaching the headwaters of the Yukon, the men with money took passage on river steamers north to Dawson City, the center of the Klondike mining district. Others built small boats or rafts and floated downstream with the current. The alternate route, easier but longer, was to go by ship to Nome or St. Michael, thence up the Yukon by riverboat to Dawson, which is 1,500 miles inland to the east. Hundreds of prospectors, unable to afford tickets on the steamers, were camped along the beach at Nome. Thousands of the newcomers were former soldiers, recently discharged after service in the Spanish-American War, who came hurrying from Cuba and the Philippines, hoping to get rich panning for nuggets and gold dust in the streams of Alaska and Canada. Others, broke and discouraged by failure to find riches in the Klondike, came drifting down the muddy Yukon in anything that would float in search of new uncrowded diggings or a chance to work their way back to the United States on an ocean vessel. These prospectors, too, ultimately fetched up on the beach at Nome, a beach that turned out to be virtually paved with gold.

All the available land for miles back from the shore had been staked with mining claims. Unless a man were able to carry his food and prospecting gear many miles inland on his back, he was out of luck. The only place open to everyone was below the high tide line where claims could not be staked. Out of curiosity someone had panned the tide flats at low water and discovered the ocean sand was rich with flakes of gold. Thereupon every time the tide went out people swarmed out onto the beaches with shovels, pans, and rockers. No matter how much gold was recovered, more was washed in from sea by every storm. It was hard work and no fortunes were made by the crude methods used, but one could earn a living.

My father gave it a try but decided that the gold he found wasn't worth the effort. And there were so many people crowding the beach that there was hardly room to use a shovel. There was much thievery, quarreling, and fighting. Supplies were scarce and prices exorbitant. My father, coming to the realization that it would take special mining equipment to mine for the gold, left his holdings in the hands of a syndicate and struck off north over the Seward Peninsula to Port Clarence. The head of the syndicate soon died an untimely death, and the holdings passed into other hands without benefit to my father. Gold seekers were already at Port Clarence, but not too many. They were generally of a better character than most of those who thronged Nome. The hardships that it took to get to the new area eliminated the less attractive element, who seemed not inclined to physical effort, preferring to live by their wits off the more industrious.

Papa liked the country around Port Clarence and Seward Peninsula. Game was plentiful, the sea and streams were alive with fish, and at Teller Mission the reindeer herds were multiplying. There seemed to be more opportunities than at any other place he'd yet seen in Alaska. As a seafaring man he was especially attracted to the only natural harbor north of Dutch Harbor in the Aleutians on the route to the Arctic Ocean. Two fine, sheltered bays, Port Clarence and Grantley Harbor, offered a protected anchorage for deep-sea vessels, something that Nome did not have. Ships there had to lie several miles out on the open roadstead while passengers and freight were lightered to shore in small boats and barges. Lives and valuable goods were often lost when craft were upset in the surf or swamped by offshore combers. There was Sledge Island offshore from Nome about three miles where steamers lay to seek shelter from the southwest gales. Papa felt that because of its good anchorage, facing on the open Bering Sea, Port Clarence was a better site for a permanent community than was Nome.

Prospectors and miners, including my father, said they'd found evidence that the surrounding mountains held a wealth of minerals such as the world had never seen. Later scientific geological studies would prove them right. The entire Seward Peninsula, which Port Clarence Bay and Grantley Harbor partly split in two, is one of the most heavily mineralized regions in Alaska. Gold was but a small part of it. Deposits of tin, graphite, copper, and other ores were found. There was jade, too—boulder-sized stones weighing hundreds of pounds that had to be broken up before they could be hauled away.

Besides the Eskimo villages of the area, the town of Teller had sprung up a few years earlier on a point of land on the south side of the channel leading from Port Clarence to Grantley Harbor. Founded in 1892 as a reindeer station, it was named after Henry Moore Teller, who was secretary of the interior at the time. Most of the newcomers who settled at Teller had their mining interests in the surrounding area, and some had married Eskimo women. According to laws then in effect, such marriages gave a white man all the rights and privileges of a Native. Although some had wives and children "Outside," they married Eskimo or Indian girls anyway. Taking advantage of their "rights," they made small fortunes hunting and trapping in areas reserved for Natives or acquiring reindeer herds in the names of their wives and half-breed children. Financially independent, they then abandoned their Native wives and children and returned to their stateside families.

Just across the mile-wide channel from Teller, at the end of the long sandspit jutting out from Teller Mission was a piece of land Papa acquired through the patent process and to which he gave the name "Nook." Nearby was an ancient Eskimo village where earlier in the century the local Natives had fought and defeated a large war party of Chukchi invaders from Siberia. When Papa settled at Nook, the ancient village had been long abandoned, being only a clutter of grass-grown mounds and ruins of old igloos dug into the ground, roofed with the curving rib bones of whales or driftwood and covered with sod cut from the tundra. In the nearby cemetery the bodies were not buried but merely laid in a hollowed-out section of ground covered with driftwood logs and whalebone to keep out dogs, wolves, and foxes. When I was a child, we used to play there. Peeking through the cracks between the weathered logs, we could see the hair and bones of our long-deceased ancestors.

During the years 1920 to 1928, Smithsonian Institution scientists dug extensively at Nook, finding many artifacts of an older culture. They took them back to the Smithsonian. Mama and her contemporaries felt a deep resentment toward the anthropologists who came to Nook. I remember these men with beards and overly warm clothes that they wore despite it being the middle of our summer. They were always armed with all sorts of instruments for measuring the depth of ground and digging, such as shovels, trowels, and some other strange-looking gear, including the ever present notebooks and expensive camera equipment which were always sheathed in black luggage-type cases. I remember when I was about twelve years old the world-renown anthropologist, Alex Hrdlička, and his group of anthropologists came to Nook, spent several hours at the old igloo ruins and the old gravesite where we used to play, and took some skeletal bones—skulls and arm and leg bones—that had lain on the scooped-out gravel bottom of the grave with the tinder-dry driftwood logs placed over them perhaps since the turn of the century, or who knows when?

Soon after settling at the Port Clarence area, my father homesteaded the land at Nook and built a large warehouse where he built his own boats, skiffs, sleds, and snowshoes. He built boats for fishing and to get around in and also to ferry travelers from Teller across to Nook. Often these were people on their way to the mining operations at Tin City, which proved to be one of the largest tin-mining operations in North America. Not long after settling in Nook, he fell in love with a dark-haired woman, just as the fortune-teller in San Francisco had predicted. Their first child, Tommy, was born in 1900. Two years later, Papa's first wife, Nellie, died while giving birth to a daughter, Margaret.

During the summers at Nook when the salmon runs were at their peak, the Natives from nearby settlements pitched their tents on the Nook Spit, where Papa allowed them to camp and catch fish to be dried on racks in preparation for the coming winter. My grandparents, Ootenna and Kina-viak, with their five children, also camped on my father's land. The second spring after Nellie had died, he noticed that Ootenna and Kinaviak had a lovely daughter. Unable to care for his young children and make a living at the same time, he was lonely and began to think about marriage again. He

Nook, Alaska, summer camp (near Teller), 1928.

noticed the young Ouiyaghasiak, eldest daughter of Ootenna and Kinaviak, and wondered if she was of age to marry. My mother was not sure of her correct age. Her mother said she was born in the fall, fifteen years after one of the worst winters they could remember. They had hardly any spring or summer that year, and there were few berries to gather for winter. My father figured that she was born in the year 1889.

In the year 1904, the hearts of the young, good-looking, blue-eyed, red-haired German, Albert Bernhardt, and the lithe, peppy Eskimo maiden, Ouiyaghasiak, entwined in mutual admiration. They were married in the fall, but not until the spunky Ouiyaghasiak convinced the young German to shave his handlebar moustache. Two years later their first child, Mary, was born. Every two years thereafter for many years, they had a new baby. After Mary, there came Sarah, who, by the way, was named after the great European actress Sarah Bernhardt. Then came David and then me. Eight children were born after me, totaling fourteen children altogether. Of the fourteen, thirteen lived to adulthood. They are, by oldest to youngest: Thomas Joseph, Margaret, Mary Teresa, Sarah Rita, David Paul, Elizabeth Wiana, Anne Sylvia, Augusta, Albert Joseph Junior, Wilhelmina, Anthony, Pauline Laretta, and Robert Aloysius.

My mother was a wonderful, unselfish woman with a great sense of humor. She was always in accord. I don't think she worried a day in her

Agnes Bernhardt (Ouiyaghasiak), Teller, Alaska, 1928.

life, except when we children got sick or hurt. Then she might as well have
been sick herself. When we girls were growing up, she would talk to us "girl
to girl," and we could tell her every little thought that was in our heads. I
never knew her to have an unhappy day. The Eskimos are superstitious and
believe in shamanism. Around the turn of the century the power and influence of the shaman was diminishing rapidly as the Eskimo people turned to
Christianity. There were many shamans in my grandparents' time, and they

believed that they could heal or change minds towards proper living. My grandparents, however, did not talk about them very much to me, probably due to my young age. Mama used to warn us that there was an old Eskimo belief about putting our clothes on inside out. She said we would have bad luck that day.

There are several major Native groups in Alaska: the Iñupiaq Eskimo along northern coastal regions and islands; the Aleut along the Aleutian chain and Alaska Peninsula; the Yup'ik Eskimo of the interior Yukon and Kuskokwim Rivers; the Athapaskan Indians also of the interior of Alaska; the Eskimo and Aleut of the Cook Inlet and Prince William Sound regions; the northern Canada Inuit and Indians; and the tribes of southeast Alaska, including the Tlingit, Haida, and Tsimpshian. Ancestral Eskimos had only one name (for instance, my grandfather's name was Ootenna and his family was known by his name).

Eskimos are a spiritual and religious people. Even to this day most Eskimos who live in the villages go to church every Sunday. In fact many of the babies born in my generation were given Biblical names such as Isaac, Jacob, Jeremiah, Luke, and Matthew for the boys and Sarah, Ruth, Magdeline, Naomi, and Hannah for the girls.

What seems to be a mystery is why the Natives from Point Hope on down to Cape Prince of Wales and King Island had quite fair skin, not dark at all, and some of the Native children with whom I grew up even had freckles, their skin being almost creamy white. My grandfather for one had quite fair skin, and my mother had the same. This leads to more of the mystery about where the Eskimos originated. Perhaps some day someone will discover a clue to the missing link in the chain as to how exactly the Eskimo race evolved.

In the reports of the Canadian explorer Vilhjalmur Stefansson about his sojourns in the Arctic regions of Alaska and Canada, he wrote about a "blonde Eskimo" race in the Coronation Gulf region of the Canadian Arctic as far back as 1904. For a whole year during this period he lived among "blonde Eskimos" who had never before seen a white man. In his report he wrote that their European characteristic (blonde hair) led him to connect these people with an early Viking colony that disappeared from Greenland between 1412 and 1585 (*My Life with the Eskimo*, 1913).

The Eskimos have no written language. Stories from one generation to another—teaching in the ways of hunting and fishing, the building of ice or sod igloos, *oomiaks*, kayaks, sleds, dog harnesses, and the making of their only musical instrument, the drum—were all handed down by word of mouth. There was a time when it was popular for Eskimo carvers to make the smiling, potbellied figure, similar to a Buddha figure, called a Billikin. It is supposed to be a good-luck charm and is carved of ivory, in just about any size desired, from a half inch to three or four inches high. They also carve masks of animals out of driftwood, which Eskimos wear during their potlatch dances. These are observed for any given occasion, such as a nice warm summer day, an especially cold winter day when they feel they need carefree light-heartedness, or the arrival of a tribe that they have not seen for some time, the success of a whale hunt, and most any time they feel jubilant about a happy event. When Eskimos did have such a get-together, they would dance and beat the drum for days sometimes, not even stopping to eat or sleep. The rhythm would reach such a crescendo and the dancers reach such a fever pitch, they finally would almost collapse to the last beat of the drummer. The most prolific in the drum and dance routine came from King and Diomede Islands. They had the biggest and loudest drums and the most enthusiastic dancers. They have even performed in the Lower 48.

In the summer of 1900 the population of Teller increased far beyond what anyone could ever imagine. At the height of its heyday, the population swelled to 10,000. There were gold-mining operations in every direction you could see, besides the tin mine going full blast at Tin City, sixty miles to the northwest. Some of the gold miners and prospectors came directly to Port Clarence by ship. Most were the overflow from Nome—disappointed people who spent all they had getting to the North, lured by greedy steamship agencies' outrageously false advertising such as: "'Nome, the New Eldorado': Thousands of people are earning $300 a day and many more than that panning the golden beaches that stretch 250 miles long! In the creek beds the diggings are yielding $4,000 a ton and $500 nuggets are common! Sailors have gotten rich from gold dredged up by the anchors of their ships!"

Nome was also described as a peaceful modern town with U.S. marshals and U.S. soldiers to keep order. There was also Fort Davis down the coast about five miles east of the city of Nome. It was quite a large army settlement in the early 1900s and up to the end of World War I. It was said that there were a number of good hotels available. By June 1898, 10,000 fortune seekers had left Puget Sound alone, and 25,000 more were awaiting passage. A one-way ticket cost $125 and freight was $40 a ton. But before long, mail began reaching the states that indicated the extent to which the truth in advertising had been stretched. The gold-bearing sands of Nome actually encompassed only a narrow strip of beach no more than three quarters of a mile long where 500 men were scrabbling to earn five to ten dollars a day, tides and weather permitting. Gold was in the hills, all right, but it was frozen solid, and coal to thaw the permafrost cost $150 a ton. Unless you were lucky enough to be where the gold was and had the equipment to work the claim, you could just make ends meet. The number of "good hotels" was a complete fallacy, as was the "peaceful, modern town." According to my father and others who were there then, Nome consisted of two streets that were "dusty when dry, muddy when wet," with crowds of idle, restless men wandering through them. Little steady work was available, and all but the worthless claims were staked. Unless you had a working claim, you would starve. Most miners who stayed over the winter had to charge the boarding house operators for meals and room till spring, when the ground thawed and they could resume their mining operations. The only year-round work available was for boardinghouse operators, storekeepers, and saloon operators, and there were plenty of the latter. Gambling and drunken carousing went on around the clock. Fights were common and men were knifed and shot by the light of the midnight sun. Few arrests were made for murder and other crimes. The law could hold criminals, if there were jails enough to hold them, until the revenue cutter arrived during its patrols of the North, for they were the enforcers of the law.

Nome, a city which has gone down in the history of Alaska as one of the wildest has also been rich in legend in the fact that the town could boast of the residency or visits of such notable and renown personalities as Billy Mitchell, the father of the U.S. Air Force; Jimmy Doolittle, a brigadier general in the U.S. Air Force and the man who led a squadron of B-25 bombers in WWII in the assault on the Japanese mainland; Jack London; Robert W. Service; Rex Beach; Roald Amundsen, the great explorer; Doc Maynard (some say the founder of Seattle); Wyatt Earp; Howard R. Hughes; Lowell Thomas; Will Rogers; and Wiley Post, just to name a few. So the city of Nome had its seamy side and its niche in history.

For three miles along the Nome beach the shacks and tents were twenty deep, and hundreds more people were arriving almost daily on every type of vessel seaworthy enough to reach Norton Sound. With no room left for one more tent, even women and children were sleeping on the damp ground out

Wiley Post and Will Rogers, Nome, Alaska, 1935.

in the open where they were bitten to distraction by swarms of vicious Arctic insects such as mosquitoes and gnats, or no-see-ums. Thousands of tons of freight was dumped on the shore just above the high tide line, where it lay unprotected from the weather and the thieves. There were no sanitary arrangements other than a few inadequate outhouses. Most of the shallow wells were contaminated, and typhoid, diphtheria, and smallpox were rampant.

Out along the creeks and back in the hills most of the wildlife was quickly exterminated by prospectors for food and skins. All around Norton Sound and far up the Yukon and the other rivers the Eskimos and Indians were without food and skins to make clothing. There was sickness and death in every village, and some were completely wiped out by disease and hunger. The meager possessions of the dead were usually carted off by travelers who left the unburied bodies to be devoured by hungry dogs and predators.

A few of the discouraged bankrupt miners were able to work their way back to the United States on ships that were shorthanded because crewmen had deserted for the diggings. Other destitutes were carried south free of charge on government vessels. Many more died, and their bones were laid in shoreside graves or washed away by storm waves and strewn along the "golden sands" that enticed them there.

The hardier ones, the people determined not to give up and go home as failures, got out of the overcrowded town with its undesirable elements and went off up the coast or into the mountains. Everything they owned was carried on their backs: pick, shovel, and gold pan; beans, coffee, and flour; a little salt and sugar; a jar of sourdough starter to leaven their biscuits and pancakes; and a knife and rifle. It was this type that generally made it to Teller—tough and industrious.

Some fairly good strikes were found near Teller on creeks flowing into Grantley Harbor, but there was little free gold in the streambeds to be had for the panning. Everything had to be thawed and laboriously hacked out of the frozen ground before the dust and nuggets could be sluiced from the dirt and gravel. The work was strenuous for the lone miner or team of partners working with hand tools to make a decent living. Soon most individuals sold their claims to mining syndicates and went to work for daily wages. The larger operations of placer mining around Grantley Harbor were at Sunset Creek, run by Charley and Frank Rice at Gold Run. Dease and Coyote Creek were run by the Tweet family—the father and his four husky Norwegian sons. The Tweet family became the last of the great gold mining era. The two youngest Tweets were still running the operations each summer up through the early 1970s. My father worked at several of the placer operations around Grantley Harbor. Later, when tin deposits were discovered fifty miles to the west near Cape Prince of Wales, he hauled supplies from Teller to Tin City by a team of horses.

Principally because of its good harbor, Teller became the hub of the Seward Peninsula mining district. Most of the buildings were sturdy, rough-hewn lumber buildings—some still standing—and they housed banks, hotels, stores, and a jail. Saloons, honky-tonks, and bawdy houses catered to the miners and sailors from the ships that called. There was even a doctor and an undertaker parlor.

The boom peaked in about 1910, then tapered off, and people began to drift away. By 1917, when most of the younger, able-bodied single men left for service in the First World War, Teller was a community of only a hundred or so. Most of those who remained were white men who had married Native women. Large families were the rule. While Papa was still a miner, during the off-season he hunted and fished to provide food for his growing family. In the winter months he trapped for furs to sell to the traders for things the land did not provide.

People bought their supplies such as flour, sugar, cloth, tobacco, tools, hardware, guns, and ammunition from the local mercantile stores or from

the trading ships that anchored in Grantley Harbor every summer. Most familiar of the trading ships of the early '20s were the MS *Herman*, under the
command of Captain Pederson; the CS *Homes*, under Captain John Back-
land; the *Lady Kindersley*, under Captain Charles Klengenberg; and also the
Effie M. Marissey, under Captain Bob Bartlett. Then in the '30s came the
MS *Patterson* which replaced the aging *Herman*; the *Nanuk*, a trading ship
of the Swenson Fur Company of Seattle; and the *Maid of Orleans* (a former
slave ship), commanded by Captain Klengenberg and his two sons, Andrew
and Jorgen, who all held large trading interests in Arctic Canada with home
offices in Vancouver, B.C. Other ships that called into Port Clarence Bay
with world renowned names included: Amundsen's *Gjoa-Maude*; the *Ghost
Ship Baychimo*; actor John Barrymore's sleek yacht; Mr. Borden's, of the
Borden Milk Company, schooner, *The Flying Cloud*; and *The Pioneer* of the
famous George Vanderbilts. Few ships went to or returned from the Arctic
Ocean without stopping at Port Clarence to trade or take on fresh water.
The historic barkentine *Bear,* a revenue cutter, and the auxiliary schooner
Boxer, operated by the Bureau of Indian Affairs, were twice-yearly visitors.
In later years, after the *Bear* was retired from service, came the Coast Guard
ships *Northland, Spencer, Haida*, and others.

Even when money and furs were scarce, Papa always bought a few special things for us: candy, gum, and a bag of oranges. He believed that a man's
first responsibility was to his family. Papa was raised in a strict Catholic
home in Germany during the reign of Emperor Wilhelm I, and he remained
a strict and straightforward man. In the winter, during which time he found
life a little more leisurely, we held catechism class in our home on Sundays.
He taught us, including my mother, all our prayers, and she learned to pray
in English as well as in Eskimo. There were traveling Catholic priests in
those days with headquarters at Mary's Igloo Mission in the interior of the
Seward Peninsula. They traveled the long hard way, by dog team. Father La-
Fortune (who translated parts of the Bible into the Iñupiaq language) would
arrive by his personal dog team to stay a week at Teller, usually near Easter
time. He held Mass every morning, and every day after school we children
would scamper off down the street to the parish hall for Sunday School. All
week we would have Sunday School after school hours. Everyone, Catholic
or not, had great respect for the priest who, though aging, traveled 150
miles or so, by dog team, in the cold snow and icy winds to spread the word
of God.

USS Northland coming into Port Clarence, 1938.

I was about two years old when we moved to Mary's Igloo, a mission village some sixty miles inland from Teller, so the older children could go to the Catholic mission school there. Father Post, the head of the school and church was from France, the brothers (or monks) were German, and the teaching nuns were Belgian. They spoke French or German among themselves, and whenever my father was visiting, they all spoke German with him in an unusual camaraderie of Europeans in an unusual setting in the Far North of Alaska. About the only thing that I recall about Mary's Igloo was a big flood and going to church in a boat. It rained so long and hard and the water rose so fast that a lot of the Christian Natives, and some of the nuns as well, thought for sure that God was punishing the earth with another deluge. They were concerned because there was no Noah with an Ark to save the righteous.

My father was an excellent cook and baker, and we always looked forward to the winter when he took a turn at kitchen duties. When we'd hear him putting the big iron Dutch oven on the stove and sending someone to the storeroom for lard to fill it with, we kids would all gather around, jumping up and down and chattering with glee because we knew that we were going to have some doughnuts. People could smell them frying all over Teller, and soon children would be hanging around outside, waiting for us to come out and play. He also made corn fritters that would melt in your mouth. He made delicious pies too. Whenever he thought that we had enough fresh apples on hand—not making us short on eating apples—he would assign one of the older girls to peeling and coring the apples. We would argue over who was going to eat the peelings and cores, for we couldn't see throwing away any part that was edible. If it was getting to the last of the crated apples, he used dried apples that he cooked first.

Papa had to teach our mother how to cook white man's food, which she learned to do quite well. But she never lost her fondness for the Native diet. She always ate sitting cross-legged on the floor. She liked boiled seal and walrus meat and dried or boiled fish dipped in seal oil. We children usually ate with Papa at the table, but if we wanted some of what our mother was having, we sat with her on the floor to share it. She liked most of the white man's food, but she did not care for beans.

In the spring we gathered the tender willow leaves when they first came out and stored them in pokes with seal oil for winter greens. They gave us iron and vitamins, I suppose, because we never did have scurvy or other vitamin-deficiency diseases. Mama called this *soo-rut*. Another plant we gathered in summer looked and tasted like rhubarb, but Mama called it "sauerkraut" because it was so sour. It was stored in a seal poke too. She showed us how to follow mouse trails in the tundra to find caches of roots the mice had gathered. They were shaped like peanuts, and she called them *pikniks*, and they tasted sweet and were sort of juicy. They had the crunch of water chestnuts. Mama said, "Don't take all the *pikniks*, you have to leave some for the mouse." Mama also taught us to pick the leaves of a small plant which looked like a stunted fir tree about ten to twelve inches tall. It was called Hudson Bay tea. She and her ancestors used to make a tea or *chi u* as it is called in the Eskimo language. It makes a spicy-tasting tea—you need very little of the leaves steeped in hot water to make a cup of tea.

In 1915 we moved back to Teller from Mary's Igloo. Our parents had had enough of the yearly periods of high water caused by the runoff from winter snows melting on the surrounding slopes of the Saw Tooth

Left to right, Wilma, Mother, Robert, Pauline, Teller, 1930.

Mountains, followed by the maddening insects that hatched out of the swamps and ponds with the first warm weather. There were plenty of bugs at Teller too, but the sea winds blew enough of them away to make life tolerable during the short, comfortably warm summers.

During the year of the big flood most of the rickety old houses of Teller, hastily built during the gold rush, washed away when the lagoon behind the town overflowed. Papa bought the best of the largest houses remaining, a former mortuary that had been empty since the boom days ended and people went back to the custom of burying their own dead. I was only four years old when we moved in, but I can still remember the red carpeting on the floor and the musty smell of the place. A sign was still nailed on the front that read, "O'Neill's Funeral Home."

Like almost every other building in town, the house was covered with tar paper to help keep the cold winds out. But all the houses had double walls with insulation in-between; if you didn't have some type of insulation, you could freeze to death. Besides a big front room and kitchen combined, there were two bedrooms, one for Papa and Mama and the youngest child, and one for the boys. We girls had one large room upstairs in the attic. In back was a big room where we stored our dry supplies such as flour, sugar, oatmeal, smoked salmon, seal oil, dried fish, and anything else that would not be harmed. We called it the "cold room." Off to the far end of this cold room was a shed about 5 x 8 feet which was used as an outhouse. In midwinter there would be a half inch of hoar frost on the walls and floor. Before you could sit on the toilet seat, you had to put down a layer of paper torn from the Montgomery Ward catalog nailed to the wall along side the commode. If you failed to do so, you would find yourself stuck to the toilet seat. In the winter time when papa was trapping, he'd skin the animals he trapped and put them on stretchers to slowly dry in the cold room. When the furs are first put on the stretchers, they are turned wrong side out so that all the remaining fatty residue can be scraped off before it gets too dried on. Each fur is dried on a frame of wood to the size of the specific animal, such as a fox skin has it's own frame and so on. When the fur finally dried, it was turned right side out and then groomed and brushed and, if need be, rubbed clean with corn meal and then brushed again.

There was an attic in this large cold room, and we younger ones had a hard time resisting the temptation to climb the ladder that led to the hatch opening in the ceiling. The hatch door was always thrown back to the open position. One day David, Anne, and I decided we would go up there and find out what deep, dark secrets the attic held. To our surprise and with hearts pounding, we discovered two new empty caskets. At this point Anne and I decided to scamper back down the ladder, but David teasingly called us scaredy-cats and in the same breath said, "Oh, look at these beautiful flowers!" With that exclamation we moved to another corner, and sure enough there were the most beautiful artificial flowers we had ever set eyes on.

There were also wide-brimmed ladies summer hats banded with velvet ribbon, lovely long gowns of silk and lace, blouses of sheer voile, and patent leather shoes that buttoned to the calf. Years later when we laughed and reminisced about the attic full of caskets, beautiful clothes, and flowers, we would say, "How come those dead people didn't haunt us for playing with their cast-off clothing?" The items we treasured mostly though were the artificial flowers. We thought they were the loveliest things we had ever seen. There were sprays, banks of white Easter lilies, roses of all colors, gladiolas, lilies of the valley, and more. They were made of fine gauze-like material with the feel of pure silk, glued to a wire frame in the shape and color of each particular flower. The stems were of a heavier wire wrapped with green tissue paper.

The next house from ours was about a half block away on the other side of the street and of the same vintage. It was much larger, more like a warehouse with a large room walled off in the back end and used for the living quarters. At the end of this large room was a shed. It had loose floorboards, and they squeaked when we walked on them. It seemed that no one owned the building for it was always vacant. When Gussie (Augusta), and Anne, and I were small, we often played in the shed of the building for the door was always ajar. One day our curiosity got the best of us and we lifted one of the floorboards, and there we saw four cigar boxes on the ground just under the boards. We picked one of them up, and it was very heavy! It was about half-full of copper pennies—a lot of them were Indian head pennies. At this particular time we were not sure what kind of money it was as we had not handled much money before, and we had never seen pennies for the least change we got from the stores was a ten-cent piece because nothing could be bought for less. We never did look in the other cigar boxes for we were content to play store with the copper pennies.

Something that was really baffling to us was grapefruit. Usually after a big windstorm coming from the southwest in the summertime, the shore at Nook would be strewn with debris of all sorts. After these big summer gales we would look forward to a long walk along the gravelly beach "oohing" and "aahing" at all the strange specimens that would be washed up on the shore. There were large jellyfish, twelve to fourteen inches across, that the storm had washed up on the beach and good fresh clean mussels that Mama steamed for supper. One of the most strange things that washed ashore were grapefruit skins cut in half. I called out to Anne, "Look at the huge orange skin I found." We had never seen any citrus fruits but oranges before then. Anne said, "They must come from another country than California or Florida" (referring to the labels stamped California or Florida on the crates the oranges came in) "for the oranges we've ever had aren't that large!"

It was a few years later when our older sister Mary married Captain Albert Walters (he was captain of the mail boat *Silver Wave*), and he would bring us new things from Nome that would clear up some of our mysterious finds. Captain Albert Walters was an import of Captain Klengenberg, who sailed his ship the *Lady Kindersley* into Grantley Harbor from San Francisco. My brother-in-law was a handsome Viking type of a man with a very masculine physique, and to top it all, he was the proud owner of the black belt from Sweden in the martial arts sport of karate. He was proud to show it, and he told accounts of his athletic career in his youth in Stockholm, Sweden. I adored him; he was sort of an idol to me. It might have been because I subconsciously admired his strong, whole body.

Like many other early Alaskans who'd come from foreign countries, Papa had not yet applied for American citizenship. Then at the outbreak of WWI, caught up in the German hatred of those days, some of his longtime friends turned against him. One day some officials came from Nome, and my father was told, "Mr. Bernhardt, we have orders for your arrest as an enemy alien and spy." I remember clearly the men, who were from the immigration office in Nome; they were robust and looked stern as they talked to Papa. We children and Mama began to cry. The smaller ones clung to Mama's long full calico skirt.

Papa said, "Why should I be an enemy and spy? My wife and children are American, and this is my country too, not Germany." It turned out that not long before this, we had had a visitor. He was served lunch with my father, and they talked about the winter's prospects for trapping furs. Papa took him to the cold room and showed him the furs he had caught so far that winter. Of the many furs hanging there the man saw three fox skins hanging side by side, one red, then a white and a black. Those were the colors of the German flag, and my father had accidently hung those fox skins in that order. When the visitor got back to Nome, he reported that my father was pro-German. Of course there was no way my father could have contacted anyone in Germany, even if he wanted to. Nor was there anything going on in our part of Alaska that would have been of interest to the Kaiser, who was having enough trouble in Europe at the time. Papa was able to convince the authorities of his loyalty and of the outlandishness of the accusation, and the charges were withdrawn.

"But you'll have to become an American citizen, Mr. Bernhardt," the immigration men told Papa. I also remember that just before they left our house, they said he would be under surveillance until he became a full-fledged American citizen.

"It will be an honor to become one," my father said. Thereupon, he got busy and studied U.S. history and the constitution. He began to take instruction under the tutelage of Mrs. Christensen, a citizen of Teller who we had known for several years by then. As the years went by, she became one of our closest friends. We grew up with her two elder children, Tommy and Karen. Finally in 1918 Papa became a U.S. citizen. He always said it was one of the most important events of his life.

3

In 1918, when I was six years old, I lost both of my legs to frostbite. In order to set this tragic event into some perspective, I must provide some background information relative to my grandparents.

Every spring after school was out and the ice on Grantley Harbor had broken up and been carried out to sea by offshore winds and tidal currents, we'd move to our fishing camp at Nook across the bay from Teller. The house that Papa had built had been added onto to accommodate our increasing family. That summer he built a house for the boys. There were eight children in 1918 when we left for Nook.

During the salmon fishing season, my grandparents, Ootenna and Kinaviak came from Teller Mission in their *oomiak* to camp nearby and fish so they could have dried fish for winter food. It gave them a chance to visit too, with friends and cousins who came to Nook every summer for fishing and trading—Eskimos from the Diomede Islands, King Island, and Saint Lawrence Island, and their Asian cousins, Siberian Chukchis. Of the Native tribes of the Bering Strait, those who had to make the most treacherous trip, a distance of about 150 miles in their open *oomiaks*, were the Eskimos from

Bernhardt family, Teller, 1918. Elizabeth is third from right, with her hand raised to her head.

Saint Lawrence Island. They would travel in a group of three *oomiaks*, full to the gunwales with tents, dogs, women, and children while the big, strong men paddled across the Bering Sea. One of the *oomiaks* had an Evinrude outboard motor, which if it wasn't broken down, would tow one of the other *oomiaks* to relieve the paddlers, although we also saw them coming in under the sheer power of the paddlers. Loaded down as they were, they would make the treacherous Bering Strait crossing in high spirits. The tribes from King Island or the Little Diomede Island most of the time would paddle the twenty miles through the Bering Strait to the mainland. They were too poor to afford the luxury of an outboard motor. The trip from Saint Lawrence Island by pure, raw manpower would take from twenty to twenty-four hours, depending on the weather. Although they were expert on predicting weather ahead of time, nature sometimes turned the tables, and it would take perhaps a half day longer. And there were times when we would see some of the women taking a turn on the paddles, and that was to give the worn-out male a rest from the grueling task.

In mid-August, before the southwesters began, which would make crossing the Bering Strait in open boats too hazardous, the visitors would break camp and leave for their homes over a hundred miles away across treacherous unprotected waters. Bad weather and oncoming wintry blasts from the north ended the fishing in late August or early September, and in 1918 we prepared to return to Teller for the winter and the opening of school. My grandparents asked if I could go with them to their village at Teller Mission as I had done before. They said they would bring me home in time for me to start school at Teller. I was allowed to go home with them which proved to be my downfall.

At the time I lived with them, my grandparents, Ootenna and Kinaviak, were still living an aboriginal lifestyle. My grandmother had three blue lines tattooed on her chin, the same as my mother had. The tatoos on the chin were to show that the woman was married and any prospective suitor who saw the tatoos would know what that meant. When my mother was growing into womanhood, the custom was fading. Their one-room igloo was atop a forty-foot bluff that sloped steeply toward the sea near the waterfall where Papa's whaler and other ships loaded water in drums to take aboard ships. Theirs was a typical Eskimo dwelling. The main floor of the earth igloo was dug about three feet into the ground. The frame was a foundation of split driftwood covered with squared chunks of tundra that eventually sodded over. On the walls hung reindeer hides that kept out drafts. A skylight and a small window let in some light and the entrance was a low door about five feet high. As you opened the door to enter, you had to step down about two steps to the main floor, which was partly boards and partly earth.

I have often wondered since I grew up, how they could they have lived in such conditions. The two windows, one a skylight, were both made of dried seal gut strips, stretched and sewn together before they were dry so one could pull the stitches really tight with the sinew that was used as thread and not tear the delicate intestines. Being transparent, the seal gut allowed in a certain amount of light. My grandmother also made waterproof parkas of the dried seal gut to be worn over a fur parka in rainy weather. Grandmother had made me one to wear when I went with my grandfather to hunt in the kayak. They used sealskin in one way or another on nearly every garment they wore. To prepare the hide they would of course scrape every vestige of blubber, then they would stretch it, and put either wooden pegs or nails at intervals to keep it taut while it dried. They also used sealskin with the hair taken off (which made it lightweight) for summer mukluks, for fancywork on parka trimmings, and for the dolls they made for their children. To get the fur off was a smelly procedure. They would soak the hide in human urine that they saved in a large galvanized tub. We used to look forward to the end of the sealskin tanning season so we wouldn't have all those smells to endure.

The sod igloo was a practical dwelling for the climate. The thick sod walls kept out the wind and made it more practical to heat. Without a fire though it became as frigid as a cold-storage room. In winter if you set a bucket of water on the floor, ice would form before morning. About four other Eskimo families lived in similar igloos in the village. There were a number of other sod igloos scattered here and there in a partly ruined state, probably vacated the generation before. Now there are scarcely any sod igloos left such as we lived in when I lived with my grandparents. Those that are left are decaying with time, just hollowed out places in the ground overgrown with tall grass, and the whalebone and driftwood frames have disappeared into splinters.

During the migration of my grandparents, they not only had to go where there would be hunting and fishing but also where they could find driftwood, for at this time in their lives the iron Lang stove was becoming much in use as a cooking and heating unit. It was a modern innovation compared with the soapstone oil lamps still in use by some of their neighbors. There is always the struggle that comes from living in a cold country of not having sufficient fuel to keep warm, but in my ancestors' day they only had the seal oil lamp made from soapstone. As they became more civilized, they began to use the iron Lang stove, but that needed wood or coal or both. The irony of it all would be that in less than seventy years the discovery of oil and gas on the North Slope would occur less than 200 miles from Point Hope where my grandparents began their migration south in their search for food and lamp oil from the whales and seals they would hunt.

Few of the Alaska Natives who now inhabit the North remember much about the early life of their parents let alone their grandparents. In the past and during my early years there was little interest in the old traditions of the parents or grandparents, especially in the villages where there was considerable western or Anglo influence. The older ones seemed to feel that the younger ones couldn't care less about their heritage, be it customs or culture, and the younger generation had a lackadaisical attitude about what life was like a generation or two ago. This happened to other aboriginal people caught in the grip of fast-changing times.

When I lived with my grandmother and grandfather, I had the opportunity to experience firsthand how my Eskimo mother and her parents lived, for they lived then just as they had for a hundred years. In their quiet, serene winter evenings the mothers would make their children toys to play with out of scraps of tanned hide and fur. One of the many things I learned to make and sew was a football such as they actually used to play in the game of Eskimo football. It was made by cutting one oblong piece of sealskin, eight inches wide by twenty inches long, then cutting two circles seven inches in diameter. You sewed the pieces together to make a ball and filled the cavity with reindeer hair. It made a very lightweight ball, and it did not make a player tired kicking it around. Another game they played during the winter months was called *munna munna*, and it went like this: There were two teams, and each team made a circle in the snow about ten to twelve feet across. The circles were about one hundred feet apart. In the start of the game the ball was set halfway between the circles. After the referee held up his hand beginning the game, one player from each side had to kick the ball towards the circle of the opposing side. The idea was to kick the ball into the circle to score a point. At the end of the game, which sometimes lasted as long as daylight allowed, the team who scored most was the champ. This game was much like basketball in the U.S. The only difference was Eskimo football was played by kicking the ball and not using the hands at all.

My grandparents loved me dearly; they had pet names for me besides calling me by my Eskimo name, Wiana (pronounced Wee-ah-nah), they also called me Nah-long-me-u, which means "white man," or King-a-lik, "the one with the high nose." Eskimo names usually were descriptive of the person named, but not always. Some names don't mean anything in particular. My grandfather would take me nearly everywhere he went. He would take me out in his kayak when he went to shoot ducks in the fall or to hunt a seal in spring. I went with him to hunt ptarmigan or Arctic hare on the tundra. Sometimes we would go to the beach below the waterfall, and I would help him gather driftwood that had been deposited on the beaches by a storm and that we needed badly for starting fires, cooking, and heating.

That year fall came early—the cold winter winds blowing down from the Arctic brought the first snowfall in September. By the end of that month the ground was frozen, and the snow was staying on the ground. October and November were usually windy and cold, and by mid-November the sea was frozen over with what they call in the North "young ice." That year the young ice was getting thicker by the day.

The fall of 1918, of course, was also when the first great influenza epidemic swept the world, taking millions of human lives. Teller was not an exception, and many there took sick and died, just as they did the world over. There was no nurse or doctor within a hundred miles, and my father and a neighbor named Jimmy LaPierre went from house to house nursing the ill. Those two, along with Bill Maloney, an Irish man who also had a large family, helped bury the dead. All of my brothers and sisters were sick too, and when the new baby was born on the last day of November, he lived only a few hours. Papa baptized him, and he and Mama named him Albert Joseph Bernhardt, Junior. Papa made him a tiny casket, and they buried him on the hill back of Teller. For some unknown reason I never got the flu, but the loss of both my feet and legs was a direct result of the epidemic.

For the first month or so after the freezing over of the bay, my grandparents had not yet sent me home. There was little concern because travel would have been foolhardy in the beastly, bitter cold weather, with temperatures dipping down to thirty-five and forty below zero and colder and gales up to thirty and forty miles an hour. Then one day the wind calmed, and the snow ceased to blow, clearing the atmosphere. On this morning my family could look out from Teller and across the new glaring ice that sealed Port Clarence Bay, and for the first time in many days see Teller Mission hills on the other shore. Papa told my brother Tommy, who was eighteen years old, to hitch up the dogs and go see if everything was all right over at my grandparents' igloo. It was not!

While Tommy was still a mile out on the ice heading for the mission, he saw no smoke rising from the igloos, and he could hear the howling of unfed malamutes. When he reached the village, the ravenous dogs lunged to the limit of their chains at him and his team as he drove by. As he passed igloo after igloo, he wondered if everyone was ill with the flu or perhaps even dead. Some of the dogs were frozen to death at their posts, some weak from hunger, and some partially covered over with drifted snow. The closer Tommy got to grandfather's igloo, the more he began to worry. He tried not to think of the consequences. It was obvious that no one had stirred around the igloo for days for there was fresh snow all around but no tracks or footprints. He had to shovel away the drifted snow from around the door of the hut before he could open it. He looked around in the dimness, for there was very little light coming in from the side seal gut window and none from the skylight in the roof as the wind had blown a snowbank clear over the top of the igloo. One of the first things Tommy thought as he entered was how very cold it was in the hut. No one was up or stirring, and it looked pretty much deserted inside.

I had been sleeping in the same bunk as my grandmother. One evening as she prepared to bank the fire with wood from the meager pile beside the stove, grandma had told me that grandpa had died in his bed. The next morning I awoke and grandma had not stirred yet when ordinarily she was up and had built a fire. I talked to her and shook her by the shoulder to try to waken her, but she was lifeless and her face was cold. So I gathered in my childish intuition that grandma, too, was dead. But I did not worry my little head for long, for I began to get drowsy, and a feeling of lethargy came over me. Whenever I would awaken, I would think about grandma again and wonder why she had died. After all she had not complained about being ill, but then grandmother did not complain about anything. She was "solid as a rock" to our clan.

I think by the next day I moved a reindeer skin and a blanket on the floor in front of the bunk where my grandmother lay and made a bed for myself. I wanted to be as near to grandma as possible. Even though I knew she was not able to give me physical comfort any longer, at least she was nearby.

I remember several times I tried to stand up, but I would fall in a heap on the floor. "What is going on?" I thought. "Why can't I use my feet?" I didn't get hysterical; I just lay back down and went to sleep for I was very drowsy this whole time. The hunger and cold I suffered would awaken me, and I would crawl on my hands and knees to the cupboard where my grandparents kept a meager supply of white man's food, such as soda crackers and dried prunes. I would eat a few crackers and some dried prunes and then crawl back to my bed on the floor. After awhile, I didn't make anymore trips to the cupboard for it was getting more cumbersome to drag my lower body to get there. Besides, I was losing strength everyday and perhaps by this time suffering from hypothermia, a condition where body and mind are too cold to function properly.

When Tommy arrived at the igloo to check on us, snow had drifted inside the door and my brother found me lying on the wood floor of the sod hut. The temperature was well below freezing, while the temperature outside was forty to forty-five below zero. There had been no fire built in the stove for several days. To Tommy it must have been like walking into a deep freeze. Near the stove was a pail of water turned to solid ice, so Tommy, putting two and two together, figured I had been without heat in the hut for three or four days. When he went over to look at the grandparents, they were frozen as solid as stone. At one point I had evidently decided that I was going to go home, for Tommy said that I had all my outdoor weather clothing on, parka and mukluks.

After surveying this horrible scene and making a plan of action quickly in his mind, Tommy dashed over to the missionary's quarters and made arrangements for them to bury the grandparents. He bundled me in reindeer skins, put me in the sled, and started his mercy mission back to Teller. After he got me home, he and Papa had to cut my mukluks down the side from top to sole to get them off my feet for my feet and lower extremities had swollen so badly, and they were beginning to turn blue-black in color as my body began to absorb heat from the room. I still have vivid memories of the horrible pain that began soon after Papa carried me into the house, put me to bed, and my limbs began to thaw. The warmth of our house and the broth that Papa was tenderly feeding me began to restore my circulation, hence my condition began to worsen almost by the hour. My feet and legs began to turn black and a new form of suffering took over my pain-racked body. I couldn't tell which was worse, freezing or unfreezing! I screamed whenever anyone came towards the bed for it seemed that the least vibration would multiply the pain in my feet and legs. In a couple of days, realizing that gangrene was taking over rapidly, my father began to make preparations to take me to Nome in the hope of saving me from complete decay. The nearest doctor was at the Holy Cross Hospital one hundred miles away over the winter trail. There were no airplanes, of course, and with the sea frozen over, navigation was nonexistent. We had to go by dogsled.

The cold weather continued with the wind drifting snow, and Papa kept delaying our departure hoping the weather would moderate. Each evening just before darkness set in he would go out and look at the sky. "Maybe it will calm tonight and we can go tomorrow," he would say to Mama. But it didn't calm. After about three days of my almost-constant screaming with pain and the odor of rotting flesh permeating the room, he said to Mama, "The longer we stay here the more she will waste away. We will have to go in spite of the weather conditions." It was a day of supreme crisis when my father and mother decided there was no other way but to make the trip to the hospital at Nome.

Papa's friend Billy Marx, another German who was the U.S. Commissioner at Teller at the time, said, "You will never get her to Nome alive."

Papa said, "God won't let her die!" Since I had been brought home he had spent a lot of time on his knees, head bowed in prayer.

Besides Papa's own team of dogs, a team was made up for a total of eleven of the best dogs in town—fast, obedient animals with the endurance to keep going long hours. A heavy freighting sled was loaded with camping equipment, supplies, warm clothes, and dog feed for a three-day trip. Mama made a reindeer-skin sleeping bag for me that was just my length. Papa dressed me in my fur parka, put me in the sleeping bag, wrapped me and my sleeping bag in heavy tarpaulin to help keep out the cold wind, and loaded me on the sled. I can still see my mother standing on the snowbank in the dreadful cold wind, eyes tearful, as we drove off in the grey overcast morning towards Cape Spencer and over the ice of Port Clarence Bay. I can still hear my father calling out to Mama, "Don't worry, we will all be back."

Tommy came with us, running ahead alongside our lead dog, Molly. After two or three miles of giving the team the usual encouraging "atta boy!" and "mush," Tommy would join Papa on the back runners of the sled, one on each side. I don't recall very much of the trip for I was in a state of delirium the major part of the time. I do recollect seeing the tops of willow branches showing above the snow now and then. I would count how many there were as we passed them, just to get my mind away from the pain in my legs, especially when the sled would bump over rough surfaces. The weather stayed around the thirty-five to forty degree below zero mark, with the windchill factor making it about fifty or sixty below zero. We were traveling in a world of complete whiteness, with a few branches of dry willows poking out here and there whenever we were traveling near the shoreline. Then traveling due south, all we could see around us were ice hummocks and snowbanks as we followed the coastline of the Bering Strait.

At first we traveled over the smooth sea ice that had been swept clear of snow by the constant wind just off the beach, and the going was fairly easy and close enough to the bluffs just south of Teller to give us shelter from the northwest wind. As we passed the bluffs at Point Riley and crossed over the land comprising Cape Spencer, we were traveling on the open expanse of the Bering Sea ice. We were struck by the full force of the northwest gale coming from the Chukchi Sea and East Cape, Siberia. The whirlwinds of blowing snow cut visibility to nothing at times. Papa had made the overland trip to Nome several times and was pretty sure where he was in spite of the blinding blizzard. At one point, believing we should be going more to the west, he called, "Gee!"—the order for the dogs to go right. But Molly, the leader, refused to go to the right and stopped and lay down on the ice. "Tommy!" my father yelled to be heard above the wind, "go find out what's wrong with that leader!" She had never disobeyed before.

The wind was blowing so hard that my brother had to crawl on hands and knees to get to the head of the team. He was trying to make Molly get up and go when there was a sudden lull in the wind and the blowing snow thinned for a moment. He saw, about twenty feet to the right, an open lead of black choppy water. Had Molly gone that way, we would have been blown into that wide crack in the ice for the surface of the ice was smooth as glass in places. With the wind blowing as it was, our sled brakes would never have held us from going right into the water, sled and all. No one would have ever found us again or known what had happened to us. When Tommy got back and reported the open water, Papa yelled, "Haw!" and Molly was ready. She led the team to the left. Soon we were off the ice and crossing the snow-covered land between Port Clarence Bay and Norton Sound. We reached the frozen sea again near Cape Douglas, where we spent the night in a shelter cabin for winter travelers that was maintained by the Alaska Road Commission.

We were thirty miles from Teller as the crow flies, and Nome was still seventy miles away. Papa gently carried me, reindeer sleeping bag and all, into the one-room shack while Tommy hurried to build a fire in the Lang stove. Tommy fed and unhitched the dogs and tied each one to a post with his own chain where they could rest for the night. By the time Papa had warmed up the stew that Mama had packed in coffee cans and cut the fresh loaf of bread that Mama also had made the day before we left home, they were almost too worn out by the strain and anxiety of the trip to eat. Papa was more and more concerned as to whether there would be a spark of life in me when we got to the hospital. The worry lines were getting deeper in his forehead, and his eyes were getting to look sunken in their sockets. The throbbing pain in my body never ceased. I had short spells of consciousness, and I recall Papa saying to me, "Take this so you can have some fluids in your body." It was a teaspoon of whiskey in half a glass of water. This may have helped my circulation and given me warmth too.

The storm was still blowing the next morning. We got an early start to try to make another twenty or more miles and reach Cape Wooley by dark.

A Protestant missionary lived there, and Papa hoped he'd be hospitable so we would have a warm place to spend the night without having to camp in a cold shelter cabin. The lay of the coastline forced us to travel into the wind most of the day. The trail was rough with the rise and fall of snowbanks that slowed us down. As dusk was falling, we saw a light ahead, shining from a window in the missionary's house. When we finally got there, he would not take us in. "There is an empty cabin a mile on down the trail," he said. "Why don't you go there." The refusal of hospitality to a traveler in need of shelter was a violation of the code of the North. Papa was not a vindictive person, but he never forgot that missionary. For the second time in his life he was punished on account of his Germanic ancestry and accent. Being that the First World War was just very recently ended, some people still entertained thoughts that he was a German spy.

Worn out by the day's hard travel, Papa didn't argue that we were desperately in need of emergency shelter for the night but continued on. Tommy and my father found the cabin in the dark, got a fire going, and warmed up the stew my mother had prepared and put in lard cans. Tommy fed the dogs while Papa tended to me. He tried to make me eat a few spoons of soup, but he said I was in no mood to eat. I had not been given any medication; there was none to give. At this point as far as my mind can recall, I had only flashes of consciousness of what was going on.

There were only four hours of daylight so in order to make time, we had to begin our travel an hour before daybreak and end an hour or so after twilight. There were no stars or moonlight to go by, just the cold and the dark. After we ate the stew, my father stayed awake all night sitting next to my bed. He gave me a few sips of water. Tommy curled up in his sleeping bag on the bunk next to where Papa laid my pain-racked body in my reindeer sleeping bag. I was drifting in and out of a coma. Although I had no feelings of fear or apprehension of my condition, my father must have because I just happened to open my eyes and I saw him looking intently at the door. I glanced over and saw two older women dressed in their parkas and mukluks. I recognized them as friends of my mother who had passed on several years before. One was standing, and the other was on one bent knee. For some unknown reason it didn't bother me even though I knew these two women were apparitions. Papa told me later that the apparitions were telling him that I was going to live through this ordeal.

We were on our way again an hour before daylight (at that time of year being about 10 AM). Unable to take nourishment I was weakening fast, and Papa was afraid I wouldn't live through each day. Nome was still forty miles away. But for a change, Lady Luck was good to us. The weather had moderated overnight and there was little wind. The trail also was in better shape and the dogs loped along at a steady clip as if they knew that we were getting nearer our destination which was the hope and special prayers of a family and the whole population of the little town of Teller. As we were nearing Nome and dusk was beginning to fall, Papa saw a man with a small team up ahead. He was coming in our general direction. Wanting to waste no time in getting me to the hospital and having no idea in what part of town it was, Papa hailed down the first man he saw and both teams stopped. "I have a very sick little girl here and must get to the hospital without delay," Papa said. "Can you direct me?" The man was friendly and willing to escort us in if we needed it, but Papa, hollered "Mush!" to Molly and with a fresh surge of hope thanked the man and drove on. As we arrived in the city of Nome, a streetlight here and there led us down Bessie Road. Papa could see the wooden cross on the spire of the Holy Cross Hospital, rising high above the surrounding snowbanks.

I have no memory at all of the last twelve hours on the trail. But when we reached the hospital and Papa took me from the sled and carried me into the hospital, I was partially revived by the disturbance of being picked up. I remember seeing a person all in white coming down the hall towards us. "I'm in heaven, Papa. I see an angel," I whispered. It was a nun in white clothes. Immediately, of course, Doctors Welch and Neuman began to tend to me. They told my father that I would surely not have lasted another day. The doctors said, as they bared my little body of its clothing and saw the condition of my feet and legs, "They must come off." And Papa said, "Then take them off."

He stood by the operating table while they amputated my right leg at mid-thigh and the left leg just below the knee. Because of my deteriorated condition only a minimum of ether was used to put me under. It was not enough for during the operation I partially awakened and started to moan when I felt my body rocking to and fro as the surgeons sawed through the bones. They stopped until I was put out again.

I was in a critical condition for several days after the surgery, and Papa would hardly leave my bedside. The nuns would say, "You must have something to eat Mr. Bernhardt," or "You must get some rest." The doctors told my father later that one of two things pulled me through: either I had a very strong constitution or the good Lord above thought I should have a longer sojourn on this earth.

When it was certain that I would live, Papa sent Tommy home with the news and to help care for those of the family who were sick with the flu. While Papa and Tommy were with me at Nome, Jimmy LaPierre spent quite a bit of time looking in on our family at home. Mary, my oldest sister, had fallen down a snowbank and broken the upper bone in her right arm. A good family friend, Sam Datos, a Greek who had been living at Teller for several years and doing some gold mining in the creeks nearby, just happened to come into town and stopped at our house to see how things were. Mama said Papa and Tommy had taken me to the Nome hospital on a mission to save my life, and here was poor Mary with a broken arm. Sam the Greek (as we called him) said, "Let me take a look and see what we can do." Then he said, "Mama, get me some wooden slats off that potato crate and some clean white cloth." The break had happened that morning, and in a few hours time the whole arm had begun to swell. Sam the Greek did such a wonderful job on Mary's arm that you couldn't tell she ever had her arm broken. In a few weeks she was able as ever to use the arm.

Once the poisons from the gangrene were out of my system, I began to get well quickly and was alert to all the strange new things around me. I never dreamed I would be in such a world as this: a real bed (we had wooden bunks at home) and white sheets to sleep in, meals brought right to me in bed, and if I needed anything at all I could ring a bell and a nurse would come. Strangers were always coming to see me. They had heard about the "little girl who was brought in by dog team from a long distance" and wondered if I had survived the ordeal. The nuns at the hospital made Christmas a special celebration for me. At home my gifts might have been an orange or an apple with some nuts and a small sack of hard candy in my Christmas stocking, and stuck in the top a comb or a colorful hair ribbon. This particular Christmas was one I would never forget—even my room had signs of a Merry Christmas. There was a bright red paper bell hanging in one corner of the room, the window was draped with red and green crepe paper streamers, and there were gifts of every description that a small girl would ever ask for, from a great assortment of dolls, to teddy bears, to books and puzzles and games. One man even gave me an RCA Victor phonograph that you cranked by hand and an assortment of records to play on it, including some records sung by the famous Caruso. The phonograph was one of those popular in that day, with a large metal horn attached to amplify the sound. When I was well enough to have visitors, the pharmacist at the Nome drug store made frequent visits to see me and brought me picture books and toys. He was later to play an important part in my life, indirectly.

The Lomen brothers, Ralph and Carl, well-known businessmen at Nome, came to see how I was progressing. They would also bring toys and storybooks, which I could not read since I had not begun the first grade of school. The four Lomen brothers and their father, Judge Lomen, were synonymous with the early history of the city of Nome, and, in fact, the whole Seward Peninsula. They held large business interests in the area and some of them became members of the territorial legislature of that generation. Another important man of the era was a second district congressman who took time out from his busy political schedule to come to the hospital to see me. He encouraged me by saying, "Bessie, one of these days when you get some new legs, I will run you a race."

But one day about a week after I was permitted to have a visitor or two, Papa said, "There's a man who would like to see you. You don't know him, but he knows all about you!" Then he told me about the man with the small team of dogs who passed us on the snowy trail on our way into Nome to the hospital. His name was Jake Kristy, a miner who lived about seven miles out in the hills in a cabin all by himself. Papa went on to explain that he was a former shipmate on a whaler in the Arctic who also stayed on in the great land of Alaska to try his luck at the mining game. The two renewed their friendship and became good friends.

When I was able to sit up in the bed, I noticed that I had no balance. I could not sit erect and kept falling backwards. This puzzled me. Then one day as I was thinking about losing my feet and legs, I asked my father if, in time, my feet and legs would grow back on. He gave me a quizzical look and then quickly said, "We will wait and see."

My father went home to Teller in January, saying as he left, "I will be back in a few weeks, and by that time you will be ready to come home." He then returned home before the spring thaw while the trail was still in shape to travel over. He had hoped to take me back home to Teller, but the doctors thought it best to give me another month or two, depending on how much improvement my right stump needed. They had to operate on it a second time. The doctors feared they had not removed all the gangrene. The doctors and nurses were amazed at the agility I was showing in getting around over the bed and how I would climb from bed to chair and vice versa, using my arms and hands for every move in transporting my body. The doctors said that if anyone believed in the evolutionary form of human progress, I was a good example of proof of it for I was "performing like a little monkey." I was ready to leave the hospital by the end of April, four and a half months after I had been admitted in such critical condition.

Arrangements were made for me to stay at the Lutheran Children's Home. I was in a wheelchair by this time and able to get around pretty well with it. Life in the orphanage was quite an experience in itself. Most of the children, like myself, were of mixed blood, part Eskimo or Indian. We all got along like one big family. I especially liked Sunday School, perhaps because we had music. There was an organ and a piano, and someone would play accompaniment while we all sang hymns. But the songs weren't like the ones we sang at Mary's Igloo Catholic church with the nuns or at the tiny Teller parsonage. One of the first things I did when I returned home from Nome was to teach my brothers and sisters the snappy church songs that I learned at the Lutheran Children's Home. I loved to belt out the hymns I'd memorized. I sure put pep into such songs as "At the Cross," "Bringing in the Sheaves," and more. I had learned the songs by heart. It used to provoke the rest of the family that I should be so enthusiastic about the whole Protestant religion. Compared to our solemn, hushed, quiet, and calm services, my father and mother felt that I was well on the way to becoming an evangelist. I felt strongly about religion, for a young child, and still do to this day.

When the ice went out in June, I was ready to go home but had to wait for a ship that was going to Teller and points north. The first one was the *Bessie B*, a small two-masted schooner named for me. The captain of the little ship was John Hegness, an able seaman who had sailed those waters for several years and a friend of my father. Years later when John Hegness became captain of the mail boat he would bring my prostheses all crated in sturdy wooden boxes to Teller from Nome where they had been brought by steamer from Seattle without the usual high freight charges, for he would say to Papa, "I want to do this for the bravest little girl in all of Alaska."

In 1919 there was no jetty at the beach at Nome as there is today. There was only a timber ramp on the beach down which boats were launched into the surf. There were a half dozen of us in the Coast Guard dory that was to take us to the *Bessie B*, which was anchored about a half mile offshore. We all wore life jackets. A Coast Guard life-saving crew assisted with the launching, and they were rowing as hard as they could to get beyond the breakers when a high wave upset the dory. I was rescued by Chief Bosun Tom Ross, then commander of the U.S. Coast Guard Station. For the third time in eight months I came near to losing my life. Perhaps my Eskimo and German ancestors, both hardy peoples, endowed me with certain elements of survival. Papa always said though that God had a divine purpose for letting me live and that I should give my life special purpose and not grow up to be just an ordinary person. He set high standards for all of us.

Once aboard the *Bessie B*, we headed northwest past Sledge Island, a shelter island used by ships when the northwestern blew hard, and then into the unpredictable waters of the Bering Strait. The next morning found us headed around Cape Spencer into Port Clarence Bay and then Grantley Harbor.

Back in Teller everyone from grownups to my contemporaries were anxiously awaiting to see what the big city had done to their homegrown girl. I never wanted anyone to think that I was any different from any of them, or especially that I was handicapped. I wanted them to know that I was able to do things for myself. The word spread like wildfire that I came home from the big city with tons of toys, and there were comments such as, "Can you imagine anyone owning thirty-eight dolls and teddy bears?" There wasn't room in our house to put all the things I brought home, so Papa and Mama put some of them in the attic of the cold room, and the rest I divided up among my sisters and brothers. Besides, by that time, I was slowly phasing myself out of the "playing house stage." I began more and more to want to play outdoors and be active with the rest of the children. Toys and dolls were for recuperating from a hospital stay.

When I left the hospital for home, they gave me a wheelchair which I learned to use with great dexterity, and after two and a half years of manipulating the wheelchair, I became quite expert in maneuvering it. I was eight years old when I entered the first grade of school, which was the year before I got my first prosthesis and learned to walk. Walter Marx, the U.S. Commissioner's son, who was a big strong boy and in the eighth grade, would carry me to school. Papa or Mama would carry me when the weather wasn't too vicious. My brother David was only ten years old so could hardly be expected to do so. I remember on stormy days when the blizzard would blow so hard, you couldn't see the schoolhouse from our house which was only a hundred yards away. Papa would tie a hauser rope from our house to the schoolhouse as a guide for us to hang on to so we wouldn't lose each other in the storm.

Until being fitted with my first artificial limbs when I was nine years of age, I got around in a wheelchair or sometimes by crawling, using my hands. It was easier and quicker to get down on the floor and scoot than to maneuver the unwieldy wheelchair around the crowded house. I soon learned to figure out the easiest and quickest way to get from one place to another for something that I wanted. I don't remember ever being sad or feeling sorry for myself because I'd lost my legs. I think it was because of my parents' attitude. When I would be sitting at the window and watching the other kids playing, I'd laugh because they were laughing and having fun.

The druggist at the Nome Drug Store had a sister in Pennsylvania who was married to a man who worked at the Union Trust Company Bank in Pittsburgh. In a letter the druggist told his sister about me and the accident that I had had. He kept them informed of my progress and my eventual release from the hospital and return home. The pharmacist's sister and her husband were Edward C. Griggs and Matilda Griggs of Pittsburgh, and they had no children. About a year after I left the hospital, my father received a letter from Mr. and Mrs. Griggs with an offer to adopt me. They told him of all the opportunities they had to offer me to make my life a useful one through the educational facilities that would be available to me. Papa answered and thanked the man for his kindness and said, "But I can't let her go. She is one of us. I'm responsible for her being here, and I'll take care of her as long as I can."

In his next letter then Mr. Griggs asked if they could send me things that I needed and pay for my education when I got ready for high school. So Uncle Ed and Aunt Matilda, as they wished me to call them, sent things that I otherwise would not have had. After I entered the second grade, I began writing little letters to Uncle Ed and he would write me in return. He became like a second father to me, and all through my adolescent and adult years, I depended on him for moral support when I needed it. I still have some of the letters he wrote me on Union Trust Company Bank stationery.

Another great man in my life was Ralph Lomen, whose family had large business interests in northern Alaska. One day when I was eight years old he came to visit my father. While they sat and talked, he saw me look-ing out the window at the other kids playing outside. He said, "Albert, isn't it about time that Bessie had some legs so she can get out and enjoy herself with the rest of them?"

"We don't have the money, Ralph. I have written letters of inquiry to two companies in the States and the price is beyond my means."

"Go ahead and order them, and I will pay the bill," Ralph said.

"I can't accept charity, Ralph. It's my responsibility."

"It's not charity at all. Consider it an exchange of favors. Someday maybe you can do something for me or someone else who needs it. After all the things you've done for others, it's time someone did something for you."

When it came time to measure me for the prosthetics, Papa laid me, undressed, on a large sheet of butcher paper on the kitchen table and drew an outline of my body on it. Every few inches he would measure the circum-ference of my stumps and write on the paper, "four inches around" or "seven inches here" and so on.

Thus, in the summer of 1920, the mail boat finally arrived at Teller. My father brought home to our summer camp (across the harbor from Tell-er), two large crates. I watched as he uncrated two large boxes made of rough lumber. As he took the crates apart, he said to me, "Here are the legs that you will walk on." My feelings were mixed as I wondered what they would look like after all the butcher paper wrappings were finally taken away, re-vealing the contents. I thought to myself, "They look like heavy pieces of machinery."

As he unwrapped one leg and then the other, they began to look better. I said to myself, "These are the parts of my legs that have been missing for over three years!" The manufacturer of the limbs was the J. F. Rawley Com-pany of Chicago. They included a short letter saying they hoped I would be comfortable in these new limbs. But before I could try them on for a fitting, my father built in our girls' room two parallel bars, or railings, made of two twenty-two foot long wooden poles fastened to the floor at each end. He set them high enough so that I could hold on to them as I walked between.

Being that there was no hospital or clinic within a hundred miles, my father had already figured out that he would be my therapist. And he was a good one. He explained to me that as a team working together, it could be possible for me to walk on this unsightly pair of manufactured prostheses.

They were quite heavy as they were made mostly of steel, wood, and heavy leather, and the feet were of thick felt. He first set a chair at each end of the parallel bars. He sat me, a tiny nine year old, at one end, then helped me in the process of attaching the prostheses to my body via straps, lacings, and braces. He had done such a good job measuring my limbs that the fit was almost perfect.

Papa was patient as he told me to walk to him at the other end of the bars. For weeks upon weeks, I practiced walking back and forth day after day. I took some tumbles, but he always encouraged me by saying, "If at first you don't succeed, try, try again." Finally, one day there was only one bar to help me with balancing and walking. I guess we were both amazed and happy that I would finally one day actually walk. After several weeks of this Papa said, "Betty, you have no bars to help you today" for he had removed the last one.

I got up from my chair and bravely, with determination, walked to my father who sat in the other chair twenty-two feet away. And I did it without any assistance. At this point in time a thought came into my mind from the Bible when Jesus said to the old lame man, "Take up thy bed and walk." From that day on I never have used a cane or crutches. I've always walked on my "own two legs."

My new legs seemed a hindrance in some ways such as scrambling up a ladder, which I could do as quickly as a monkey without them. But soon I was just as rough and ready as the rest of the kids. We used to slide down snowbanks in the wintertime on a small piece of reindeer skin. My right leg had a bolt of steel to make a knee joint with a nut on the end to hold it together. Sometimes when I was playing, the nut would come unscrewed and the bolt would fall out. The lower half of my leg would go sliding down the snowy slope. I'd take off after it, find the nut and bolt, put it back together, and go on sliding or playing "King of the Mountain." There were times too when a strap would break while I was out playing, and I would make a quick repair—enough to get me home in order to do a better job. In the spring it was worse for it was disastrous if and when I got my feet wet. The glue they used to put the toe-part of the foot to the main foot (which was of heavy, solid grey felt) would get wet, and it took a lot of drying out to put it back together. After a couple of years of hard usage, the artificial legs that Mr. Lomen had bought were ruined by my playing in the wet snow. I was also outgrowing them.

I had been writing to Uncle Ed and Aunt Matilda since I was nine years old, which was my second year of school. My Uncle Ed was smart when he insisted to my father that I write to him at the beginning of my education even though I could write only a few simple lines at first. In that way he kept up with the progress I was making in school. This also gave him an idea of what made me tick. And, I suppose, to see if I would be worth sponsoring in the furthering of my education. He often complimented me on my interesting letters and said I seemed very "observant." Uncle Ed and Aunt Matilda never had children of their own, and I may as well have been their adopted child for they wanted to do so much for my welfare.

In one of my many letters to Uncle Ed, I mentioned the fact that in the wintertime we received wonderful radio reception at Teller, and some nights we could get just about any large city in the Northern Hemisphere; Russian, German, Japanese, English, and some large broadcasting stations in the United States came in clear as a bell. Every Saturday night, on our old battery-run Philco, we listened to the National Barn Dance from KNX Los Angeles. And we nearly always had a roomful of neighbors. I especially pointed out to my uncle that we could receive KDKA, a powerful Westing-house station in Pittsburgh, on certain nights. He was pretty excited about this news, and right away he wrote back and said he knew the people who owned the station. Since we received it so clear, he suggested, "Why not make an appointment to say a few words to you over the air?"

The appointment was made over a month in advance. One night in February 1929, we, at Teller, Alaska, sat ourselves down near the old Phil-co with the dial set on the spot where KDKA Pittsburgh would come in. Squeaks, squawks, and interferences of all kinds nearly deafened our ears! But we didn't give up. Papa was the engineer at the radio, and he tried every-thing to find the station. Nothing but interference! I guess, according to the powers that be, I was not supposed to hear my uncle's voice, let alone know him in person, which never happened.

4

Although Teller was more or less isolated in the years I was growing up, as was most of the northern half of Alaska from the mainstream of travel in the world, interesting and historical events always seemed to be happening there. During the early 1920s, while the Russian Revolution was still going on over in Siberia, refugees would cross the Bering Sea by open boat in summer or escape the encampment at Big Diomede Island, which was a possession of Russia and only a mere twenty-one miles across the Bering Strait from Cape Prince of Wales, practically next door to my hometown of Teller. Or they would trudge the forty miles over the frozen wastes of the Bering Strait in the wintertime. For some years my father was deputized by the U.S. Marshal's office at Nome, and when Russian refugees showed up at Teller, he would take them into custody and keep them at our house until they could be turned over to the federal marshal at Nome. He nearly always handcuffed them for we didn't know what kind of people they were or whether they were spies or saboteurs. One of my father's good friends, Pete Paulsen, went into Siberia to trade and was captured and held prisoner in 1918. His ship was lost in the ice and its cargo confiscated by the

Russians. Paulsen escaped two years later and returned to Nome. He bought a trading schooner in 1920 and named it the *Trader*, appropriately. He plied the northern Alaska waters from the Yukon River to Nome and on to Point Barrow for many years. I remember when he would come to our house to visit with my father, he would give each of us a fifty-cent piece and tell us to buy some candy. Sometimes he would come and give us a whole big bag of mixed hard candy and a whole-dozen packet of chewing gum for Mama. We felt like millionaires receiving those gifts.

Some of Papa's friends who operated trading ships along the Siberian coast turned to gunrunning and whiskey smuggling during the revolution and made big profits selling illegal weapons and ammunition and cheap liquor to both sides in the conflict. Some lost their ships and others their lives, but those who stopped at Teller on the way back to the U.S. had some real horror stories to tell about things they'd seen and heard about "on the other side of the Bering Strait." One captain told of sailing down the coast in his schooner and having people come out in boats or signal from the land to be picked up. Starving and terrified, entire communities came aboard and begged to be taken to the U.S. or China or at least be allowed the safety of being on a ship that flew the American flag.

The revolution caused a complete breakdown of government and commerce in Russia and for several years few of the trains traveled over the Trans-Siberian Railroad to Vladivostok, the principal port on the Siberian east coast, that normally would have carried goods to be transshipped to vessels serving the region northward to the Arctic. So by the early 1920s, about the only food and other supplies to reach the area came from the few small trading ships that came each year during the short summer when the Bering Sea was free of ice. The Natives, who knew how to live off the land and sea, did not suffer greatly, but the hordes of refugees, many being upper-class and professional people who had walked across Siberia to avoid being murdered by the Bolsheviks, starved and froze by the thousands.

A Captain Thomson, who lived at Nome for several years, told of losing his schooner and how he and his family just barely escaped with their lives. He traded along the Siberian Arctic coast for many years. On one of his expeditions he met and later married a young Russian woman who was the governess for the children of an official in a community on the Gulf of Anadyr. He did not bring her home to the United States at the end of the navigation seasons, but each year when the ice went out, he would stop and pick her up and take her with him on cruises into the far Arctic. With her knowledge of the language and dialects of the Chukchis and his reputation for fair play, they did well financially and the northern villagers would often save their furs and ivory until Thomson's ship returned because he generally paid a better price and his trade goods were of the highest quality. By 1923 they had two sons—Mikhail was five and Constantine about three.

By then the revolution was just about over and the victorious Reds were in command of practically everything. They had seized the naval vessels and were methodically visiting the towns and villages on the Siberian coast, executing everyone who'd been remotely connected with the old regime and seizing their possessions. With no wireless on his vessel, Captain Thomson was unaware of what was going on except what he heard by "mukluk telegraph"—the word-of-mouth communication system where bits of news and rumors were passed on from person to person.

Late in the summer returning south, driven from the Arctic by the advancing ice pack, the schooner became fogbound and becalmed for several days in a small bay on the Gulf of Anadyr, 300 and some miles across the Bering Sea from Nome. One morning a skin boat paddled by Chukchis loomed silently out of the surrounding mist and came alongside the vessel. The Natives came aboard and warned Thomson that a Russian gunboat manned by revolutionaries was on its way up the coast and was presently creeping through the fog just a few miles away. One Chukchi put a hand to his ear and said, "I can hear its engines now. They are coming here to kill you and steal your ship."

While his young wife Mary bundled up the children, Thomson launched a dory, put aboard a few cases of canned goods, some blankets, and an old sail, and then, with his family in the dory, abandoned the schooner with its valuable load of furs and trade goods. Helped by the current of an ebbing tide he took to the oars and rowed out of the bay. In later years Mikhail Thomson said he could remember little of the trip except hearing the engines of the gunboat and seeing its shadow going by in the fog a few yards away as they passed it in the channel leading to the sea. He could remember being cold and miserable and sipping condensed milk from holes punched in a can during the stormy voyage while his father rowed all the way to Nome.

❊   ❊   ❊

When I was small the Chukchis were still coming over from Siberia each summer to fish at Nook, our summer camp, and socialize with the Alaskan Eskimos, as they had done for ages. The Chukchis didn't seem to go any place but the Seward Peninsula, probably because it was the closest point to Siberia. They came mainly to Teller but hardly ever to Nome. It is the unwritten law of the Arctic to extend hospitality to friend and stranger alike, but when it came to dealing with the Chukchis, the traders from Alaska who went to the coastal villages in their schooners had to think twice before dispensing good will towards them. My mother used to tell my father to watch out for the Chukchi for he can lie and steal. My grandparents encountered the Chukchis in their great skin boats along the coastal walrus hunting areas of Alaska when my mother was a little girl. They are more tall and brawny than their Alaskan counterparts with a marked Mongolian strain. They inhabited the west and north coast of Siberia and were a wandering type of people. Once when my father made a trip to Siberia with a trader in the early 1900s, he told how the Chukchis came out to the vessel and clambered aboard without a word of greeting or an invitation from the skipper. They spoke an entirely different tongue from that of their fellow Arctic dwellers.

By the white man's standards my grandparents and their neighbors were considered awfully backward but smart in natural instincts. Compared to the Chukchis, however, even the poorest of our Eskimos dressed well, with reindeer parkas and sealskin boots and pants and whatever they needed for the winter. Most of the Chukchis we saw wore ragged skin and fur garments and castoff white men's clothing such as Melton jackets worn thin and faded with large holes in the elbows. Some of them wore a parka-type tunic, but without the hood, made of dried bird skins, such as murres and puffins, with all the feathers left on. Their footwear was very worn and made of some sort of tanned hide, like a moccasin. Some of the men wore cutoff rubber boots worn thin of sole and cut down like a slipper. The women wore calico parkas that were usually patched with every kind of cloth they could find or had on hand, even pieces of gunnysacks. They loved to trade our Natives for tobacco, tea, and bars of Fels Naptha soap in return for a martin or weasel skin. They said soap and tobacco were very scarce on the other side. We heard that a lot of what they wore had been stripped from victims of the revolution or dug from graveyards when the White Russians were driven from their homes or murdered by the Reds.

Some of the men's heads were shorn clean and other men wore their hair as my grandfather had, with a thick fringe around the head and the crown shaved like a monk's. Others had several strands of long hair hanging down the sides of their faces to their shoulders, such as I had seen in pictures of old Chinese men of the Ming era. Some men, as well as some of the women and girls, wore earrings. One man had a tiny silver bell, about an inch and a half high, sewn to his parka hood. They used metal trinkets in any fashion that entered their minds.

The Chukchis would usually show up in early July, soon after the Bering Strait was free of ice, in a small fleet of two or three *oomiaks*. We'd see their shabby old sails coming over the horizon, their great skin boats loaded down to the gunwales with young and old, camping equipment, and things to trade with the Alaskan Eskimos for necessities unavailable in Siberia.

Deep in the long ago, before *kabloona* (the white man) came to the North, there was much commerce between the Natives on both sides of the Bering Strait. Nook was the gathering place where the tribes would meet each summer to fish and barter and palaver. Each group had something that the other could use. The interior Indians would come too. They were quite a different people with a culture and habits distinct from the coastal Eskimos and Siberian Chukchi. They paddled down the rivers in canoes or walked through the mountains over ancient trails, carrying the meat and skins of land animals on their backs. Our people had fish and dried fish, seal skins and oil, whalebone, and whale oil. The stock-in-trade of the Chukchis was often commercial items that had come into their hands from Chinese traders who traveled up their coast in junks or overland by camel caravan in summer. The first metal objects possessed by Alaskan Eskimos came by this route—pots and pans, knives, fishhooks, and muzzleloading muskets.

The principal item of trade the Chukchi brought was a blue bead which was used as a form of money by the Chinese. The Chukchi women wore necklaces of blue Peking glass beads or milk-white Russian porcelain beads and both were popular trade goods in the mid-1800s. These bright, transparent beads were made of what was called Peking glass. The Chinese traders gave them to the Chukchis for their furs and ivory. They, in turn, swapped them to the Eskimos and Indians—a few beads for a rabbit or dried fish, maybe several for a seal skin or a poke of seal oil. Such beads could be dug up almost anywhere around Nook and Teller. We would find them eight or ten inches down in the sand and gravel as we played. I've never seen such a beautiful blue as was in those Peking glass beads, especially when you held them up and let the sun shine through them. My sister and I would string them and make bracelets for ourselves.

The Chukchi men who came to Nook when I was young wore earrings made of those Chinese beads. The faces of the women had blue tatoos on them, some had them on the cheeks and on the chin not unlike those of Mama and her mother, who both had blue chin tatoos. The chief of their tribe wore the remains of what had been a ship's officer's cap—just the headband and visor with his bald, shaven crown showing through the top. He wore the cap proudly and with authority. It set him apart from his people. It gave him an air of prestige.

The Chukchis ate differently than the Alaskan Eskimo. One thing they dearly loved was rotten seabirds. On their way over from Siberia, they'd stop at the Diomedes and King Island and trade with the Natives there for the puffins, kittiwakes, murres, and other birds that flocked there by the millions every year to nest in niches in the barren cliffs. Captured in nets and killed with sticks, nothing was done to preserve them. By the time the Chukchis got to Nook those long-dead birds would smell to high heaven. They'd just peel the skins off, feathers and all, boil and then devour them, while they all sat on the ground in a circle.

There was one little Chukchi girl about my age who I became quite friendly with, and every summer I looked forward to seeing her again. Though she spoke no word of English, and the Eskimo tongue that I knew could not even come close to her Siberian language, as with most children, we had little difficulty in understanding one another. I could not pronounce her Native Siberian name, but we called her "Twenty Cents" because she wore dangling earrings made of American silver ten cent pieces, one on each ear. Her ears were pierced as was the custom for most young Native girls of the Bering Strait. Twenty Cents and I would trade things back and forth. She wanted my Aunt Jemima rag doll for which she gave me a few blue glass beads, for that was all she had. She had not a semblance of a toy of any kind. I don't think she knew even what a toy was.

One time when the Siberians were camped at Nook, my father gave me a tin pipe tobacco box that he had just emptied and said, "Here, Bessie, use this for your sewing box." Those Velvet tobacco and Prince Albert tobacco tins in those days were made much like a lunch box, with two handles that folded down and a lid that opened on hinges. They were bright red or green with colorful pictures on the outside and bright gold inside. Long after they were emptied, they retained the fragrant smell of fine tobacco. That day I was proudly showing my brand new tin sewing box to Twenty Cents, and right away she wanted it. She began dickering as to what she would trade for it. She begged and pleaded, but I would not let her have my shiny new tobacco box. She let me know that she would give me all her beads for the tin box. She motioned for me to come over to her place to see what she had to give me for it. Her house was a ragged tent and her family's *oomiak* turned over on its side and propped up with their handmade paddle to make a shelter from the wind. They were camped a couple hundred yards from our house. My parents had warned us not to go in the Chukchi tents for they were dirty and full of lice. We were never allowed to go into anyone's house unless asked in by the head of the family, which could be either the mother or the father. It was an awfully hot day, perhaps seventy-five or eighty degrees, and it was beginning to get muggy that afternoon. Big black clouds began to hang over the mountaintops behind Teller Mission.

The Seward Peninsula seems to be a breeding ground for violent summer thunderstorms. One was waiting in those black clouds over to the northwest, and it broke on us just as we got to the Chukchi camp. The lightning flashed, the thunder rolled, and warm rain poured down in torrents. The Siberians were terribly afraid of electrical storms, and at the first flash and rumble Twenty Cents ran to her tent and crawled under the bedding, which consisted of deer hides and seal skins. Even after the storm had passed and the sun came out, she would not come out for fear the storm would start again.

✳   ✳   ✳

The writings in journals, discovered with the remains of the starved and frozen dead, relate the sufferings of human beings caught in Arctic misadventures. My own experience is proof enough to me of the unforgiving nature of the frigid Arctic. One can but guess at the details of mishaps that have befallen hunters, traders, miners, and explorers who set out in the North one day and were never seen or heard of again. The harsh climate, unpredictable weather, forbidding land, treacherous seas, and shifting ice packs can fatally trap even the hardy and experienced. The careless and the greenhorns, *Cheechakoes* we call them in the North, seldom have a chance, and few are granted another chance or the opportunity to make more than one mistake.

When I was just a small girl, one of the great tragedies of the Arctic happened just 500 miles from Teller on Wrangel Island, a chunk of rock lying about a hundred miles north of North Cape, Siberia, in the Chukchi Sea. We knew the sole survivor, Ada Blackjack, a full-blooded Eskimo woman who lived at Nome. Born Ada Delutuk in about 1899 in a Native village some miles east of Nome, she was educated in a mission school and married an Eskimo trapper, Jack Blackjack. Not long after their son Ben was born, her husband was drowned. Ben was a frail and sickly child. Being unable to support him, Ada put him in a mission home.

At this time the Canadian explorer Vilhjalmer Stefansson was organizing an expedition to take possession of Wrangel Island in the Arctic Ocean for the British Empire. He proposed that it be used as a steppingstone for future polar air routes. Since 1849 when Captain Henry Kellett, an Englishman searching for the Northwest Passage, claimed to have sighted Wrangel at a distant across the ice pack, ships from other nations, including the United States, Canada, and Russia, had put parties ashore and claimed the 3,400-square-mile island for their countries. In 1916 the czar of Russia informed the world that Wrangel Island was part of his empire, period! Stefansson ignored the claim, and after the Russian Revolution, he sent off the 1921 expedition to confirm possession for Great Britain.

He picked four men to do the job, one Canadian and three Americans. Allen Crawford, twenty, of Toronto, was appointed commander because he was a British subject, and Englishmen were putting up the money for the venture. He'd had no prior Arctic experience. Lorne Knight, twenty-eight, from McMinnville, Oregon, had been with Stefansson on a prior northern voyage. Frederick Maurer, twenty-nine, of Ohio, was a survivor of the shipwreck of Stefansson's *Karluk*, crushed by ice near Wrangel in 1914. And a nineteen-year-old Texan, Milton Galle, had been Stefansson's secretary.

Before departing Nome on the schooner *Silver Wave*, Ada was hired as a cook and to keep the men's fur and skin garments repaired. They didn't tell her much about the expedition, just that they were going to an island up north and intended to stay one winter. Her pay was to be $50 a month, and she hoped to earn enough to take Ben out of the mission home. She was told that an Eskimo family was to go along and that she would live with them. The Eskimo men were to hunt game to feed the expedition, and the women would do the cooking and sewing. When it came time to leave Nome, the family, if there ever was one, hadn't arrived, and the *Silver Wave* sailed without them.

Landing on Wrangel Island on the fifteenth of September, 1921, the young explorers signed a proclamation taking possession again for England and sent it back to Stefansson on the *Silver Wave*. The schooner returned to Nome, leaving the five to be picked up by a relief ship the following year.

It never arrived. Joe Bernard, master of the schooner *Teddy Bear*, tried to take his ship to Wrangel Island in 1922 to rescue the party but couldn't make it through the ice pack. The summer passed and with the approach of winter the situation was extremely serious. There was practically no food left, and wild game was almost nonexistent, notwithstanding the fact that Wrangel Island was the summer nesting ground of great flocks of snow geese. The geese must have been there, but no one seems to know why the explorers didn't shoot a few hundred for the coming winter. Perhaps by the time they'd given up hope of being rescued that year, the birds had departed for their wintering area in farmers' fields in the state of Washington. Or maybe the rich, oily flesh of geese was too much for the white men's stomachs.

Faced with starvation, in early January of 1923, Crawford and Knight tried to cross the frozen Chukchi Sea to the Siberian coast to look for help, but the ice was too rough. Knight became seriously ill with scurvy, and they returned to Wrangel two weeks later. On the twenty-eighth of January, Crawford, Maurer, and Galle took five of the sled dogs and set out again for Siberia. Knight, too sick and weak to travel, was left behind to be cared for by Ada Blackjack. The three men were never heard of again. "I don't know what happened to them," Ada said afterward. "Maybe they fell through the ice, or they could have been killed by a polar bear or Russians. I don't know."

She fed and nursed Lorne Knight, but he grew weaker. "It was a bad time," she said when she was interviewed many years afterward. "I don't like to talk about it." A .22 rifle and a shotgun had been left with her. "We needed food, but I didn't know anything about how to shoot. I was scared to death, but I had to learn." And Ada Blackjack did learn. She shot seals and ducks and snared foxes. She cooked eider ducks for broth to feed the sick man. Soon he could not even swallow. "He never complained," she said. "He knew he was going to die." She would read the Bible to him. One day she couldn't read because her eyes were so filled with tears. He asked her what was the matter, and she said she thought he was going to leave her, then she began to cry. He told her to hang on some way until the rescue ship got there. He died during the night of June 22, 1923.

She left Knight's body in the tent. Even if the ground had not been frozen too solidly to dig a grave, she couldn't have buried him because she was sick with scurvy herself. Several days after his death Ada managed to shoot a seal, but before she could get to it, a female polar bear with a cub made off with it. "I was getting pretty weak, almost starved to death, I guess," she later said. "All I had left was a little hardtack and some tea." Doubting her own survival, she wrote a note giving the circumstances of what had become of the others and how Knight had died. She never gave up hope of being rescued though she doubted that she could make it through another winter. "I think I would have died, too," she said. "It's hard to talk about what you feel when someone dies and you are alone. But the Lord took care of me."

The *Donaldson*, a ship hired by Stefansson, arrived on the nineteenth of August and found Ada. She'd been on Wrangel Island almost two years, the last two months alone with the dead man in the tent. Aboard the rescue ship were twelve Eskimos who Stefansson had sent along to found a permanent colony on the island. Also on the ship was Harold Noice, an adventurer who'd been hired to command the rescue expedition. After Lorne's body had been buried, Noice left with Ada, taking the diaries and documents of the other members of the expedition. The Eskimos who remained behind were later captured by Russians from the gunboat *Red October* that arrived in the summer of 1924 to take possession of the island for Soviet Russia. The colonists were taken to Vladivostok, where three of them died. They were later sent to China, the survivors finally reaching Seattle on a Japanese freighter. They returned to their homes in Alaska in 1925. The Russians established a colony of their own on Wrangel Island that apparently is still there.

Even after her rescue Ada Blackjack's troubles were not over. With her earnings from the expedition, she was able to take Ben from the mission, and they visited the United States. When she returned to Alaska, she married a George Johnson. They had a son named Billy, but the marriage soon broke up. Unable to earn a living, she put Billy in the Jesse Lee Home, a Methodist orphanage and school at Seward, Alaska, where I later went to high school. As part of my job at the school, I attended to Billy and the rest of the little ones of his age group. When Billy was nine, Ada took him out of the home, and in 1947 they went to Seattle where they lived for fourteen years. "I had a hard time in Seattle," she said. "There was no money, and I had to have surgery. The welfare people told me to get out and go to work. About the only work I could find was berry-picking in the summertime."

Worse, she was hurt very deeply by articles that Noice sold to a newspaper syndicate. First he pictured Ada as the heroine that she was, but in later stories he made slanderous statements about her that were entirely false. He even mutilated some of the pages in the Wrangel Island diaries and records so the true entries could not be read. Stefansson defended her, as did Knight's parents. "My mother was terribly hurt," her younger son Billy said, "but she knows that she did all in her power to save Knight's life. She stayed with his parents later and they knew the truth, too." Billy said that Noice wrote such things about his mother just for money. "He made good money from the articles, but then the story started dying out. We think he invented lies about her then to revive the story and get more money."

Stefansson's book about the expedition, *The Adventure of Wrangel Island*, was published in 1925. Although Ada had been promised royalties from the book, she never received a penny. In 1974 at age seventy-five and living in Anchorage, she said, "Stefansson was a good man." No one knows what ever happened to Harold Noice, but Alaskans and others who know the true story of Ada Blackjack say she is the greatest heroine in the history of the Arctic.

❊   ❊   ❊

My father had a German sea captain friend named Charlie Klengenberg who he hadn't seen in a few years. So in the year of 1924 on his way from San Francisco to the Arctic on his ship the *Maid of Orleans*, Captain Klengenberg stopped in at Teller and made a point to visit my father. They swapped stories and had coffee and ate smoked salmon and homemade bread as they lunched together at our house. We had not seen the *Maid of Orleans* every year as we did most of the other trading vessels. Her area of operations was the northern coast of Canada and the Arctic islands, where she visited the remote villages of the Kogmollik tribe along the ice-jammed channels of the Northwest Passage. Captain Klengenberg's home was at Coppermine Northwest Territory on Coronation Gulf, more than 1,000 miles east of Point Barrow. His wife was a Kogmollik Eskimo, and they had a large family. He would remain in the Arctic for several years at a time. When he was out of trade goods and supplies, he'd point the *Maid of Orleans* bowsprit westward, work her through the Beaufort Sea ice pack, round Point Barrow, and head south for Vancouver, British Columbia, Puget Sound, and San Francisco. He'd sell his furs and ivory, refit his ship, and load up for another long voyage. In the Arctic, the waters were open for navigation only about three months of every summer. The remainder of each year the *Maid of Orleans* would lie frozen-in at Coppermine in Coronation Gulf.

Returning to the North in 1924, Klengenberg stopped to visit my father and buy dried fish and smoked salmon from him and reindeer skins for clothing from the reindeer herders at Teller Mission. His first mate was a husky young Norwegian named Henry Larsen. About twenty-five years old, Larsen had spent most of his life at sea as a North Sea fisherman, a cadet in the Norwegian navy, and a mate on transatlantic liners. On sealing expeditions to frigid Greenland waters he'd acquired a love of the North and was uncomfortable elsewhere. Blonde and blue-eyed, he was a true Norseman. Henry Larsen fell in love with my sister Sarah, who was sixteen then, and wanted to marry her. Papa said, "No, my girls can't marry until they're eighteen, and then only if the man will stay here with them."

That rule put an end to a lot of love-at-first-sight situations that came our way when we were approaching maturity. There was a good reason for it. Half-blood girls are often quite attractive, especially in the eyes of virile young men far away from home. My parents were well aware of what usually happened to such marriages. Either the girl was abandoned when the husband decided to return to his home, or if he took her back to the States, the Native wife was often deserted with a child or two and no friends or means of support in an environment she did not understand. The result was usually tragic—hungry children with a mother hanging around the skid rows of seaport cities. Mama and Papa weren't about to let it happen to us. It caused us a few minor heartbreaks, but we were better for it.

Another practice that began with the whalers, explorers, and traders, was to anchor off a village, pick up a few young Native girls and take them away on extended cruises as temporary wives. Many were never seen again, having died or been dumped off in foreign ports. Those that were brought back when the vessels were homeward bound were usually pregnant, infected with venereal diseases, or both. Crews of fishing boats, tugs, and even ocean freighters would pick up footloose girls at their first port of call in Alaska and keep them aboard until the ship was ready to return to its home port. For many such Native girls, it was their only opportunity to have a few days of decent food, a warm, clean place to sleep, a new dress or pair of shoes, or a little spending money.

Had any of us girls fallen by the wayside, it would not have been because we hadn't been warned against it. When ships anchored in Grantley Harbor, the officers always came to visit my father because he was well known from Nome to Barrow and greatly respected for his knowledge of the North. While the captains, mates, and engineers sat and talked to Papa, the younger sailors would make eyes at us. A lot of them had the idea that it was always open season as far as Alaskan girls were concerned. But they were wrong about the Bernhardts' daughters. Mama really patrolled us! If anyone got out of her sight when there was a ship in the harbor, she came looking. She trusted nobody, male or female!

But we were only human, and blooming feminine instincts were easily fired by the presence of good-looking, clean-cut young men. We used to resent the caution and distrust of our parents, but recalling some girlfriends who were not so carefully guarded, we were the fortunate ones. In nearly every seaport about the time of the breakup every spring, a fair-skinned baby or two could be expected to be born as the result of shore leave granted to seamen during the previous summer.

In 1926 Mama really had her hands full keeping us out of mischief. The dirigible *Norge*, after a flight over the North Pole from Spitsbergen, Norway, landed and then collapsed on the ice of Grantley Harbor at Teller. No one was injured, but for weeks afterward Teller was full of handsome European strangers. With four girls of the perilous age, it was impossible for our mother to be everywhere and see everything going on all the time. I was only fourteen but certainly old enough to bear watching.

About a month before the flight, my father talked to a traveler who said that a dirigible was going to fly over the North Pole from Spitsbergen to Nome, under the command of Roald Amundsen, the famous Arctic explorer and discoverer of the South Pole.

"Why, Amundsen is a good friend of mine," Papa said. "I met him back in '06 when he went through here in the *Gjoa* after coming through the Northwest Passage. I saw him in 1920, too, when he sailed the *Maud* over the top of Siberia. He used to come to my house for Mama's homemade bread, coffee, and smoked salmon. When are they going to start?"

"Supposed to be early in May," the traveler said.

Raold Amundson, captain of *Norge*, Teller, 1926.

"I hope I have a chance to see him again. We'll have to keep our eyes open. Teller is on a direct line between the Pole and Nome. Maybe they will fly right over."

The airship *Norge* had been built in Italy for the Norwegians, and the expedition would actually start in Rome. Amundsen was the commander, but the actual flying of the airship would be done by the Italian aviator, Colonel Umberto Nobile, and a crew of his countrymen. There would be other Norwegians aboard as well as the American sportsman and explorer Lincoln Ellsworth.

Commander Nobile, diri-
gible *Norge*, Teller, 1926.
Note on photo reads, "The
commander of the Norge.
the ˙Mascotte. and the
˙Fascio of Rome: on the
frontal part of the disassembled cabin. –26 6 . . .
May 1926."

    Papa told us about the proposed flight, but we didn't think too much
about it. We'd never even seen an automobile or an airplane, except in pictures, so we had no idea what a dirigible was. One evening a few weeks
later—it was May 13, 1926—Sarah was doing the supper dishes, and she
looked out the window toward the north and saw what she thought was an
odd-looking cloud above the Lost River Mountains. It was dark grey and
shaped like an egg. She called to Papa, "Look at that funny dark cloud over
there. I wonder what it means?"

Every different kind of cloud had a meaning for my father. He was quite an expert at predicting the weather, as most sailing ship men were, and you could depend upon his observations. He looked out the window for a few minutes, then said, "That is a funny cloud. It could almost be a tornado." We all began to be a bit concerned, including Mama. Everyone was watching the "cloud," and it seemed to be getting bigger by the minute. Papa walked the floor a bit, as he always did when he was thinking. When he looked again the cloud was quite a bit larger and closer. "I'm going to go see Henry Müller," he said.

Müller was a neighbor and one of several other Germans who lived at Teller. Most were married to Eskimo women and were close friends. So Papa walked down the street to Müller's, and we saw them standing looking out toward the strange-looking cloud. Then Mama said in Eskimo, "I'm going out and see what's up."

Just about the whole town had gathered outside by then—maybe a dozen men and boys, several wives, and lots of kids. They were all looking out over Port Clarence Bay, and that "thing" was getting bigger and bigger all the time.

"That's not a cloud."

"It's a flying whale!"

Soon we could hear the hum of motors.

Finally Papa said, "It's the airship! It's Amundsen."

The whole town was out on the ice—storekeepers left stores unattended with the doors wide open. Everyone dropped what they were doing to investigate the strange sight. All eyes were focused in the northwestern sky. Of course we did not realize at the time that this was a once-in-a-lifetime event.

The sound got louder and the dirigible got bigger until we could read the name *Norge* on it and see the gondola and engines hanging underneath. The closer it got, the lighter became its color—first a charcoal gray, then silvery. You would have thought the world was coming to an end because the kids were all so scared. Anne and Gussie and I always were quite close, and we hung onto each other and to Mama in our fear and excitement. As the *Norge* passed over Teller, the sound got almost unbearable, and we put our hands over our delicate ears to shut out the noise. We weren't used to all that racket. In the quiet life we lived up there the loudest sounds we ever heard were outboard motor noise and steamer whistles.

Then we three girls panicked and ran home as fast as we could, me taking up the rear on my wooden legs. We hid in the clothes closet. I was the oldest of the three and finally, when the sound began to fade away, I said, "We can't keep hiding here, let's go see what's going on." So with curiosity overcoming fright, we went out again and down onto the rim of the ice on Grantley Harbor where everybody else was.

The first and only lighter-than-air craft to fly over the top of the world and its landing at my little hometown surely put Teller, Alaska, on the map. It was the first lighter-than-air craft to make a successful flight over the North Pole. Later Amundsen told Papa they had a magnetic compass in the gondola, and it became erratic as they neared the magnetic pole. They found out that the north geographic pole and the north magnetic pole do not lie at the same place on this earth as the lay person would surmise. The north magnetic pole lies almost 1,400 miles away from true geographic north.

The engines of the airship were idling, and the propellers just barely turning over. Moving slowly, the dirigible was dropping down and circling low enough that we could see people peering down at us. Then a window opened, and we heard a voice up there in the sky, speaking slowly and distinctly through a megaphone.

"We are going to try to make a landing on the ice."

"That's Amundsen!" Papa said.

"We will drop our mooring ropes, and I want every able-bodied man and boy to come out and grab a hold of them and hang on!"

"Let's go, fellows! We've got orders from above," Papa said.

While they were running out onto the ice to catch the ropes, the wind came up and the *Norge* circled again out over Port Clarence. It was coming back when something fluttered down from the gondola. At that distance it looked to be only about an inch square, and we thought it was a piece of paper. It landed on the ice between Teller and Nook, and my father said to my brother, "Dave, run over and see what that thing is."

A bunch of boys raced out, but David got there first, picked it up, and brought it back to shore where the crowd had gathered. It was an aluminum door from the gondola. Later, when Papa tried to give it back, Amundsen said to keep it. We had it for many years until Papa gave it to the Alaska museum at Juneau.

The wind, which had been blustery all day, died down and the dirigible slowly came down. Helium was released, and the *Norge* settled down

Dirigible *Norge* landing, Teller, Alaska, 1926.

Deflating *Norge*, Teller, 1926.

on the ice. The *Norge* had seventy-two helium tanks, thirty-six on each side, built into the framework and connected by aluminum catwalks. Helium is a colorless, odorless gas that is lighter than air. It is nearly twice as heavy as hydrogen, but it has 92% more of the lifting power of hydrogen. Its inertness makes it safer to use in balloons, blimps, and dirigibles than the highly explosive hydrogen. Several times the *Norge* almost got away from the men as they pulled down on the mooring ropes. Later, some said that they were lifted off their feet as they pulled on the ropes and had to let go to keep from being hoisted aloft. When they got to within eighty or a hundred feet of the beach, they could pull the *Norge* no further because of the rough ice piled up against the shore. Boat anchors were put out, one at the bow and one at the stern, to keep the airship from drifting. The crew disembarked. Amundsen wore an old parka, and Colonel Nobile was dressed in his high-ranking military uniform with shiny brass buttons, beribboned medals, and knee-high shiny black leather boots. In his arms the Italian officer carried an excited and trembling tiny white terrier. He held her close to protect her from the biting cold, calling her "Titina" and speaking softly in Italian to calm her nervousness. Titina had on a coat of wool tailored to her size. Amundsen's narrow face and long thin nose gave him the appearance of an eagle or a hawk. He and Papa shook hands and said a few words in German. Then my father asked, "You're here and you made it over the pole?"

"Yeah, you bet we did."

"I heard you were going to land at Nome."

"We were scheduled to, but we were getting low on fuel. We made the 2000 miles from Spitsbergen to Barrow in only 46 hours. Then we ran into headwinds, and it took 26 hours to come the last 500 miles. We're lucky to even be here."

The wind began to blow in gusts harder than ever. The dirigible bucked and plunged at the end of the ropes, as if the whale it so resembled was trying to free itself of harpoon lines. Suddenly it was pushed by a tremendous gust, smashed down, and rolled over onto the ice. As it struck, it made a noise as if a million tin cans were rattling around inside as the metal girders and catwalks collapsed. The noise was deafening, like a giant chivaree! As we girls stood in awe of such a huge hulk being reduced to a heap of twisted metal framework, the silver cover fabric draping grotesquely, our first thought was that it might explode. Frightened and confused over the whole calamitous event unfolding before our eyes, we three girls again scrambled for the comforting confinement of our old house. After the noise had subsided and the excitement calmed down, it seemed obvious that the airship was a complete wreck, the whole 320 feet of it. After an historic 72 hour flight over 2,700 miles of treacherous and vast icecaps at the top of the world, they should come to this end? We had a feeling of compassion for the crew who were scrambling around in a state of confusion but were nonetheless happy to be alive.

One member of the crew, whom we later learned was foreman rigger Renato Alesandrini, had gone back aboard for something, and when the airship collapsed, he was caught inside. But he had a knife and was able to cut his way through and free himself without injury. To us little girls it was complete chaos, with groups of people here and there speaking Norwegian, Italian, French, and some German, with a little English thrown in. After awhile the crew began passing out fresh oranges direct from sunny Italy and transported over the North Pole. We could never have gotten them fresher than that—they had been grown and picked in faraway Italy only a few days earlier. They were sweet and juicy. Soon came more goodies—wonderful cookies from Norway and Sweden and the best chocolate bars you ever tasted, which had come from Europe. It was just like Christmas all over again. That very same evening there were toasts of Italian wine and champagne at the Waldhelm's and Peterson's stores.

I said to the other girls, "Oh, now how is that poor man going to get back to Italy?" as Colonel Nobile walked by.

Nobile turned and said in fine English, "Don't you worry, little girl. I'll get home all right."

Besides Amundsen, Nobile, and Ellsworth, there were fourteen others aboard the *Norge*. Several were Norwegians, two were Swedes, and there was one little Frenchman no more than five feet tall. The rest were Italians. After the landing and before the crash, we noticed that the Norwegians and Swedes kept to themselves and that the Italians stayed at Waldhelm's Store. Amundsen told my father that he and Nobile were not on speaking terms, having quarreled throughout the flight about who was the commander of the expedition. Because he had organized the expedition and raised the money for it, Amundsen assumed that he was in complete charge. He felt that Nobile and the others were merely a hired crew whose job was to fly the airship wherever he directed. In addition, the explorer was very vain and self-assured, not inclined to share glory with anyone.

It would probably have been impossible for there to have not been a personality clash between the two. Umberto Nobile, famous in his own right as an airship designer and the world's foremost dirigible pilot, was an idol of the Italian people. Vain himself, he was not a person to play second fiddle to anyone, not even to the man who'd been first to navigate the Northwest Passage and first to reach the South Pole. His logic, considered faulty by many, was that as chief pilot, he was responsible for the navigation and a safe flight. He felt he should be the overall commander. And though the *Norge* was owned by the Norwegians, it had been designed and built by Italians in their own land. Had it not been for Nobile and his countrymen, he reasoned, there would have been no airship and therefore no polar flight could have been accomplished. The honor should be his and Italy's. By such reasoning, Lincoln Ellsworth could also have laid claim to the leadership. The wealthy son of an American millionaire, he'd put up most of the money to buy the dirigible and finance the expedition. Had it not been for him there certainly would have been no flight. But as a devoted admirer of Amundsen, Ellsworth kept in the background and had little to say. The principals, all dead now, faded into history, but the dispute never has been settled. There were two stores in town, Peterson's and Waldhelm's. Each owned a general store and had living quarters upstairs for the use of travelers. Amundsen and the other Norwegians and the Swedes stayed at Peterson's. Nobile and his Italian crewmen and the Frenchman took rooms at Waldhelm's. Publicly, Papa didn't take one side or the other, but I heard him tell my mother, "Amundsen isn't an easy fellow to get along with at best, but I think he's right. He told me that if he'd trusted Nobile's navigation, they would have never even made it to the North Pole and would be down on the ice pack somewhere now. Amundsen said he caught three bad mistakes that Nobile made, so after that he plotted his own courses and made the crew steer them."

"You think Amundsen is the boss then?"

"You bet he is the boss. It's just like with a ship—the owner is the boss, and the captain and crew do what they're told and no monkey business about it."

But Papa appreciated the Italian's point of view, too, even though he disagreed with it. "Something like this happens sooner or later in isolated places," Papa used to say about the feud. "You get to know each other too well and get on each other's nerves, then something like this comes and whenever there's glory or distinction to be shared by more than one in command, there's bound to be friction and differences."

He didn't let his longtime friendship with Amundsen interfere with his passing the time of day with Colonel Nobile whenever they met. During his stay in Teller, Amundsen came to our house to talk with my father. Nobile never did, although he took a walk past our place every morning carrying Titina. We could tell when he was coming and followed his progress up the street just by listening to the clamor of the village dogs. Big ravenous malemutes, chained behind their owners' houses, they'd have gobbled up poor little Titina in one gulp had she gotten within reach.

A slender man, dark-eyed and clean-shaven, the colonel was a striking figure in his military uniform and boots, especially when compared to the weather-beaten Amundsen with his grizzled handlebar mustache and worn, rumpled Arctic clothing. We girls always found the handsome Italian to be warm and friendly, a much easier person to like than his aloof adversary. The Norwegian never smiled, and his blue eyes seemed to reflect all the years they'd looked upon the Arctic ice packs and the snowy mountains of Antarctica.

A few days after the crash Amundsen and Ellsworth hired a dog team and sled to take them to Nome. When they got there, hardly anyone would speak to them. Nome had been let down. Ever since word was first received of the proposed flight, the town had been preparing for the arrival of the dirigible. Reporters, photographers, and newsreel men were flown in via Fairbanks to await the big event. This would really put Nome on the map. A landing area was laid out, a mooring mast erected, and the town decorated in honor of the polar flyers. "Rome to Nome" banners were strung across the narrow main street, and all the flags were hung out. When news of the landing at Teller reached Nome, the decorations were torn down and the welcoming committee was disbanded. Completely overlooking the uncontrollable weather factors that had forced the airship back to earth short of its intended goal, the citizens of Nome were piqued and resentful because little who-ever-heard-of-Teller had gotten all the publicity. Where formerly we were said to be seventy-five miles northwest of Nome, now Nome was seventy-five miles southeast of Teller.

Until the crash of the *Norge*, hardly anyone but sea captains even knew that Teller existed. Then, overnight, the whole world was hearing about us on the radio, and only because the airship lacked the few gallons of fuel needed to get to Nome. While circling to land, a wireless message had been sent saying they were coming down on Grantley Harbor. Immediately the

First airplane to arrive at Teller, Joe Crosson, pilot, 1926.

newsmen who'd been waiting at Nome and Fairbanks took to the sky in chartered airplanes and headed for the scene. In those early days of Alaska flying, and with the airplanes that they had, the 550-mile hop from Fairbanks to the Bering Sea was almost as hazardous as the *Norge's* flight from Spitsbergen, on the other side of the world, to Teller, Alaska, had been.

The first to arrive was a single-engine biplane with a wooden propeller, piloted by the pioneer bush pilot, Joe Crosson. He had a newsreel cameraman aboard from *Pathe News*. It was the first airplane that any of us had seen, but in the days that followed airplanes became quite common. After photographing the wreckage with everyone in Teller standing around it, and taking shots of Amundsen and the crew and Nobile with Titina, Joe and the newsreel man roared off for the return to Fairbanks. Soon other airplanes landed with reporters and cameramen. We were interviewed and photographed and later saw our pictures in Seattle newspapers that were flown in by Joe Crosson on a later trip from Fairbanks. One picture, captioned, "Eskimos at Teller looking at the wreckage of the *Norge*" shows Gussie, Anne, and me, with our backs to the camera, staring at the crashed airship.

The ice in Grantley Harbor normally broke up and went out about the middle of June, so anything that was to be salvaged of the dirigible had to be taken to shore immediately because the thaw had already set in. Every day the crew would go down and work at dismantling the twisted girders, crating the engines and other equipment, and dragging everything up onto solid land. Anything too badly damaged to be worth shipping back to Italy was given to whomever wanted it. The fabric cover was ripped off and thrown aside. It was quickly latched onto by the women and girls, and soon everyone in town it seemed was wearing garments made of airship silk.

The airship was covered with three layers of fabric, each of a different material. The outer ply was a tough, silvery material, the second was of brownish oiled silk, and the inner layer was like very tightly woven linen. We kept only the brown oiled silk material. It was quite dark to begin with, but someone discovered that the oil could be soaked out with kerosene or vinegar. This took away most of the brown color, and it came out a beautiful light creamy yellow. It was easy to sew, and we made dresses, blouses, and underthings. We were really the ladies, all decked out in silk. I still have a blouse that I made from that airship silk, and it's just as good as new. It still fits me, and I wear it occasionally. I like to think that I have a blouse that flew over the North Pole!

I had always believed that my blouse and the gondola door were probably the only things remaining from the flight of the *Norge*. One day recently, however, I read an article by Stanton Patty, a Seattle newspaperman, about a retired Coast Guard man who owns a bottle of fruit juice that came over on the dirigible. Dale McCulloch was a twenty-three year old radioman on the Coast Guard cutter *Bear* when he and a shipmate came ashore at Teller a few weeks after the flight and the crash. Going into one of the stores, they saw two unusual bottles in a showcase and asked the storekeeper what they were.

"Oh, that's wine that came over the Pole with Amundsen."

"How much do you want for it?"

"Thirty-five cents a bottle."

They bought both bottles, and his buddy opened his and drank it. He said it tasted like raspberry wine, but the label indicated it was fruit juice. McCulloch has saved his and planned to open it on his fiftieth wedding anniversary on New Year's Day of 1975. However, then he changed his mind and thought that it should go to a museum.

I don't recall that particular incident, but I do remember my father having brandy with Amundsen and that some of the Italian flyers were sharing wine with their new American friends. We had some great times while those European flyers were at Teller. Of course, we always had a dance and

This page and facing page: crating *Norge* to ship back to Italy.

entertained visitors whenever a ship was in the harbor and the crew was ashore, but usually they'd be gone after a day or two. The crew of the dirigible were in Teller for about a month, and we made the most of it. Lincoln Ellsworth had heard about how I had lost my legs when I was six years old. He told my brother David, as he handed him a box of expensive Norwegian chocolates, "Give this to your sick sister."

The dances would be held at The Woodbine, a big empty warehouse owned by Jimmy LaPierre, a jolly, round, plump French bachelor and a good friend to everyone. He was the young people's favorite person in our hometown. He had a cozy little house situated between our house and the Müllers, who were the two poorest families with the most kids. He was our everyday Santa Claus, Godfather, Uncle, and just about any other affectionate name you could think of. For a bachelor, he was crazy about children and drew them like a magnet. They in turn had great admiration for him. He always had homemade cake or cookies or wonderful ice cream on hand to pass around. We used to love to spend an hour or so in his warm cozy house, and he was always so full of interesting conversation. He especially showed tenderness towards my younger sister Anne. He always called her his *tingmee-ak*, which meant "little bird."

Jimmy would play his fiddle for the dances, Papa and my brother David would play their accordions, and Mr. Tweet and his sons would play harmonicas. Also Mr. Tweet would "rattle the bones" with a couple of sticks or click two spoons together to keep the beat for the music. David had an old guitar that he would strum when he wasn't playing accordion. Sometimes the dances would be to the music of a windup phonograph. There'd be schottisches, polkas, square dances, Virginia reels, and all the other old-time dances.

There was always the request for Papa to play the "Blue Danube" waltz on his accordion. Besides my memories of the music and the faces of happy people enjoying themselves and one another, I can still hear the sound of the dancers' feet shuffling the cornmeal that had been sprinkled on the splintery warehouse floor to counteract some of the roughness. Sometimes girls would dance with girls while the boys stood by, too shy to ask. But there was no lack of courage as far as the Norwegians and Italians were concerned. When the flyers would ask the older girls and women to dance, we younger ones would blush at the thought of being held close by a handsome stranger from the other side of the world.

I recall several of them well: Natale Cecioni, the chief mechanic; Renato Alesandrini, who'd had to cut his way out of the wrecked *Norge*; Ettore

Vincenzo Pamella and Attilio Caratti, *Norge* crew, Teller, 1926.

Arduino; Attilio Caratti; and Vincenzo Pamella. Pamella fell in love with my sister Sarah, whom Henry Larsen, the mate of the *Maid of Orleans*, had wanted to marry. She was a very attractive girl, and someone was always proposing to her. And so did Vincenzo Pamella. "I want to marry her and take her back to Italy," he told my parents. Sarah was seventeen—not old enough by Papa's rules to marry, so he put his foot down about her going off to Italy. "If you marry her, you must stay here."

Pamella loved his country and had a deep sense of loyalty to his commanding officer. "Colonel Nobile is going to design and build another airship to fly over the North Pole again, this time for Italy, and he will need me," he said. "Maybe next year, or the year after that, we will come back here again. Then I shall marry her and stay."

Sarah was in love with Vincenzo, too. He was a very nice-looking, clean-cut fellow who had a nice smile. He had beautiful blonde curly hair and the bluest eyes you ever saw. He was a blonde Italian! When it came time for them to leave, we all especially hated to see Vincenzo go; he was such a pleasant person. But he promised that he'd be back again some day, and we were sure he'd keep his promise, if only just for Sarah. In June the crew of the *Norge* left for Nome to catch the steamer *Victoria* to Seattle and home.

In 1928 two years after the *Norge* had made the historic flight over the North Pole and landed at my hometown of Teller, we heard that Colonel

Umberto Nobile had become a general and designed and built a new dirigible as Vincenzo Pamella had told us he would do. Nobile planned another flight over the top of the world. The airship was named the *Italia*, and the venture was sponsored entirely by the Italian government. Most of the crew would be those who'd been with Nobile on the *Norge*. The plan was to fly from Spitsbergen to the Pole, then back to Spitsbergen, but we all, and especially Sarah who'd been mooning about the handsome Vincenzo Pamella for the past two years, hoped they'd change their minds and come to Alaska again.

As we were to learn later, had the dirigible continued on to North America, the flight would probably have been successful. It wasn't. After circling the vicinity of the North Pole, the *Italia* turned back toward Spitsbergen but encountered strong headwinds that blew her off course. Finally, short of engine fuel, she was forced down onto the ice pack far to the northeast of her goal in a crash landing that tore off part of the gondola. Ten of the crew, including Nobile and his dog Titina, were thrown or jumped from the *Italia* on impact and were seriously injured. One man was instantly killed when an engine crushed him. Lightened of the weight of the ten men and the gondola, the out-of-control dirigible was lifted by its internal hydrogen bags back into the sky and blown back toward the Pole again, carrying the remaining six crew members, most of whom we'd known. Pamella, one of those thrown clear in the crash of the gondola, escaped injury. Later though, he and several other survivors died of starvation and exposure while crossing the ice pack trying to reach Siberia.

Upon learning that the *Italia* was missing, Roald Amundsen put aside his bitterness toward Nobile, chartered a French seaplane, and with a crew of Frenchmen took off from Tromso, Norway, to search for the Italians. They were never heard from again. Some weeks later a pontoon from their seaplane was found floating in the Arctic Ocean west of Norway.

Nobile, who'd been badly injured in the crash, and Titina his terrier mascot were rescued by a Swedish air force pilot who got drunk and wrecked his plane while making a second landing to pick up other members of the marooned expedition. The survivors, after spending seven days on the drifting ice, were found by a Russian icebreaker.

Though we never saw these beautiful European people again, they left a warmness in our hearts that we would never forget.

5

The last summer that my father worked at hauling freight to the Tin City mine was 1918, the summer before the fall of my accident. Taking care of seven children was just too much for Mama to handle with help only from the older ones, along with fishing, berry-picking, preparing skins, sewing, and all her other duties. Papa's presence at home was more important than the cash he earned at the mines.

It was over fifty miles from Nook to Tin City, and if anything happened while he was there, it took too long to get home—a two-day walk down the beach. It would have been quicker to go by sea, but it was just too dangerous to travel to Tin City by small boat because beyond Point Spencer was the open Bering Strait with no protection from westerly or southerly winds. There were no inlets along the way where one could run for shelter in case of a sudden blow. All the way to Cape Prince of Wales it was one long, straight stretch of treacherous beach toward which the never-ending rollers came sweeping in from the ocean to trip on the offshore shallows, tumble, and break their backs in booming, windblown surf. So to get to Tin City, or back to Teller, you either walked, rode horseback, or went by a horse team and wagon that the company owned.

We had a telephone that was a one-party line that ran from the Tin City mines to Nook. It was the old-fashioned kind where you cranked the handle to make it ring at the other end. Once, when my father was at Tin City, we got to roughhousing and a rifle was knocked from the gun rack and cut a deep gash in Mary's scalp. I can still see my mother, after she got the blood stopped, going to the phone, turning the crank, and asking the person at the tin mine to have Albert (she called him "Albut") come home because one of the girls had been hurt. He called back, and a couple of days later he was there. With seven lively kids, too many things could happen while he was away.

Papa had a graphite mine up the Tuksuk River which he and Tommy worked on part of the time. I remember how they used to have several gunnysacks ready for Captain Pederson when he stopped by in the fall to pick up Papa's barrels of salmon for the San Francisco markets. After quitting the tin mines, Papa worked for several seasons on his own near the Rice's gold mine up Sunset Creek. The diggings were only about six miles from home, on the other side of Grantley Harbor. By 1930, most of the worthwhile deposits of gold in the area had been worked out and the mines shut down. From then on we had to live off the land. It wasn't too difficult if a person had a capacity for lots of hard work, and both of our parents certainly had that. Still, it wasn't as easy to do as it had been in the early years of their marriage when they were much younger and there weren't so many young mouths to feed. In about 1920, a law was passed that took away the aboriginal rights of white men who were married to Native women. After that Papa and several of the neighbor men could no longer legally hunt, trap, and fish without regard to season or region. The restriction didn't bother us too much because the laws specifically stated that it was lawful to kill game out of season when in need of food. And what family in the North wasn't always in need of food?

Papa would often come home from the trap line in the wintertime with his moustache and eyelashes fringed in frost. He would stomp his feet as he came in the door "to get the circulation going," and then take off his heavy fur clothes, muskrat parka, fur cap with ear flaps, mukluks, sealskin pants, and fur mitts. Sometimes he would get stormbound at his trap line cabin up the Tuksuk for several days, and Mama would worry about him. It wouldn't have been so bad if he could have just phoned us and said, "The weather up here is not fit for an animal to be out in," but we just had to wait and worry. By the grace of God and thanks to his trusty dog team, he always made it home. I can remember many times when Mama would walk the floor when a blizzard came up by the time darkness fell, and Papa had not yet come home. She seemed instinctively to know that he was safe in his cabin and would be home as soon as the weather permitted. But they both knew that that was part of the ordeal of making a living in that "god-forsaken" country, as I have heard it called many times. Living in the Far North had many discomforts, but in many ways it was sweet and there were compensations.

Whenever the vicious winter storms kept my father home from his trap lines, he did what he enjoyed most to do for us, and that was to bake pies or make doughnuts. I still think to this day that he made the most delicious apple pies that anyone ever baked, and the doughnuts he made were out of this world. Another specialty that my father made often in the wintertime was corn fritters. He still remembered the recipe his mother made back in the Old Country. We ate them hot from the iron kettle with syrup or molasses.

Another thing that he liked to do for us was play his accordion. He loved music, and he wanted us to appreciate it too. He played all the Strauss waltzes, German polkas, and schottisches, mostly music from the Old Country. Sometimes he would say, "Gussie, you and Albert get up and dance while I play a waltz," and he would play "The Blue Danube," "Tales from the Vienna Woods," or "Wiener Blut," just to name a few.

Where fish and meat were concerned, hunger was not a problem at Teller unless a person was downright lazy, a drinker, or both. The wildlife that had been so decimated by the whalers, sealers, and the gold rush hordes had come back dramatically since the turn of the century. All one needed was a rifle and ammunition or traps or snares to take squirrels and rabbits, ptarmigan, emperor geese, ducks, and other waterfowl. The reindeer herds had multiplied greatly, too. They were the private property of individuals, families, and the Lomen Reindeer Company, but one could always trade something for a carcass—or perhaps even poach an unbranded animal now and then.

While the Natives could and did live on meat or fish alone, the eating habits of the white man, which he passed on to his offspring, made it imperative that he have a source of cash or something of value to sell or trade for the flour, sugar, salt, beans, rice, and canned goods; the kerosene and gasoline to light his house and run his boat; the coal to feed his fires; and all the other items such as tobacco and matches, guns and ammunition that were necessary to adapt the basic Arctic environment to the minimum that his civilized tastes required.

After the mining dwindled down, Papa managed to earn money one way or another. After the freeze-up and the snows came, he would go out and mark the winter trails for the Alaska Road Commission. He used red flags that were fastened to five-foot wooden laths. We all pitched in to point the stakes and tack the flags onto them. Even the youngest ones had a hand in this task. In the spring after the ice went out, Papa would sound the channel and rechart the passage between Port Clarence and Grantley Harbor and set marker buoys for the government so ships entering and leaving would not run aground. He also tended the lighthouse at Nook, which marked the narrowest point in the channel between Nook and Teller. In the summer, he had his business of ferrying people and supplies on their way from Teller to Tin City, which was the only route of getting supplies overland to the tin mines. He was deputized as a U.S. Marshal for many years in the early part of the century. He also was an outspoken member of the school board for more years than anyone else at Teller. He built his own boats, of which some were dories, and he also built some made to order for people in the general area or from Nome. He made his own nets for fishing salmon or herring or to seine for fish. Whenever the nets needed mending or repairing, he did that too, and sometimes I would help him; he taught me how to use the shuttle to make the knots. Our father was a practical man, and he made do with what others would throw away.

Our mother was also affected by Papa's practical ways. She baked sourdough bread three times a week, tanned the skins that were made into parkas and mukluks, dried and made the sinew into strands with which she sewed the skins. She taught me how to do all this because I could not go out and do the outside chores that the able-bodied ones had to do. Also, with the yarn that Uncle Ed sent me, I knitted socks, mittens, scarves, and other useful items. In the winter months, Mama's evenings at home were spent making clothing and parkas out of fur and hide. There were definite styles to the parkas for men and women. The men's parkas were not made quite as fancy as the women's were, and as for mukluks, the men's were made with intricate fancywork around the top and more wolverine trim. The men's could be made of reindeer calf, sealskin, squirrel, or Arctic hare, with fancywork made of small squares, oblong or triangle pieces of black and white tanned unborn reindeer calf skin, sewn in a pattern. The reason they used this kind of hide for the fancywork was that it was more pliable and the hair was fine and short and therefore much easier to sew the little designs together with sinew. I helped my mother make many of these strips, which she would then use around the cuff parts of the parkas and also around the bottom edge of the parka. The parkas were made like a tunic with a hood, and their hem came halfway between the thigh and the knee of a man. After the front and back were sewn together, the sleeves were sewn in and then the hood; finally, the fancywork at the cuff of the sleeve and the bottom edge of the parka itself was sewn. The finishing touches were the narrow strips of wolverine edging around the bottom of the tunic. Last but not least was the most expensive piece of fur—the ruff, or the thick grayish-white scruff of wolf fur around the face of the hood. The Eskimos never used wolf hide for garments, only for trim, and the wolverine fur the same way. The wolf head skin was used for the topside of mittens. Many Eskimo men had two sets of parkas, one made of the heavy reindeer skins with much more wolf trim for winter wear, and the other a parka of lighter weight fur such as squirrel or reindeer calf. For summer wear, they had parkas made of duck, a heavy cotton material, or of just cotton calico. In winter, the men who had to go out for meat wore both winter and summer parkas together. The summer weight one was worn under the heavier winter reindeer parka in order to withstand temperatures of minus forty degrees or colder.

The old style of the women's parka was the slit up each side about to the knee, with the front and back panels rounded. The women's parkas also had more fancy strips, such as the insert from the front of the hood down to the breast. That part would be made of black and white designs of the unborn calf of the reindeer. After the early 1920s, the women's parka style changed to resemble the men's somewhat in that they no longer had the slit sides. I also helped my mother make mukluks, the footwear which everyone in the family wore. The tops were made of seal or reindeer calf, and the soles were made of walrus hide, for it was thick, tough, and would wear for quite some time.

Papa believed cleanliness was next to godliness. About once a week, we girls had to take turns scrubbing our wooden plank floors with strong brown soap and water and a stiff brush. We would scrub the plank floors until they were almost white. Mama saw to it that our bodies were clean—if we didn't wash our hair as often as she thought we should, she put herself to the task for us. We didn't have fancy soaps and shampoos. We used Fels Naptha soap for baths, shampoos, and laundry. One thing Papa could not tolerate was long hair on the boys. On a Saturday, he would get out his barber shears, a stool, and a towel, and would line the boys up, each one taking his turn in the chair. We girls, however, all had long hair, which we wore in braids with the ends tied with ribbon or yarn, and if we went one day without redoing our braids we heard about it from Papa. He not only reprimanded us but threatened to shave all the hair off our heads if we neglected to keep our hair clean and neatly done. Our oldest sister, Margaret, had the longest and most beautiful hair of all of us girls. When her hair hung down her back, and was not done up, it would almost reach the floor when she sat in a chair. My mother had shiny black hair which was always clean, and she kept it in two neat braids. She was slender in build, small in height, and I don't think she ever weighed more than one hundred ten pounds. Of any of the girls in the family, I came the nearest to resembling my mother, in height, weight, and appearance. I also resemble my maternal grandmother, Kinaviak, in many ways—she also was slender and agile, and there was not a lazy bone in her body. I have known three generations, including myself, of my Eskimo ancestry, and they were all on the lean and slender side.

As the younger sisters and brothers were expected to arrive into the world, my mother would begin walking the floor and Papa made sure that he was not somewhere on the trail, or over across the bay in the boat, but that he was near enough to hear if she should call to him. My father was present at all our births, either in the capacity of midwife or assisting the midwife, and we all saw the first light of day at our own home. My father, being a staunch Catholic, baptized each and every one of us at birth as soon as he and Mama could bathe our little bodies and wrap us in warm blankets.

I remember when my oldest sister's twins were born. My mother and a midwife and the mother-to-be were in a tent, for we were out camping near the Tuksuk River to pick our winter supply of berries. My mother cleared us all out of the big tent, made sure there was plenty of hot water, some clean towels, and a blanket, and then she and the midwife proceeded to walk the floor and wait it out. Then they started to work strenuously over my sister, talking to her encouragingly, and hours passed before we heard the cry of her firstborn, a girl. Mama bathed the baby, wrapped her in a clean cotton blanket, and doing so said to the midwife, "I think there is another one to be born." The woman answered, "I have the same feeling that there is another baby there." Soon another muffled cry came from where my sister lay, tired and weary. My mother said, "Let me take it and see what I can do for she is going limp." We had no idea that an emergency had arisen. But my mother told us later that the second twin was almost stillborn, until my mother put her fingers down the little throat and pulled out some thick phlegm which was choking the little one. That was only one of the times that I was glad that my mother had such great intuition and instinctively knew what to do in dire situations. I have thought many times that the Almighty above answered her prayers for I knew when she was praying fervently.

*   *   *

Before airplanes became common in the North in the 1930s, few visitors came to Teller between the freeze-up in October, when navigation ended, and the June breakup when ships could get in again. Each month a dog team driver brought the mail from Fairbanks, down the frozen Tanana and Yukon Rivers to Norton Sound, up the coast to Nome, then over the winter trails to Teller, Tin City, Wales, and Kotzebue. Father LaFortune, from the mission at Pilgrim Springs (which was called Mary's Igloo), usually came at Easter, before the thaw, while good dog team travel was still possible.

Everything slowed down during the winter months, but there was little idleness. The reindeer herds had to be cared for, men trapped and hunted, and the women and children fished through holes in the sea ice. I would often go out with Mama onto the frozen bay, where we'd sit for hours on a deerskin on a sled, fishing for sole and tomcod through the ice. The sole is a flat fish, and the tomcod looks like a little shark with a black back and white belly. It is not the smartest fish around and can be easily caught. It swims straight ahead and snaps at anything that gets in front of it. If you jiggle the line, you can't even feel a tomcod on your hook. You have to "weigh" the line with your hand, and if it feels a bit heavier than the bait, you pull it in and usually have a fish. Every few minutes, you must scrape the scum of ice that forms on the surface of the water. Mama had an instrument that my grandfather made for her for that purpose. The handle was long, made from willow driftwood, and the end was carved flat like a spoon, leaving just a frame—something like a tennis racket only much smaller—which then was woven with strips of rawhide to make sort of a latticework effect.

Where we fished, the water was about a hundred feet deep, but generally we only let our line down about ten or fifteen feet, and at the most twenty or twenty-five. Sometimes we would catch the bottom fish like sole, rock cod, and lots of bullheads. We used just ordinary twine for fishline, and made our own hooks from the soft iron wire that came around kerosene and potato cases. We'd use two sticks to wind in the line so we wouldn't get our mittens wet, which would have caused our hands to freeze in an instant when it was twenty-five or thirty below zero. I had one advantage out there fishing on the ice—my feet didn't get cold.

We all had chores. After Tommy went to sea, David was the big brother of the family. He loved the outdoors and was hardly ever inside except to eat and rest or get dried out and warmed up so he could go back out hunting or fishing or doing things with his friends. He seemed to be more Eskimo than any of us. His chores were caring for the dogs and hauling ice. In summer the dogs were fed fish heads and tails and guts. They got dried salmon and dried tomcod in the winter. Also, Papa cooked cornmeal with fat to feed the dogs, as they needed fat for energy. David had to bring the dogs out of their inside stalls to chain them to posts outside of the barn so they could get fresh air and exercise everyday. If a blizzard was blowing, he had a day off from that job. In winter, when the wells were frozen solid, David would take the team and sled and go out to the lake back of town and cut blocks of ice about eighteen inches square and haul them home to be melted in buckets and tubs for drinking and cooking. It gave us the purest water you ever saw. There was never a speck of anything in it, clear as crystal. We kept a bucket on the back of the stove into which a block of ice was put to melt so there would always be drinking water available. Behind the stove was a 55-gallon oil drum with the top cut out. My father had rigged pipes to it from the firebox of the stove and this was kept full by adding blocks of ice. There was a brass spigot at the bottom of the drum from which water could be drawn for washing clothes and bathing. When the fire was banked for the night, that big barrel of hot water helped keep the room warm until the stove was rekindled in the morning.

Sarah and Anne cut kindling wood and stacked it behind the kitchen stove. They also hauled a couple of sacks of coal at a time on a small sled from the warehouse to the entry shed. This made it easier to fill the coal scuttles for the heater and the kitchen stove without having to go across the street to the warehouse when there was a blizzard or snowdrifts outside almost concealing the door. There were times after a three or four-day blizzard when we had to use a side entrance door to shovel away the snow that had completely blocked our main entrance door. Sometimes the windows would also be completely covered over with snow and had to be swept off. After a fifty or sixty mile-an-hour gale had blown the snow and compacted it so hard against the doors and windows, you had to use an adze to chip it away. It would be packed onto the door or window as if a mason had cemented it on.

Sometimes a winter would set in early and last longer into the spring than usual, and we'd run short of coal. Then Papa would go out in the tundra and cut chucks of sod about eight or ten inches square that would just fit in the firebox of the cookstove. These oil-soaked chunks of sod would smolder all night long, just like peat. Except for a little stunted willow and alder that grew along the creeks, we had no wood other than the driftwood that washed ashore after every summer storm. When the wind and seas had moderated, everyone with a boat would be out along the coastline from Nook Spit to Cape Spencer to the Brevig Lagoon grabbing up the driftwood as fast as it came in. There was never enough, and people would almost pray for another storm so they could get more of the wood. Most of it had been carried down to sea via the Yukon and the Kuskokwim Rivers and other streams that drained the timber regions of the interior, but my father said that a lot of the driftwood must come from rivers in Russia and the Kamchatka Peninsula, drifting north and northwest to our beaches.

We had a natural cold storage—an excavation under our house at Teller with a hatch lid for an entrance. During the dead of winter, Papa would keep a kerosene lantern down there to keep the chill out so the food would not freeze but would stay at a temperature of about thirty-five to thirty-seven degrees. This underground storage space was about five feet from floor to ceiling and perhaps ten feet wide by fifteen feet long. That is where we kept our perishables such as crates of eggs and potatoes, onions, sacks of carrots, and also cases of canned goods. I remember the tasteful cheeses in a wheel—Papa made sure these were kept in a large tin can with a tight lid so that the mice wouldn't get into them. Even though we would get down to our last few potatoes—flour and sugar were low and coffee and tea almost had to be rationed—we were by no means in danger of starvation. There was plenty of dried fish and salted and smoked salmon, and the new runs of smelt, herring, and salmon would have begun. Reindeer and seal meat were plentiful and available when you had the ammunition.

In the spring, my brothers brought home brant and emperor geese, nice and fat and right for roasting. I remember one time when Tommy was about sixteen years old, he brought home a swan that he had shot, and Mama baked it, but it was so tough it was like eating shoe leather. It must have been an old one, for they are reputed to live nearly a century. That incident happened before the swan became an endangered species. Those were the days when we used to see flocks of trumpeter swan, about ten or fifteen in a flock, flying over in the early spring, their long wings making a slow sweeping motion as they made their silent journey to the tundra flats north of Nook where they would nest. They have not been seen in that area since the early 1920s, but a few are still found to breed in the tundra flats of northern Canada. We also saw many birds that are now endangered, such as whooping crane, whistling swan, brant (a species of geese which I don't think even exists anymore), and some that are not endangered but were more plentiful fifty years ago, such as emperor geese, pintail, Arctic tern, jaeger, and more.

The Natives used every part of the animals that they killed, nothing was thrown away. The meat was eaten, fresh or dried, and some of the bones were used for tools. I can remember my grandfather having snow goggles made of two pieces of ivory the size of a fifty cent piece each. They were thinner than a fourth of an inch, each with a slit an inch and a quarter long and not wider than an eighth of an inch for the opening. These were fastened with a piece of rawhide and tied around the head. A person would get snow blindness if they didn't have such gear when they hunted seal or rabbits or other game in the winter. There were days when the sun would shine so bright that it made your eyes water, and you couldn't stay outside very long without snow goggles. There was one delicacy that my grandparents and my mother relished and that we younger ones learned to really like as well, and that was bone marrow. My mother used to bake skinned reindeer legs, the shin parts, until they were nice and brown, and after we had eaten the roasted meat from the bone, she would crack the bones so that we could scoop out the delicious marrow which we spread on bread as you would butter. When we ate an Eskimo meal with Mama, we would eat while sitting on the ground outdoors. These meals were mainly boiled or dried fish with seal oil, *soorut* greens, and berries. While Mama would drink tea, we had cool clear water from an artesian well. When Papa ate his lunch or dinner inside with the boys at the dinner table, he would have fried or boiled fish, boiled potatoes, some boiled dandelion or wild onion greens with vinegar, or fresh greens from our little vegetable patch, such as radishes, leaf lettuce, young carrots, or turnips.

❊　❊　❊

About forty miles directly east of Teller was a place called Hot Springs or Pilgrim Springs. That was the same area where we lived when I was three years old. Then it was a Catholic Mission called Mary's Igloo. It was protected by the Saw Tooth Mountains and far enough inland to be more or less free from the northerly winds blowing off the ice packs. There were natural hot springs or geothermal areas where the mission monks (or brothers, as we called them) cultivated beautiful vegetable gardens. They made even broader use of the geothermal activity by building a spa where people from all around, including my father, used to go to soak their tired stiff muscles. Papa made at least one trip every winter to soak away the pain of his rheumatism. He would come home feeling fresh and supple. He and Father LaFortune, a French priest, and Brother Wilhelm, a German monk, would relax in the hot baths for hours, chatting in German and reminiscing about the Old Country.

All of the staff at Mary's Igloo Mission were either German, Belgian, or French. Everything was immaculate and run on an orderly basis. The main vegetables that they grew were spinach, Brussels sprouts, celery, carrots, cabbage, rutabagas, and several varieties of lettuce. All this produce grew fast and big in the short but intense growing season of twenty-four hours a day of sunlight during the summer. What they didn't harvest for immediate use, they stored in frost-proof root cellars, and when Papa visited the mission during the winter, he'd always take along smoked and salted salmon for the staff and the children, and he would come home with a sack or two of vegetables.

He never forgot the children, some of whom were orphans. He always brought them a bucket of hard Christmas candy that he had saved especially for them. Some of our neighbors' kids were not as fortunate as we Bernhardts. Almost every family in Teller had lots of children, and if the father was sickly, lazy, a drinker, or a gambler, they had terrible times and would have starved without the charity of others. There were no welfare programs then, of course, and those who were more provident and had a little extra would help care for the dependents of those who were not. Papa would always give someone less fortunate a helping hand; he would say, "You can't let children suffer just because their parents are no good." There was one old fellow, also married to a Native woman, who never seemed to be able to put by enough food to see his large family through the winter. I'd see him measure out the food, and if he spilled just one bean or one grain of rice, he'd pick it up and put it in the pot. He seemed to work hard enough but apparently was not the manager that my father was. Papa was known as a good provider and never were we cold or hungry or without proper clothing, even after a season when the fish runs had been poor or bad weather interfered.

One of Papa's favorite foods was eggs, but they always were a problem to keep. No matter how he tried to keep them fresh longer, by the end of winter any that hadn't been used would have spoiled. Some egg-starved people, who couldn't wait for the arrival of supply ships, would go to offshore islands in the spring and rob the nests of seabirds on the cliffs. Such eggs had a strong fishy taste that got worse with age. We gathered sea gull eggs, which we thought delicious compared to some other birds. The eider duck eggs that we gathered in the marshy places were nearly as big as turkey eggs and dark of yolk but good eating. We also found ptarmigan eggs, which we thought the closest thing to hen eggs, for they could be used in baking cakes. The chicken eggs we got at home arrived on the MS *Patterson*, and by the time they reached us in July, they would already have been weeks away from the chickens that laid them. Stored in the cellar at thirty-nine degrees and the cases turned over every few weeks, made it possible to have eggs at Christmas as well as a few even for Easter.

Papa made it a point that we would observe Easter Sunday with joy and happiness. He believed very strongly in the resurrection, as he did in the other Catholic doctrines that he taught us. He would bake hot cross buns and a couple of apple pies, and for Easter breakfast he would make us corn fritters. Easter and Christmas were two big holidays at our house. Papa and Mama would go all out to make them memorable for all of us. Easter time meant excitement not only in our immediate family but also the two other Catholic families in Teller.

We also knew that Father LaFortune, our traveling priest, would be arriving any day as near to Easter as the weather would permit him to travel with his dog team, for he had a rough trail of more than fifty miles over frozen lakes, rivers, and snow-packed terrain. He would spend about a month traveling to out-of-the-way settlements to minister to the sick, comfort the aged, perform the baptismal ceremony to the newborn, and give the last rites to those at death's door. He spoke fluent Iñupiaq and even said Mass in Iñupiaq for the Natives in the most remote places. He also advised young people about adolescence and what marriage should mean.

My parents especially loved to make Christmas a time of happiness for us. They seemed to enjoy the season, the preparation, and the meaning of this great day. We children believed in Santa Claus when we were small, and I still remember when I found out who Saint Nick really was. Mama would set a plate with cookies and a cup for coffee for Santa as he would be cold and hungry when he dropped down from the North Pole. One Christmas Eve, when I was seven or eight, Anne and I, who slept together upstairs, had been giggling and whispering until late, too excited for sleep. Then we heard the jingle of bells outside. A few minutes later there was the sound of paper bags being opened and our parents talking in low tones. Slipping out of bed I made my way in the dark to the door where I could see my parents putting things in our stockings. Those long black cotton stockings that we wore would be hung on the ladder that led to our sleeping quarters in the garret.

The only gifts we received were the contents of the stockings, which consisted of a small bag of hard candy, an orange and apple, some mixed nuts, and an inexpensive trinket. But how happy we were to receive even that much. The boys might get a harmonica or pocketknife; we girls got a comb or barrettes for the hair or one of those little pink celluloid dolls with the arms and legs that could be twirled around and around and would fall off when the rubber band that held them together was wound too tight and broke.

Right after the stockings were distributed and a special breakfast of eggs and oatmeal was over, Mama would put a big reindeer roast in the oven, to be served with potatoes and carrots sautéed in the juice of the roast, rich brown gravy, and canned peas. For dessert we had Papa's homemade apple pie. One time Papa ordered a turkey from one of the markets at Nome, and it came frozen via dog team a week or two before Christmas. We did not like it for we thought it tasted fishy. Not that we disliked fish, but it being a fowl, we thought it should have a somewhat different flavor.

The only and biggest social event of the year was the Christmas program presented by our school. It meant excitement, cheerfulness, and good will prevailing at every turn. Expectations were high throughout the days of preparation for the big day. We children would begin to get nervous about our parts in the Christmas play.

There was no such a thing as wearing a bright new dress every year—perhaps the dress we wore last year just needed lengthening at the hem or the side seams let out a little. It was too nice a dress for just any occasion, even if it was made of calico. If last year's dress did not fit, even with the necessary alterations, it was handed down to the next in line. We never expected our parents to furnish us with dresses of silk or satin or rayon for we instinctively knew we had to be satisfied with things as they were.

Our teachers put every effort into making it as happy and exciting as they could for us all. Despite the lack of many things in the Arctic that in other parts of the world make the Christmas season a merry and enjoyable one, we made substitutions wherever we could. We had no fir trees to decorate in our homes or schoolhouse. But our teacher would have the older boys go out and chop the biggest alder or willow they could find. My brother David, Tommy Blatchford, and Heinie Müller would take our sled and go to the end of the big lake back of Teller where there was a willow grove in the lowland and where the ground would be swampy in the summertime. First the boys would have to shovel the snow away from the trunk, which was buried deep. They would find the sturdiest one with the thickest trunk, at least six feet tall and perhaps two and a half to three inches in diameter.

While the boys were out in the cold selecting the willow tree, we girls were in the warm schoolhouse popping corn on the old potbellied heating stove, and we would string the popcorn to be part of the decorations for the tree. The smaller boys and girls made daisy chains out of colored paper to be draped around the tree. All the decorations were handmade by the students, with whatever material was available. The willow or alder tree was usually sparse of branches so the boys would also bring home extra branches cut from other willows. The boys would then drill different sized holes in the trunk of the willow or alder at scattered intervals and then stick more branches in these holes to make the tree a little fuller. Then the whole trunk and all the branches would be wrapped with green crepe paper. By the time the tree was decorated with everything we could make, and the teacher had put up the handmade star that we had covered with chewing-gum foil, we were pretty proud of the tree. Everyone at school had a hand in the completion of the Christmas tree, and it was really something to behold for our eager eyes. It lifted our spirits no end.

After completion of the tree, the schoolroom was decorated with red and green crepe paper streamers. Then the stage platform was set up, complete with curtains hung on heavy-duty wire strung from one end of the stage to the other. And finally came the climax to our labor of love, the taffy pull. Our teacher furnished all the supplies, and what fun we all had.

Discipline in our small school was excellent, and we respected our teachers. We were all so eager to learn and felt so fortunate to have a schoolhouse and a teacher that we would stay after school to help her clean the blackboard and the erasers or any other jobs she had for us. All eight grades were taught in one room.

* * *

In the spring, after the ice started breaking up in Grantley Harbor and pan ice, or ice floes, began churning around in Port Clarence Bay, we began to get anxious to move to the Nook, which meant also that school would be out. We would load the scow, which Papa had built for the purpose of moving us to Nook and back to Teller in the fall, with household goods, clothes, and bedding. Papa steered a straight course north with the forty-horsepower Evinrude motor straining at the stern of the scow.

Most of the time in early June, the ice pack would move back into the harbor, and with the force of the incoming tide, it would pile the beach high with icebergs. As if by some giant hand playing jackstraws, the bergs would be deposited grotesquely on top of each other. When icebergs are adrift and the two main forces are present—wind and current—they can be seen moving against the motion of the surrounding ice pack. If the current is southerly and the wind northerly, the two motions of ice oppose each other, and the icebergs pile up with giant roars and squeaks as they buckle and snap. When the pressure ridges get fifteen or twenty, even thirty feet high, the topmost cakes of ice come tumbling down with a horrendous crash.

David was always the instigator of bold ventures. He would dare Sarah and Anne to jump from the shore ice to a loose cake of ice. Then he would see how far he could travel along the shore ice with the tide without going so far from shore that he couldn't make it back by hopscotching on cakes of ice. That was just one of the daring feats that David used to do. I'm sure that boy had no fear of nature. While my siblings were testing their skills on the ice floes, I would stand on the shore ice, after carefully plotting my course so as not to slip, and breathlessly watch the proceedings from there. Almost constantly, we could hear distant sharp squeaks or a low hum, almost like a human voice. They were the seals and whales calling to each other out in

Port Clarence Bay as there were many open leads past the ice floes. If you put your ear to the surface of the ice, you could hear an eerie underwater symphony.

From the early 1920s onward, Papa supported his family principally by trapping fox and fishing. The first fish to arrive after the breakup were harbor trout, smelt, and eulachon, the fat candlefish that everybody called "hooligans." Caught with fine-meshed seines, the first few messes of trout and smelt tasted wonderful after a winter of salted, dried, or smoked fish, tomcod, and reindeer meat.

When the smelt runs were over, huge schools of herring came swarming into Grantley Harbor. The water would be just black with the fish, an almost solid mass about three feet deep, twenty or thirty feet across, and hundreds of yards in length. From a long distance you could see that the herring were coming by the ripple they made while swimming just below the surface. They seldom broke water unless pursued by salmon or belugas (small white whales), and then many of the fish in the school would jump all at once. Falling back into the sea, they made a sound like gravel being dumped on a tin roof. The herring were harvested by net or seine. One end of the seine would be held by people on the beach, while the rest of it was paid out of a dory in a half circle around the milling fish. Having cork floats on the topside and lead sinkers on the underwater side, the net hung upright in the water like a fence. It was then pulled onto the beach. Sometimes 300 or 400 pounds of herring would be caught in a single haul. Beluga whales would be right behind the school of herring—many times we could see the mother whale surface with a baby whale lying on her back. The herring were a delicacy. Papa salted them in barrels, smoked them, or pickled them with vinegar and spices. Sometimes he preserved them Eskimo style by putting them into a pit dug six feet or so into the permafrost where they were preserved in nature's cold storage to be eaten later. Smoked, baked, fried, or boiled, they were real good eating.

King salmon, weighing up to fifty pounds, showed up with the herring runs late in June. The kings were often gorged with the smaller fish they had just eaten. Accompanying the migrating kings were immature salmon that we called "salmon-trout" or blackmouths. These were another delicacy sold fresh to those who weren't fishermen. The salmon were caught in gill nets. One end of the net, which was fitted with floats and sinkers as the seines were, would be tied to the beach and the other end anchored in deep water so that it formed a fence-like barrier extending in a half circle out from shore. The openings in the mesh were about four inches square, allowing smaller fish to pass through but entangling the larger ones about the gills: hence the name "gill nets." Several times each day the nets would be checked for salmon.

Papa got the surprise of his life one morning when he and Albert, who was ten years old at the time, went out in the dory to get the salmon catch from the net. He noticed that one part of the salmon net was being weighted down more than ever. He thought there might be a seal entangled in the net, as sometimes was the case. When he got the net partly in the boat, he found that he had caught a ninety-eight pound king salmon. Up to that time, it was the largest king salmon caught by net.

The moneymakers were the sockeyes or red salmon. They came in July. Not a large fish, weighing on average about six pounds apiece, the bright reddish flesh and delicate flavor of the sockeye made it one of the most desirable of commercial fish. Over the years, my father developed and improved processing methods that made his salmon so popular on the San Francisco market and in New York delicatessens that he could never satisfy the demand. He also had a commitment to supply his Nome customers, businessmen and store owners.

After the sockeyes had been caught and butchered, several things could be done with them. A delicacy favored by Scandinavians was the bellies, a narrow strip of fat flesh that was salted in kegs with a dash of brown sugar added to sweeten the brine. The remainder of each fish was dried or hand-canned. Papa's major product, though, was fillets of salmon salted down in barrels. He tried to have at least 500 barrels filled and ready for shipment south at the end of every season. Sacks of rock salt were imported via the *Patterson*, Captain Pederson's ship from the States, as were disassembled staves and hoops and barrel heads to be coopered together as needed to make barrels.

Papa smoked about half of the king salmon that he caught. They'd be cut in strips, soaked overnight in a light brine, hung on racks outside to partially dry, then put in the smokehouse and smoke cured. He used slow fires of green willow or alder, which gave off a dense, moist smoke that seasoned the already tasty fish with a pungent, mouth-watering flavor. Some of the smoked king salmon was spiced and canned in olive oil and produced the greatest tidbit of all.

Sherman and John Reimer Sr. looking at Yukon River salmon trap, 1958.

In August and September, after the king and sockeye runs had moved on up into the spawning streams beyond the Imuruk Basin, the silver salmon, or coho, appeared from the sea. Then came the dog salmon, or chums, and then the pink salmon also called humpies. The silvers and dogs were quite a bit larger than the sockeyes but not so valuable commercially. These were usually split and boned and hung on wooden racks to dry, rock-hard, in the wind and sun, to feed our dogs or to sell to other dog owners. Occasionally, an exploration ship going into the Arctic would stop and buy our dried salmon for expedition dog teams. The Royal Canadian Mounted Police (RCMP) bought a lot of Papa's dried salmon for dog food as they stopped at Teller on their way to Herschel Island and points north in the Canadian Arctic.

We also seined for tomcod in late August when the schools would be almost as thick as the herring. These we dried for winter use and for dog feed as they were more plentiful than salmon. When the Tomcod runs came, Papa would build us a shelter of a tarpaulin hung over a frame as a windbreak from the sharp fall winds and rains. There we would spend most of the day cleaning and stringing tomcods on a length of wire. When the length of wire was full of cleaned tomcods, perhaps twenty or thirty, we would fasten it into a ring so the fish could be draped over a wooden railing to dry. About four of us girls would be assigned this task as long as the tomcod run was on, which could last two or three weeks. Sometimes we would get so tired by the end of the day that we would start getting playful and silly and throw tomcod guts at each other. Some would land in our hair and some square in the face, and the girls making the bull's-eye would laugh the loudest. Soon, the bickering would start, and then Papa would have to step in and settle things. We got our share of whippings when the punishment was due. I can still recall seeing that big black leather strop hanging in his closet, and we all dreaded the times when he would go to the closet to get it.

We didn't always fish at Nook. Sometimes the salmon runs didn't remain long in Grantley Harbor but migrated directly to the Tuksuk River, a narrow, winding tidal channel leading to the Imuruk Basin, which we called the "Salt Lake" but which was actually a landlocked bay. When fishing was poor at Nook and salmon were jumping in the Tuksuk, Papa and Mama, kids, dogs, and camping equipment would be loaded into our big power launch, the *Devil Whale*, which Papa had purchased in 1925. With a dory carrying the fishnets and other gear towing astern, we'd go chugging off up Grantley Harbor, probably looking like a tribe of Chukchis on the move.

Through the years, Papa owned many boats—some he built, but the *Devil Whale* was his favorite. Captain Pederson brought it up one year on the *Patterson*. "I got a good deal on this boat in Frisco," said Captain Pederson. "It looked like just what you could use up here so I brought it along." The boat was lowered into the water, the diesel engine started, and Papa fell in love with it immediately. A deal was made with Pederson, and we had a fine boat that lasted many years. She was about thirty feet long, had a good seaworthy hull, and was large enough for our entire family to travel safely in at one time. There was a small cabin with bunks and a place to cook. Nothing fancy, but as far as we were concerned, it was a yacht. In a local fleet of Model T-type skiffs and dories, the *Devil Whale* was a Cadillac. We had great times with it.

Mama especially liked it when we went to fish the Tuksuk where sometimes we'd spend a whole summer. As soon as camp was set up, she'd take us girls out picking berries. The first of the season were the big, yellow, juicy salmonberries which grew on low bushes. Later came the blueberries and blackberries and red cranberries. The blackberries weren't the blackberry that we know in the Lower 48, being more like a currant and resembling a little black bead. They were sweet and filled with tiny seeds and grew on a low vine that crawled in the tundra moss. Scandinavians said they were similar to the lingonberries they'd known in the Old Country.

Being the only fruit that grows in the Arctic, wild berries were the only source of sweetening and flavoring in Mama's Native diet. She gathered them diligently. The different varieties were not always kept separate but were all put together in a keg or sealskin poke. Stored in a cool place, they never spoiled or fermented and would keep until they were all used up by midwinter. We ate them plain or with sugar and canned milk like Stateside people do strawberries and cream. A dish that contained berries that we all liked was *kamahmuk* or "Eskimo ice cream." With her hands, my mother would mix reindeer suet and a little water in a bowl until it was soft, then whipping it with her fingers, she'd add a few more drops of water at a time until it got fluffy like whipped cream. She'd then add a bit of sugar, mix in the berries, and we had our *kamahmuk*. The mixing had to be done slowly and just so, or you'd end up with an inedible mess of lumpy grease. Sometimes Mama would crush boiled tomcod liver to a paste, add a bit of sugar, mix in the berries, and this we would have as a dessert that we relished. This was called *ugrupuck*.

One misconception held by the white population is that seal oil tastes and smells like fish. This is far from true. If properly cared for, it has no odor and has a buttery flavor. When it gets old and rancid, like any other oily substance, it does get a potent smell to it and gets dark in color. An uninitiated person, wanting to get the oil from a piece of blubber, might put it in a kettle over a hot fire and render it as he would hog fat for the lard. If one did seal oil by that method, it would get an unpleasant taste and smell. Seal blubber must be allowed to render itself in a cool place. Mama had an *ulu* (pronounced oo-loo) which she used to scrape the layer of blubber from the seal hide as soon as the seal was killed. An *ulu* is a woman's cutting knife, usually made from the steel blade of a saw, cut in the shape of a half-moon with an ivory or bone handle. She also used it in cutting the furs she made into parkas, mukluks, and other clothes. When she scraped the blubber, it would come off the carcass with the skin, in a blanket two or three inches thick. After being separated from the skin, the blubber was cut into strips, put in a keg or five-gallon tin, and stored in a cool, dark place for a few weeks during which time the oil gradually seeped out of the blubber. Rendered in this manner, seal oil is almost colorless and has about as much flavor as olive oil. Light and warmth affect it, and so does time. As it ages, it turns a dark yellow, then brown, becoming thick and rancid, perhaps from bacterial action. Sometimes, such older oil could or would be used by the elderly Eskimos, for that was all they had left until new oil was made during seal hunting time in the early spring.

After we moved to Nook in the spring, and Mama had some fresh seal oil on hand, she would tell David to build a fire outside on the gravel in the yard. She would put on a large iron pot half-full of seal oil and begin making what we called "Eskimo doughnuts." She had her own recipe for the dough made from sourdough, but she never rolled out the dough or used a cookie cutter to cut out the rings. She would pinch off a small amount of dough, poke her finger through the center, and drop it into the hot seal oil. She would turn them as they got a lovely brown and use a forked twig to dip them out. I've never tasted anything so good made from scratch!

When all the oil had seeped from the tissues of the blubber, there remained a pinkish fiber the Eskimos called *tung yuq*. They would put this in a seal poke with some fresh seal oil and *ugruk* meat—young walrus meat that has been partially dried, then boiled, and then cut into three- or four-inch pieces. This was served along with *soorut* (tender young willow greens) and made a fairly balanced meal. I had such a meal many times with my grandparents and also with my mother, and it was very good.

Though some seals were speared during the winter months when they poked their heads from breathing holes in the ice to fill their lungs with fresh air, most were shot in the spring when they hauled out of open leads to bask on the ice in the bright sunlight. Most common was the harbor seal, also called the leopard seal because of its spotted coat. Seal liver was considered to be a delicacy in our part of the country. The flavor is very delicate, and it is as tender as chicken liver. Even Europeans, once they've tried it, say it's the best liver they've ever eaten. It is said to be very high in vitamins and certain minerals. The old-time seamen and explorers who ate seal liver never had scurvy or other vitamin-deficiency diseases. After the main ice fields had broken and leads appeared, boatloads of hunters would go out to the open sea and kill the big, fat walruses as they slept on drifting ice floes. Weighing as much as a ton and a half, these largest of the northern seal furnished, in addition to meat and blubber, tough skins for mukluk soles and *oomiak* hulls, and ivory from their tusks for carving and trading. The walrus uses its tusks for digging clams and mussels at the bottom of the sea. In very early times, the walrus hunter would slit open the stomach and scoop out the partly-digested shellfish and devour them with relish, a gourmet item.

Except for the beluga, or white whale that would become entangled in fishnets while following herring and salmon runs, few whales were taken in our region of Grantley Harbor. The Native whalers at Point Barrow paddled many miles from land through the shifting ice pack in search of their quarry. Often we would be surrounded by the gray whales as we rowed our skiff or dory to Teller, crossing the channel from Nook. They would surface near our boat, and sometimes we saw a mother whale carrying her baby on her back. In the summertime, there were schools or pods of beluga whale all around the channel. They seemed to be migrating up to the Tuksuk for we would even see them up in the Tuksuk River as we picked berries up on the bluffs. The hillsides were very steep in some areas, affording a view where we could look down and see the forms of white whales swimming under the surface.

From these animals and skins, Eskimos made clothing, tents, and boat covers, and from reindeer and caribou legs came sinew for thread, cord, and bows. They used beluga whale and caribou sinew to sew walrus hides that are the covering over the driftwood frames of *oomiaks* and kayaks. The skin covering the frame of the *oomiak* is so tight that it gives and rebounds when it bumps the ice cakes. They used strips of rawhide left over from the hull to lash the hide to the framework. Hunters used the bladder of the seal, or the whole sealskin, which they inflated and then fastened to a line attached to a spear that they shot into the seal; this kept the seal afloat until they could get to it. The harpooning instrument they used is an ingenious combination of a harpoon head mounted on a bore or ivory fore-shaft lashed into a socket fixed to the end of a wooden shaft. When the head of the harpoon had gone into the hide and blubber of the animal they were hunting, the foreshaft separated from the head, which remained in the animal, and the shaft floated free, while the hunter held his catch on a line connected only to the head of the shaft. For hauling up a walrus or whale which he had killed, the hunter used a pulley attached to the shore ice.

My father also loved the land that we homesteaded at Nook, and he even tried a bit of agriculture on a small scale. The hardy vegetables, such as radishes, green onions, leaf lettuce, and carrots, we had no difficulty raising; the twenty-four hours of daylight that time of year matured the vegetables in almost half the time that it takes in the Lower 48. We kids couldn't wait to raid the garden; before the radishes and carrots were even half-grown, we would be munching on them as we played. Every spring, one of Papa's regular orders of the day was that we go out and gather the wild dandelions and wild green onions, which grew profusely everywhere. These we would boil gently and serve hot with a little vinegar. Papa said we had to have a certain amount of fresh greens to help keep us fit. We had them with our lunch or dinner nearly everyday while they were in season.

Also during the early spring and summer, one could see blue seas of forget-me-nots, orange-yellow poppies, purple hyacinths, white daisies, fox-gloves, wild sweet peas, and bluebells, which grew in areas where it was sandy, such as between the beach and the flatlands. There were wildflowers of every color for as far as the eye could see.

We got to know quite well the officers and crews of most of the ships that came to the North each year, beginning with the famous revenue cutter *Bear*, which made history in Alaska and in later years in the Antarctic. In her forty-one years of service, she helped shape the history of Alaska during the time that it was a United States territory and even years before when Alaska was under the jurisdiction of the treasury department. She enforced the law and order of the U.S. government. She patrolled the Bering Sea and Arctic Ocean for about seven months of every year for all those many years. From the bleak shores of the Bering Sea, from the Aleutians to the Bering Strait and the Arctic, Eskimos, missionaries, teachers, criminals, senators, and high government officials stood on her decks as passengers. She was a sight to behold when she came into Port Clarence Bay, all decked out in her best, and her white sails bellowed out as she came gliding into her anchorage. Admiral Byrd took her to the Antarctic in 1933 and again in 1939. After that, she briefly became a museum. I have a brother-in-law who served on her during her last years on the Bering Patrol. Her days of glory still ring in the hearts of those of us who remember.

The prestigious *St. Roch* was another ship that called into Port Clarence Bay and also made history. She, under Captain Henry Larsen, was the first ship to circumnavigate the Northwest Passage, that is, to make a path around the North American continent by traversing from east to west and vice versa. Her captain Henry Larsen, was a very good friend of my family. Another noteworthy ship was the USMS *Boxer* in the service of the United States government through the interior department (Bureau of Indian Affairs), which had almost direct control of the health and welfare of the Alaskan Natives. There were also freighters of all kinds, scruffy little trading schooners, and the boats that carried the mail during the navigational season.

Our best friend and our mail link with the outside world was the MS *Patterson*. An aging sailing schooner, powered by a diesel engine, with a sawed-off bowsprit, ice-gouged hull, and cluttered decks, she was anything but a beauty. But never mind her dirt and rust and ugliness, she was the magic craft that brought us the products of a world we could only dream about. She was Easter, the Fourth of July, Thanksgiving, and Christmas all rolled into one. Captain Pederson was our Santa Claus because it was he who brought, in late August, the gifts we got at Christmas and most of the makings of our Christmas dinner. He also brought us *muktuk*, which, when fresh, is a layer of grayish-black fat just beneath the black outer, shiny skin of the whale. Eaten raw, *muktuk* is considered by the Eskimos to be the very best food that comes from the sea. It may sound outlandish to some, but to us it had the flavor of coconut. He also brought gunnysacks full of cracklins, which were rendered-out bits of whale fat, nice and brown and crunchy. Each fall we couldn't wait until Captain Pederson would stop by to bring us such goodies.

The *Patterson*'s home port was San Francisco. After a winter at dockside being overhauled, painted, and refitted, she'd load with supplies and trade goods and head for the North in late spring. Before sailing for the Far North, she'd take on a deck load of sacked coal, drums of oil, cases of tinned gasoline and kerosene, and stacks of lumber for transport to Arctic regions barren of such items.

Teller was one of the *Patterson*'s first ports of call when she returned to the North. Sometimes the open sea beyond Point Spencer would be free of ice while Grantley Harbor still had floating bergs, some as large as a football field. We'd see the ship lying out on the horizon, waiting for an offshore wind to move the ice and open up the anchorage. By now, we would have been down nearly to the end of everything. We had the necessities for existence but were short of the little extras that added spice and variety to our everyday existence. Dried beans, rice and macaroni, oatmeal flour and sugar, yeast, baking powder, salt, pepper, and other spices, canned and dried fruits, crates of eggs, potatoes and big, brown-skinned onions—all our staples, supplies, and fuel came from the Lower 48 on the *Patterson*. Then there were mysterious boxes that vanished to some hiding place we never could find—gifts that would turn up in our stockings at Christmas. But we could always find the boxes of dried prunes and apricots, figs, Fig Newtons, and Eagle Brand milk, which we loved to get into. My father always got a few

SS *Victoria* and US Coast Guard *Bear*, 1920.

extras for our wintertime treats, such as a few boxes of apples, two crates of oranges, assorted cookies, and wooden buckets of hard candy and mixed nuts for our Christmas stockings. I don't know how my father did it. He'd spend everything he had on food and clothing for his family. If we needed something that he didn't ordinarily have on the order, he'd sell a skin or two to one of the local stores and buy it.

In the fall, driven from the Arctic by the southward creep of the ice pack, one of the *Patterson's* last stops en route home to San Francisco would be Teller. Our *muktuk* was unloaded, and Papa's kegs of spiced herring, barrels of salt salmon, and cases of tinned and smoked salmon were taken aboard. The fur skins he'd taken the past winter would be shipped off to a St. Louis fur company. Just before the battered old schooner sailed, Papa would give Captain Pederson his order for groceries and supplies to be brought north on the next voyage in the early summer. And Captain Pederson would always say to Papa, "Albert, do you suppose you could put up a bit more fish this year than you did last season? These people down in San Francisco can't seem to get enough of it, especially your smoked salmon." The San Francisco outlet would send some to the New York City delicatessens, especially spiced herring and cases of smoked, kippered salmon put up in olive oil. Of course, the size of the runs and the fishing weather were the controlling factors, but each year, Papa tried to put up a few more kegs of herring, a few more barrels of salt salmon, and a few more cases of smoked salmon packed in olive oil. His fields were the sea, his crop was fish, and, like any good farmer, he harvested everything he could.

✳   ✳   ✳

It was the practice of the early Eskimos that the father, who was the hunter and provider for his family, was always fed first and got the choice skins for his clothing. The mother was next in line because she was the preparer of the food and maker of the clothes. Then came the older boys. Next to be fed and clothed were the nonproviders, the girls and small children or old grandparents. It was a brutal system, but one that insured the survival of the family. If the hunter did not have strength and protection from the weather, he could not go in search of game to feed the family, and all would perish.

Mama and her contemporaries had known hunger at Shishmaref and Ikpek. She remembered when all they had left were a few pieces of seal meat in the poke and a few frozen tomcods. Everything else had been depleted months before they would be able to trade a fox skin for some flour and tea from the traders, who would come after the breakup of the ice that had locked them in for as long as eight months. The arrival of spring meant not only that the traders would arrive with badly needed staples and goods, but that the gathering of fresh greens would be possible and a welcome supplement to the meager diet of fish and meat. Summer would bring berries to be put up for winter use. Sometimes, however, summer would be cool and not warm enough to produce all the leaves and greens they needed to harvest for use during the long cold winters. They had to harvest whatever they would need to tide them over the foreboding winters for they had no corner grocery store. In that land, in those days, you gathered the edible commodity while the gathering was good. When my mother was a young child, she saw the deaths of starving babies, and she saw old people, the ill and feeble, using the last of their energy to plod out onto the sea ice or off into the tundra to die alone rather than be a further burden on their families. Even when she was a young woman, she used to hear of the strangulation at birth of baby girls in the more remote tribes. A baby boy was an asset because he'd grow up to be a hunter, a provider. A girl would only produce more mouths that could not be fed in a land where the game in the lean years could not be found. The struggle for survival was first and foremost, as it always has been in any frontier life.

Mama, having been born into the old culture with its shamanism and superstitions, believed very firmly in the supernatural, and these beliefs stuck with her in spite of being a converted Catholic. She had a strong sense of what is called extrasensory perception, seemed to know of things that were happening some place else, and often had forebodings of the future. If my mother had a hunch something was going to happen, it generally did, and we would hear of it later. She could feel things when we could not.

An example of this was a human-like creature reportedly seen in the early 1920s by Eskimos up near Mary's Igloo, around the Imuruk Basin, the Tuksuk River area, and other nearby places. Mama saw it a couple of times while picking berries. Once she got within twenty feet of it, and she said it walked upright like a man. It was peeking at her from behind some tall willows. Its face was thin and bony with dry wrinkled skin covering it. It wore a ragged fur parka with a fringe of ragged fur around the head. Whatever the thing was, it never spoke or made any human noises, but it whistled and made sounds like the bird that people called *tuva* in Siberia. It was occasionally seen taking salmon from drying racks or meat from caches. It was considered to be harmless by those who saw it, and there was never a posse organized to go out and kill or capture it, as there might be if such a thing were reported around a modern community. Some thought it was a ghost or apparition, a specter visible only to Native eyes. Nowadays, it might be thought of as the Himalayan abominable snowman or yeti, or, as in the northwest United States, a sasquatch or bigfoot. Or was it a refugee from Russian Siberia, who did not want to be found out so he would not be deported back to the Siberian salt mines?

In northwestern Alaska, the Eskimo call it the "hiding man" or *inoo-goorock*. Tales about the hiding men are numerous from Bristol Bay to Barrow and all along the Bering Sea coast to the Arctic Ocean. From the time that I was a little girl, I heard sketchy stories about hiding men from my grandmother and my mother. Their recollections were possibly recounted from their own mothers and grandmothers. All my life, I have heard mothers say to their children, not only my mother but other Native mothers, "If you don't be good little boys and girls the *inoogoorock* will get you." Or if a child was afraid of the dark it was because the hiding man would get them.

The mysterious hiding man of northern Alaska goes many generations back in history. There were definite sightings when my mother was growing up. Her mother told her of strange characters dashing into willow groves when spotted by a human. They were from all reports always thin in stature, with the skin on their face dry and wrinkled, not from old age apparently, but sort of weather-beaten. The ones who were sighted appeared to be about in their forties or fifties in age, for they were very quick and agile. Their clothing was usually well-worn, ragged, and faded whether it be of cloth or hides. Their lower extremities were never seen, except from long distances; consequently it could not be said for certain what sort of footwear they had. But in the summer, when tracks could be seen in the sandy river beach of the Tuksuk River, there were barefoot prints, and in the winter in the snow they had some sort of footwear for the tracks that were made were not from bare feet.

I had a strange experience of my own when we were camping one summer up near the Tuksuk River. While we all slept in our tent one night, I was awakened just before dawn by the sound of voices speaking in some foreign Native language. Perhaps, I, too, possess a trace of a supernatural sense. Or maybe the ones I heard were actually Russian refugees. The very way they giggled and laughed, they sounded like children, perhaps two or three of them. Their voices sounded similar to the way a 33 LP record would sound if played at 45 speed. When I heard the voices, in a vague way I said to myself, "Gee, the rest of the kids are up already and playing outside." I rubbed the sleep from my eyes as I raised my head from the pillow to see if everyone was accounted for. They were all still sound asleep; after all it was still dusk outside. I heard muffled laughter and chattering but could not understand a word that was said. "They" were laughing and playing on the side of the tent where I slept with Anne and Gussie. I slept near the outside wall. The antics continued for several minutes, and my heart was pounding in my throat. I was so frightened. Soon the playfulness faded away. I really didn't go back to sleep, for I couldn't wait to tell Mama and the rest what I had heard while everyone slept. As soon as everyone was awake and we were rolling up the bedding, I told them what I had heard in the wee hours before daybreak. We wasted no time going outside and found evidence of playful activity in the sandy ground outside the tent. There actually were scooped out places, footprints, and general disarray in the sand. Later that day a neighbor who was camped a hundred yards away said some of their dried salmon was missing from the racks, and footprints of people could be seen as if there had been a scuffle. We thought they could be extraterrestrial beings or visitors from outer space.

My father, who was quite a practical person and not given to inventing tall stories, had some experiences that are hard to explain unless one believes in sasquatch or other beings of such types. He had a hut out on the Tuksuk—similar to an igloo, dug partly into the ground and roofed with sod—where he stayed when hunting and trapping in the winter. Several times while spending the night there he heard something walking about near his cabin. The thing would walk on the snow-packed roof of his cabin and stomp its feet. The snow would crunch under the heavy footsteps, and his dogs would become nervous and bristle and bark in a manner that indicated a fear of something they did not quite understand.

Another time, while gathering driftwood at Brevig Lagoon, he had taken along my younger brother Tony and my two younger sisters Wilma and Pauline. They were sitting on a log near the shoreline eating their lunch when the younger ones noticed Papa stand up quickly to get a better look at something that he thought was a human. For some minutes, Papa's gaze was fixed on the being as it walked upright at first, then got down on all fours and scampered along that way for awhile, then stood up like a man again. It came within a hundred yards of him, but always stayed partially hidden by some willows. The younger children seemed unaware that Papa was getting quite concerned at this creature playing hide-and-seek with him. They were too busy playing and horsing around. As dusk began to fall and a souther began to whip up, Papa said, "Come, let's start for home."

In his meanderings around the wilds of Alaska, even in some places where no human had been before him, he encountered at least four unexplainable creatures. They were always alone, and he never could get up close to them. They had a way of eluding a man. I guess that's why we always called them hiding men.

6

No more children were born to my parents after Robert came into the world in 1928. Albert Junior, who was given the same name as the one-day-old baby boy who had died during the flu epidemic, came along in 1920, just two years after the previous Albert Junior. Five children were brought into the world between 1920 and 1928. By this time, the four eldest had gone away from home with Papa and Mama's good wishes, which left nine of us still at home. We were a lusty crowd and sometimes Papa had his hands full keeping us in line. When bickering started, he'd stop it by separating the ones responsible for it rather than try to find out who started it since both sides would say the other one had. If my father saw anyone sitting around looking lazy while there was still something to be done, he would see that our minds and hands were kept busy as he believed in the old adage "idle hands wrought no good."

David, being the oldest and biggest one at home at this time, always seemed to get everything he set his mind to. For instance, at the noon recess from school he always got home first and therefore got the mush pot left over from breakfast, which we always fought over. There was not much to eat that was already cooked, and there was no such thing as leftovers at our house. So whoever was unlucky enough not to get the leftover mush, had to be satisfied with smoked or dried salmon and homemade bread with peanut butter. David, of course, got the Eagle Brand milk too. There were no such snack foods as sandwich makings or potato chips that are available to the schoolchildren now. Nor were there drive-in hamburger stands.

Mama's mild manners and lightheartedness stemmed from her upbringing. The Eskimos of that era were mild-tempered, and the families were closely knit. Their ways blended into a gentle and indulgent pattern in their everyday lives. Mama left the discipline up to Papa for he was the boss, and we all knew it. What my father said, he meant, and we knew that he was not going to tell us two or three times. If you didn't do what you were told the first time he said it, you got a good preaching that you never forgot. I don't recall ever seeing or hearing of an Eskimo child being chastised by his parents. But the Eskimos never thought Papa was a mean man because he spanked his children. They knew that he was strict. He expected us to understand the meaning of his teachings and preachings in order that we would become respectable and responsible citizens as we grew up into manhood and womanhood. He wanted us to know right from wrong. He could not tolerate a lazy person. He instilled in us a sense of being useful human beings. Papa was a firm believer that you can do anything in the world you wanted to, no matter what, you just had to stick with it. He not only was a good father, he was our teacher, doctor, counselor, psychologist, minister, and ideologist.

All the boys in the family were natural musicians. They all mastered and played any musical instrument that came into their hands. The oldest brother Tom played the violin; David, the second brother, played the accordion and mouth harp; Albert, the guitar and accordion; Tony, the guitar and accordion too; and Robert, the youngest boy in the family, played anything from piano to guitar and accordion to drums. When Robert was in the army in the early 1950s, he put together a band, and they played in several night spots in Anchorage.

My father was revered by the Eskimos because he was intelligent and kind to everyone. If he had ever done anybody wrong, he would have had a bad name. The Natives thought very well of him because they thought he did things in just the right way. They even looked up to him as a kind of wise chief and would come to him for advice and help in all kinds of

Brother Albert, with guitar, and friend, Teller, 1920.

matters. He made friends with everybody. I don't think Papa ever had an enemy, although there were some people he did not like for good reason. If anybody was hungry, he gave them food. He would loan his boat or his sled if a man had to go get food or fuel for his family. He would do anything if there was a legitimate reason for it, but he didn't want somebody to just come along and say, "I want to use your boat" or "Can I borrow your gun?"

If the reason was good, he'd say, "Sure, you can have it, but bring it back at such and such a time." He took good care of everything he owned and expected others to do likewise. If a person borrowed his dogs and abused them or was careless with his boat or rifle, they never got another chance.

When anyone was sick or hurt, they'd send for Albert Bernhardt, and he'd always go at once and see what they needed. He would tell the parent, "That child has a high temperature. Make her stay in bed and give her lots of liquids. No solid food as long as there is a fever." And when the temperature had gone down, he'd say, "Now you can let her have a bit of soup or stew until she is stronger." About the only medicine he had available to prescribe was aspirin or whiskey. He could set broken bones and stitch up wounds. He often said that he wished he had been able to become a doctor. I think he would have been a good one. He was gentle and understanding, and people loved him, and he loved them. There was no unpleasant task he would not do if called upon. If a person died or was killed, he would help prepare and bury the body.

Other than his desire to have been a doctor, I never heard my father express an indication that he would have cared to have done something different with his life. But he used to do a lot of silent thinking, and I've often wondered what his thoughts were then. The first thing in the morning he was always quiet and moody and had little to say. As soon as he was dressed, he would go down to the water's edge and stand for a time with his hands behind his back looking out across the bay toward the ocean that could lead one to anywhere in the world. Maybe it was just a sailor's habit that he'd developed in his years of standing shipboard watches, but whatever went on in his mind down there on the beach always made a different person of him. He'd come back to the house full of life and anxious to get on with the day's activities. When he came in, he'd give his predictions for the day's weather. "The wind is going to blow southeast this evening" or "There's a ring around the sun [or moon]—that means rain is coming." He was usually right about the weather as with most other things.

He and Bill Maloney and also Jimmy LaPierre were the doers of Teller, but Papa was the leader. Whenever a problem came up, whether it be with the school, sickness, disasters brought on by natural causes, or whatever, Papa always began the initial act. Whenever the schoolhouse needed a new rope for the bell, which was the kind that you rang to call the students to class, Papa would make the rounds of the parents to find out who would help to replace the old weather-rotted rope. Although Teller had a territorial school at the time we attended, Papa couldn't see waiting till they could submit a request to Juneau for this needed part of the upkeep that the territory was responsible for. Whenever there was an outbreak of a communicable disease, Papa saw to it that the ones involved, whether in our family or others in town, were made aware of the proper care for their recovery. Whenever the lagoon back of Teller was about to flood our town in the spring, Papa got the men and boys together to sandbag the banks. These are just a few examples of the foresight that our father had.

Every moment that he could spare from his busy and sometimes action-filled days, he spent reading. I remember such periodicals as *The Pathfinder, The Manchester Guardian, Reader's Digest,* and more, which he acquired from the captains or members of the crew of the many ships that stopped at Port Clarence. To him they were a precious commodity, and he would stack them in his closet or on a shelf near where he did his reading. Whenever an occasion came up that we had to have an explanation about something, he would say, "I just read the other day about why that is" or "According to an article in *Reader's Digest,* it happened this way." He always gave a sensible answer or an explanation that we could understand to any question that we might ask him. The main rules he lived by were cleanliness, honesty, and trust in God.

Our house was lighted by a gasoline lantern and kerosene lamps. The gas lantern was used mostly in the main room of the house where our parents spent most of their time during the winter months. My father did his usual reading while Mama sewed on furs. The kettle on the stove sang in high monotonous tones and the wind outside howled in the dark night. The kerosene lamps, with their flaming wicks, made a reddish light that was hard to see by. We would study or read at one long table with a lamp in the middle, the boys at one end and the girls at the other. It was hard to see if the lamp was too far away, and we'd start bickering about who should be closest to the light. Papa often had to quiet us down several times during an evening.

In later years he installed a small gasoline-powered dc generator in a little shed outside, and we had electric lights. What a blessing compared to the dim reddish light of the kerosene lamp. We thought we were in high society with electric lights. Then in the later 1930s he built a windmill to generate power. My father believed in solar heat and energy from the wind.

Papa's social time involved playing the card game whist at the Tweets. They would have a series of these games going that would last for days, and the only time-out would be for the participants to go home and tend to a few chores. Then they'd resume the intense game again the following evening.

The Tweet family was one of the wealthiest at Teller for they owned two prosperous mining interests in the Teller area, one at Dease Creek and the other at Gold Run. They had four husky Norwegian sons, and they did not hire any outside help to work their gold mines. Papa and David were the only members of our family who were ever inside of their house. Besides Papa playing cards at their house winter evening after evening, David would stop by to get the boys to play a game of Eskimo football, or *munna munna.*

Another popular sport in the winter was ice sailing. Walter Marx, the Tweet boys, and my brother David all had their own rigs that they built themselves. The rig was a pair of skis fastened together, then a pole with a sail attached. They would sail them on the glare ice on the big lake back of Teller whenever the wind blew, and they could travel at times up to thirty miles per hour.

The Tweet boys were always shy of us girls whenever they came to our house. They never spoke about how prosperous their mining interests were, but the way in which they lived showed that they were among the wealthy folk of Teller. They ate like kings and always had baked hams, turkeys, chicken, and beef roasts, while we, the poorer families, subsisted mostly from the land, sea, and rivers—nature's breadbox.

There was no such thing as racial discrimination at Teller—everyone intermingled without a feeling of inferiority even though there were all the ingredients to make such a condition exist since there were Natives, half-bloods, and the rich whites. Papa always said that the situation that breeds racism is the overabundance of money, or in other words, the rich. He said they more or less buy their station in life, and therefore, they get the idea that they are better than others. He said, "Not that their bodies or minds are any better than ours." One of his favorite quotes is from the Bible: "For the love of money is the root of all evil" (I Timothy 6:10).

For recreation Mama loved to play the outdoor games that the young folks played, and she played just as hard as the kids. Her favorite winter pastime was Eskimo football, *munna munna*. It was similar to soccer and played by everyone from grownups to older children of both sexes, out on the smooth sea ice of the bay or on the hard, crusted snow on the lagoon behind the town. Because of the scarcity of wood there were no goal posts. Circles were cut into the ice or snow and the ball had to be kicked into one of them to score. It was an age-old game, played by Eskimos longer than anyone could remember. Mama said that in her young days in the wintertime when the moon was full, everyone in her village would be out kicking the ball. The ball they used at Teller was exactly the same as the ones used by the early-day Eskimos, cut out of sealskin, sewn together, and stuffed with reindeer hair. I made many of them at home. It was amazing how far such a ball could be kicked, and how much bounce it had. And how our mother loved to join in the game. Weather permitting, Saturdays and Sundays were football days. She loved natural things and the outdoors. About the only time she ever sat still was to eat or sew.

She also liked to be social with people of her age group. There were about four or five Eskimo families who lived in Teller regularly (I mean they didn't move from one village to the next like the more nomadic Natives liked to do). She and the older family members loved to play cards during the dark, stormy evenings of winter. They had their own version of poker and one game sort of like gin rummy. There was a lot of competition; you could tell by the way they played and all the enthusiasm they displayed. There was a lot of hilarity and merriment during the progress of the card games. They would play until the wee hours of the morning. We never saw anyone get angry.

Sometimes, when Mama had a few moments to just sit down and relax, she would tell us an Eskimo story, something like an Aesop fable in the Eskimo tradition. One that I remembered through the years was the one about how there came to be polar bears and black bears. This story I remember well as I wrote it down on March 22, 1935, for our journalism class when I was a student at Edmonds High School.

This legend concerns the Eskimo dogs, which are the Eskimos' only beasts of burden and are capable of doing about fifty miles a day for many successive days. These wolfish animals, according to the early Eskimos, used to stand about four feet high, with features resembling those of a bear more than the diminutive wolf-like type of dogs today.

The Beginning of Two Bears

One cold clear day in midwinter a certain huge bear-like dog was the proud parent of two clumsy little animals as much different from one another as if they were not of the same parentage. One was as black as night, and the other was as white as the surrounding snow-covered country. They grew up and finally came to the stage when their mother told them they had to seek their own foraging for food and shift for themselves. She took them out early one morning and directed the black one, which as it grew up resembled a black bear, and told him he had to inhabit the inland. Then she took his brother, the white one, and pointed out towards the ice floes and icebergs and told him he was to make his home among the floating masses of ice and snow. So, they claim, that's how there came to be black bears and polar bears.

My father always talked things over with my mother, which I understand was not customary with many old-time Germans. In some ways Mama was still like a child and eager to learn. She'd ask questions, and he'd explain things to her, part in English, part in Eskimo. He even taught her to speak a little German, and now and then she'd use a German word in conversation. She may have thought it was an English word because when he was teaching her English, he'd sometimes accidentally throw in a little of his native tongue. The Eskimo he spoke was actually more of the pidgin-type or a jargon containing parts of many languages. He could communicate well with non-English-speaking Eskimos but understood much more than he could speak.

Mama had quite a sense of humor and could be a real comedian at times. Once one of my older sisters came back from Nome wearing make-up, silk stockings, and high-heeled shoes. We were sitting in the kitchen chatting when we heard a clumping sound, and here came Mama with the silk stockings and high-heeled shoes on, her ankles wobbling. She'd smeared some of my sister's rouge on her cheeks and daubed on lipstick. "Look at me! I'm a flapper from Nome," she giggled. We girls had a big laugh over the outfit our mother had put on.

Mama adhered to many of the old Eskimo customs. One was the manner in which she cared for her babies. The youngest, until it was big enough to walk, was always carried on her back in her parka or *umuk*. I suppose to the baby it was like being in a perpetual motion cradle, probably like still being in the womb, absorbing the warmth of its mother's body and comforted by her movements. Babies carried in this manner seldom fretted. I don't remember there ever being any "accidents." The Eskimo mother seemed to sense by the baby's movements that it was time for it to "go." I've heard Mama suddenly say, "Hold it, hold it!" and whip the little one out of her hood and onto the coffee can, or whatever was being used for a potty, always just in the nick of time. There were some close calls though.

✳   ✳   ✳

It seems when the aurora borealis was active in the northern sky at night, the radio and communication by shortwave were drastically disrupted. We would gather outside the house and stand, mouth agape, at the antics the aurora borealis displayed. In all colors of the spectrum it would form all sorts of shapes and dash here and there like a giant whip wielded by an unseen hand. It would come in the shape of a bell, then a streamer of ribbon, then Santa and his reindeer, and just about anything you could imagine. We would whistle and make it dash even faster across the sky—it seemed to come from all directions as we whistled in sharp staccato. All my life I have wondered just why it is that the auroral displays seemed to activate when we would whistle at them. Perhaps the scientists know the answer to that.

And then there was the radio. The first ones, bulky battery-operated sets with a half dozen or so dials, first showed up at Teller in the mid-twenties. Reception was poor in the summer, but in winter when it was cold and clear and when there where no northern light displays to cause static, stations were often picked up from everywhere in the world. We had one of the first radio sets at Teller, an old Philco battery operated. One station that came in loud and clear was KNX in Los Angeles. Many Saturday evenings we listened to the National Barn Dance and other popular programs of those days. The first set that Papa bought was a six-tube Philco with a crooked horn loudspeaker. Saturday evening was radio night at our house, and it was almost impossible to get us away from the set as long as the batteries held out. Mama wasn't especially interested in what came over the air. Often when we'd be glued to the speaker listening to some program from far away, she'd say, "You can have your old radio. I'm going over to visit with so-and-so," and she'd be gone for the evening.

As Sarah, Anne, Gussie, and I reached our teens and began blossoming into womanhood, one of us was always getting a proposal of marriage. Back then marriageable women in Alaska were outnumbered by bachelors by about ten to one. Under such conditions of no competition a girl didn't have to be very bright or pretty to get a man. But looking through old family pictures taken in those days, we appear to have all been quite attractive. We had dark eyes, shiny black hair, straight white teeth, nice figures, and we were always clean. So Mama watched us like a hawk, especially when a ship was in the harbor.

When the Coast Guard cutters came north each year for the Bering Sea and Arctic Ocean patrol, they always anchored just offshore. We used to think it was so the officers could come ashore and visit with our father, but now I think it was mainly because of all the girls Mr. Bernhardt had. When we were older, the four of us slept in a separate little house of our own, and our parents and the younger children lived in the larger house. The walls and ceilings were papered with old newspapers to help keep out the drafts, and you could read the details of the news highlights of those days. Prominently displayed were the trial and conviction of the famous murderess Winnie Ruth Judd, other sensational crimes of the 1920s, the flights of Charles A. Lindbergh and other famous transatlantic aviators, and the front page from a Seattle paper, showing a picture of several of us standing in front of the wrecked dirigible *Norge* lying on the ice at Teller.

Just because we lived far off the beaten track didn't mean we were out of touch with the rest of the world. In the summertime we were almost constantly in contact with the crews of ships that just ten days or two weeks earlier had been in such ports as Vancouver, B.C.; Seattle; or San Francisco. We learned the latest songs from the sailors and picked up all the new expressions that they used. Our parents didn't always approve of some of the slang the visitors taught us, even though it was perfectly harmless. I guess it was just the Eskimo's natural resistance to change. We had a generation gap in those days, too. Some phrases and slang we heard in the late 1920s were "High old time," "Sez you," and "So's your old man." My sisters were taught to dance the Charleston, which was a dance craze at the time.

Our parents liked to see us have a good time, so when the sailors were ashore, the big room in the main house would be cleared, and Papa would get out his accordion and play the music that my sisters and the sailors danced to. We had some wonderful times, even if our mother didn't trust us out of her sight. Nowadays a girl will say to her parents, "You don't trust me," as an excuse for being allowed to do as she pleases. Of course, we weren't trusted, nor should we have been. Our parents would have shirked their responsibilities had they given in and let us do whatever we wanted. With very little stimulation young emotions can quickly become uncontrollable. So I'm glad now that Mama didn't trust us. She probably saved us from a lot of heartaches.

There was a young good-looking, red-headed Greek in Teller named Mike Ganitos who used to come to our house. He had a small gold mine and also a jade mine and was considered to be quite well-to-do. At about thirty-five, he was very handsome with his beautiful red hair and trimmed mustache. And he was about the cleanest man you ever saw. We girls thought he liked Mary Müller pretty much, and I believe she liked him a bit, too. When I was about sixteen years old, Mike used to say, "Bessie, when you get older I'm going to marry you." I thought that was the rudest thing a grown man could say to an innocent young girl, and it used to burn me to a crisp when he'd say it. I thought he was only kidding me, and marriage was something you just didn't joke about. Then, when I was seventeen, he said, "Bessie, would you marry me if your father said you could?" I knew then that he was serious. I'm sure he would have been a very good husband, but I was not about to become "Mrs." to anybody. I said, "No!" and resentment welled up inside of me.

Then one day he got me in a corner and handed me a gift-wrapped small package and said, "Here is something for you."

"What is it?" I asked.

"Open it and see."

I opened the box, and there was a beautiful ruby ring, my birthstone. That ruby was a jewel to behold. But I shoved him away and threw the ring at him. "I don't want it!" I said. "Give it to someone else!" I was deeply insulted that a man old enough to be my uncle would want to marry me. I couldn't conceive of a marriage between a seventeen-year-old girl and a thirty-five-year-old man. I had no intention of getting married at the time. I'm glad now that it worked out the way it did—it wasn't meant for me to settle down and raise a family, as probably would have happened. I really couldn't see it that way. Some of the girls thought I was crazy. There I had a chance to marry a wealthy man. I know he would have been good and kind to me, and I could have had about anything I wanted. I threw it all away, but I'm glad I did. At that time of my life, I didn't know what love meant.

Later that year, when he got back from his mine, Mike Ganitos came to our house and handed me a gold wristwatch. Again I refused his gift. He told me, "I want you to have it, no strings attached. I am just giving it to you because I like you as a friend."

"Well, I'll have to ask my father first," I said.

After he had gone, I told Papa that Mike had wanted to give me a beautiful gold watch.

"Why didn't you take it? You're going to go away to school soon and you probably won't ever see him again, and a watch will come in handy when you're at school," Papa said; he was a practical man.

So the next time I saw Mike, I told him that it was all right for me to accept the watch, and it made him feel good that I accepted his gift. But I never did like it because it came from him, the man who had marriage on his mind. I don't know why I had such an aversion to him, unless it was the difference in our ages. I didn't want to be thought of as the years went by as an old man's darling. I liked him as a family friend, and he was always the perfect gentleman. After I had been away at school for several months, I traded the watch for another one from one of the girls. I guess I didn't want to have a constant reminder of Mike Ganitos.

✳   ✳   ✳

Early in 1928 my father got a letter by dog team mail from Henry A. Larsen, the Norwegian mate who'd been on Klengenberg's *Maid of Orleans* back in 1924 and who'd wanted to marry Sarah. He wrote that he had joined the Royal Canadian Mounted Police and was the sergeant in charge of a patrol schooner being built at North Vancouver, British Columbia. The vessel, to be christened *St. Roch*, would be ready to leave for the Arctic in late June, and he expected to reach Teller several weeks later. Larsen wanted to know if Papa could have a ton or so of dried salmon to sell to the mounted police. It would be for the dogs they would use on winter patrols in the Far North while the ship was frozen-in. Papa answered that the dog feed would be ready when they arrived.

The school year ended, the ice went out, and we moved back to Nook for the summer. The runs of smelt, herring, and salmon came. No matter how busy we were at fishing and taking care of the catch, we all kept an eye seaward, anxious for the first glimpse of the expected vessel. We girls wondered if Henry Larsen would still be in love with Sarah and would the mounties be as handsome as the pictures we had seen of them. Would they be wearing their broad-brimmed hats, scarlet tunics, riding breeches with gold stripes, and black shiny boots?

Then one day in mid-July when a brisk onshore wind was blowing, a two-masted schooner, with jib and foresail and mainsail bellied before the westerly, hove into view around Point Spencer. Papa watched her through his binoculars for a time. "That's got to be her," he said. "She's flying the Union Jack." We saw few sailing ships anymore and thought she was a beauty, heeling to the wind and with a white wave at her bow. But Papa, old sailor that he was, was critical of her rig. He shook his head and said, "She looks like a powerboat that's had sails put on as an afterthought. Her mainmast is too tall, and she ought to have topsails." By this time most of the older schooners that we knew had been converted to motor vessels, the bowsprits cut off, the canvas removed, the masts shortened, and the booms added for hoisting cargo. As much as my father loved sailing ships, in his opinion the approaching craft had been de-modernized. "Don't those Canucks know the days of sail are over?"

The stubby little ship, about a hundred feet long, was painted gray with a white stripe from stem to stern. Amidships the deck was piled high with sacked coal, oil drums, and lumber. She rode deep in the water from the heavy load she carried. The pilothouse and cabin were in the after portion of the vessel. As she drew nearer, we could read the black lettering on the bow, *St. Roch*. The closer view was not as impressive as the distant one. The odds and ends of supplies on deck made her appear almost as unkempt and cluttered as the MS *Patterson*, which had come and gone a few days earlier, bound for Herschel Island.

As the schooner approached its anchorage near the Grantley Harbor entrance, some of the crew clambered over the cargo to the stays, the canvas was dropped, and the vessel lost the glamor of the sailing ship and became just another powerboat, chugging along with black diesel engine smoke trailing from her stack. No one who watched the *St. Roch* that day would have guessed from her appearance that she would one day become the most famous ship in the history of the North, and that her captain, Sergeant Henry A. Larsen, would be one of the great Arctic navigators. The *St. Roch* was the only craft to navigate the ice-jammed Northwest Passage in both directions. In 1940 Larsen and a crew of nine sailed the Northwest Passage all the way to Halifax, the first ship to accomplish this. Four years later Henry A. Larsen sailed the ship back through the Northwest Passage to be the first man to sail a ship from east to west.

Papa and David piled into the *Devil Whale*, our launch, and shortly after the Canadian police schooner had dropped anchor, they were alongside. Sergeant Larsen was standing in the open pilothouse door looking the same as when we'd last seen him four years before—stocky, blonde, blue-eyed, and ruddy-faced. Most of the crew were young men, handsome in the eyes of teenage girls. But not a one was wearing the famous uniform of the R.C.M.P., being garbed in the ordinary clothes of working seamen. But when off duty, they were something to set eyes on in their traditional red tunics, black trousers with a gold stripe down each leg, snappy stetson hats with the gold cord around the crown, and black boots.

"Hello, Henry!" Papa called. "Long time, no see!"

"Hello, Albert!" his voice still carried a Norwegian accent. "Is our dog feed ready?"

"Come aboard, and I'll take you to Nook and you can see it."

"If you say it's all right I'll take your word for it," Larsen said.

"Come along anyhow, and we'll have a mug-up. I got a pretty good smoke on my kings this year."

At the mention of smoked king salmon, Larsen was over the side and into our boat. The chief engineer, a corporal introduced as Jack Foster, and one of the younger constables came along. Chugging back to Nook in the *Devil Whale* Larsen asked, "Where is Sarah? Is she married yet?"

"Oh, she got married a few months ago."

"I hope she is happy and has a good husband," he replied.

Larsen inspected the salmon dangling in the wind on the drying racks. "Looks pretty good. How much you got here?" he asked Papa.

"About a ton and a half."

"We'll take it all," Larsen announced.

Mama poured strong, hot coffee, sliced warm fresh bread, and put a big dish of smoked salmon on the table. We kids all sat back listening to the men talk, and we girls returned the admiring glances of the twinkly-eyed engineer, Corporal Foster. In his late twenties, he had a way of looking at a girl that made her feel that she was the most important person in the world. Mama kept an eye on us girls, noticing that we were stricken with amour in our eyes.

At first the conversation was about Amundsen. "I never had a chance to meet the man," Sergeant Larsen said, "but he came from the next town from where I was born in Norway."

"Do you think there's a chance that he's still alive up there in the ice pack somewhere?" Papa asked.

"Not a chance, Albert. If he was in a ship or was driving dogs, I'd say yes, but with an airplane there's too many things that could go haywire and that he had no control over. No, I think we've seen the last of Roald Amundsen."

They discussed some of the missing explorer's famous expeditions, dwelling at some length on the three-year voyage through the Northwest Passage in the old fishing sloop *Gjoa*. "If he had had a ship like the *St. Roch*, he could have made it in one year, I'll bet you that."

"How do you think your ship will stand up in the ice pack, Henry?"

"None better was ever built. Her hull is as round as an egg and that makes her a miserable rolling brute in the open sea, but if she ever gets in a squeeze she'll pop up out of the ice and not be crushed like a better sea boat might. And you never saw such timbers in a ship her size, Albert. No ice will ever sink the *St. Roch*."

"She's way underpowered, though," Corporal Foster said. "She has only a 150-horsepower engine when she should have at least 300."

"Why did they rig her for sail, anyway?" Papa asked.

"That's those old fogey politicians in Ottawa," Larsen said. "They say that wind is free and diesel oil costs money. I know, and you know, what's going to happen when we get in the ice, Albert. We'll just sit and stir up the water and get no place, even if there is a wind."

"As I remember the *Gjoa*, she didn't have much of an engine, either."

"A thirteen-horsepower kerosene engine is what she had. Her tonnage was less than fifty, ours is eighty. She was an old, old boat, ours is brand new. Yeah, if I had the chance, I'll bet you I could take that *St. Roch* through the Northwest Passage myself, and maybe in just one season, too, if the ice and the weather were just right."

David and the young constable came in, smelling of dried salmon. "It's all in the boat and ready to go, Skipper," the mountie said.

Mama poured more coffee, and the conversation continued. My father wanted to know all about the schooner and how much use it would be in a region where the navigation season seldom lasted more than ninety days, and some years even less than that on account of the ice conditions.

"Our patrols will be from Herschel Island," Larsen said, "just east of the Alaska border near the mouth of the Mackenzie River, all the way to Cambridge Bay on Victoria Island at the other end of Dease Strait. We plan to visit all the major villages and as many of the small ones as we can every season. Some of those tribes up there have been having a lot of starvation and sickness. People have started coming in by airplane to places that never saw a white man before. It's not been good for the Natives."

"Same old story," Papa said. "Get in, get it, and get out."

"There are tribes up there, like the Kogmolliks, that live just as their ancestors did a thousand years ago. They still use seal oil lamps and hunt with bows and arrows and spears. As long as they are left alone, they get along all right, but a couple of white men in an airplane can doom a whole village. They'll connive them out of their furs and ivory for practically nothing or give them some disease they have no resistance against."

"I'm glad to hear that the Canadian government is trying to do something to take care of their Eskimos."

"It's about time. They're wonderful people, but a little longer and it will be too late to save them. One good measles epidemic could wipe out every Eskimo up there."

"And you say you're going to freeze-in for the winter?"

"Yeah. When the ice starts to move south in August, we'll find a sheltered bay, freeze her in, and make winter patrols by dog team. We expect to be icebound about nine months of every year."

"Enough to drive a man crazy, eh, Henry?"

"Oh, there will be plenty to keep us busy."

"I suppose your boys will do a bit of hunting and trapping?"

"Yeah, lots of fur up there: fox, wolf, polar bear, muskrat, rabbits, caribou. You ever been in the Canadian Arctic, Albert?"

"No, when I was on the whaler, we didn't get beyond the Beaufort Sea, but I've heard stories from people who have been there. Sounds like great country."

"If you're tough and know how to take care of yourself, it is. No place for a cheechako, though."

David had been sitting quietly, fascinated by the dialogue between Henry Larsen and our father. During a break in the conversation, he said, "I sure wish I was going with you, Sergeant."

"How old are you, David?"

"Eighteen."

"Can you drive dogs?"

"I've been doing it since I was a little kid."

"We're allowed to hire Native guides and dog team drivers as special constables. If you'd like to come along, I'd be glad to have you."

David got excited. "Can I go, Papa?"

My father puffed on his pipe for a few moments and glanced toward Mama before answering. "You know the rules, Dave, you boys can't leave home until you're twenty-one."

"Can't I go just for the summer?"

"They won't be coming back this season, are you, Henry?"

"No, not until fall a year from now."

"I could come back on the *Patterson*; she'll be up there, too."

Papa glanced at Mama and right away knew her answer. "I'm sorry, Dave, but there's too much work for you to do at home. We can't get along without you yet. Albert isn't big enough to take over your jobs."

David didn't argue but you could see him swallowing hard to keep a lump down in his throat. He was terribly disappointed, but disobedience was unthinkable. We had been taught by our Eskimo mother that the good of the family always came before anyone's personal wishes. In the harsh life of her youth and that of her ancestors, the selfish act of an individual could destroy the family unit.

Sergeant Larsen slapped him on the shoulder. "It's only a couple years, Dave, and you've got a long life ahead of you. We'll be coming out next year and going North again the year after that. You'll be of age by then, and you can sure go with us if you want to." He emptied his coffee cup, complimented Mama on her baking and Papa on his smoked salmon, then got to his feet. "I guess it's time we got that dog feed aboard and our anchor up."

"What's the hurry, Henry?" Papa said. "The ice usually doesn't go out at Barrow until the first of August."

"It's five hundred miles to Barrow, and we don't go very fast. I talked by wireless to the Hudson's Bay company ship *Baychimo* this morning. They said the ice went out once already, but the last storm brought it back again. The *Boxer*, the *Patterson*, and the *Baychimo* are anchored down the coast waiting for it to go out again, and I want to be there when it does. It's another twelve hundred miles to Cambridge Bay, and we have a lot of stops to make." He paid for the ton and a half of dried salmon.

That evening we crossed over to Teller where a dance was held at Jimmy LaPierre's Woodbine hall in honor of the Canadian visitors. This time they were in uniform, and all the women and girls in town fell in love with the handsome mounties. The whole town turned out for the dance. Papa played the accordion, Jim LaPierre his violin, David his guitar and mouth harp, and old man Tweet put his musical talent in by clicking his musical spoons. A wonderful time was had by all.

When the sun set at half past midnight, the dance was going full swing. It was still going strong and noisy at sunrise three hours later. At the finish of a piece of music Sergeant Larsen went to the center of the floor and said, "I hate to stop the fun folks, but it's almost high tide. Time to go, boys." We all went down to the beach to see the mounties off to their little ship. "I sure wish I was going with them," David said. As they were about to shove off, Corporal Foster recited a little poem:

We left our horses far behind,
And took to the open sea,
For we are the men of the horse marines,
But they call us the R.C.M.P.

The *St. Roch* sailed away with her ambitious and courageous crew for the ice-locked ports of call. In return for the Alaskan husky Larsen bought that year, he brought Papa a McKenzie River husky a year later. She was a beautiful animal.

For the remainder of the summer of 1928 and the winter following the departure of the *St. Roch*, David talked about little else than what he'd heard Henry Larsen say about the wonders of the Canadian Arctic. He found an old map of the Arctic Regions and spent long hours pouring over it. He borrowed every book in town that had any reference to the Canadian Arctic. Then, the following year when Captain Pederson of the *Patterson* brought our supplies, David pleaded with our parents to be allowed to take a summer's job on her to Cambridge Bay in the Canadian Arctic and back. He was still two years shy of being twenty-one, but Mama interceded for him and said, "He has always been a good boy, Papa. We won't need to worry about him." We girls promised to pitch in and do his chores so he

David, my older brother, on his trading schooner in Canada's
Northwest Territories, 1933.

could make the trip. So David was allowed to go with Captain Pederson in
the summer of 1929.

When the *Patterson* returned in the fall, my brother was not aboard.
"He wanted to spend the winter at Bathurst Inlet in Northern Canada," the
captain said, "so we left him there. But don't worry about that young man.
He's a natural for the country and everybody likes him."

We never saw David again. He has lived for many years at Coppermine,
Northwest Territories. He married a Canadian Inuit girl who died, leaving
him with four children. By a later marriage he had two more children. During the years when the *St. Roch* was wintering at Coppermine, David worked

as a special constable, as an interpreter, for the mounted police under the direction of Sergeant Henry Larsen. He also spent time at court hearings in different parts of the Northwest Territories interpreting for jurors. The Royal Canadian Mounted Police hold court in that province, and they are the judges at those hearings.

I have some correspondence which I received from Henry A. Larsen in the early 1950s, after he became superintendent of the G Division of the Royal Canadian Mounted Police in Ottawa. When Sergeant Larsen was in charge of the RCMP barracks in Vancouver, B.C., I wrote him as I had not a word from my brother David in almost a year. Sergeant Larsen wrote back to me and said he had sent Corporal Cormier to locate David. He said David was in fine shape and busy fur trapping and trading from village to village in his schooner.

After many years of patrolling the Arctic, in 1940 Sergeant Larsen was ordered to attempt a voyage through the Northwest Passage. Following Amundsen's route, it took two and a half years. The *St. Roch* got to Halifax, Nova Scotia, on October 11, 1942, becoming the first ship in history to sail from west to east through the Northwest Passage. Two years later, in 1944, returning by a more northerly route, Larsen was favored with ideal weather and little ice, making the trip from Halifax to Vancouver, B.C., in eighty-eight days. In later years she traveled from Vancouver B.C. to Halifax by way of the Panama Canal, thus also becoming the first ship to circumnavigate the North American continent. Larsen, Foster, and most of the crew who were on the famous voyages have passed on, but their sturdy ship, long since retired, sits on permanent display in a dry dock at the maritime museum in Vancouver, B.C.

7

With the coming of aviation to remote regions of Alaska, the demand for dried salmon for dog feed began to dwindle as dogs were no longer needed except for local travel. By the early thirties mail and supplies began to come to us by air, and long trips by dog team were getting to be uncommon. Before the airplane, summer travel was mostly by water because overland treks were virtually impossible. The way was blocked by the countless lakes and ponds and mosquito-breeding swamps that filled the valleys between impassable mountain ranges.

In the winter it was easier. There was a network of trails all through the North with roadhouses about every twenty to twenty-five miles, or a day's travel apart. A fast trip from Teller to Fairbanks, over 500 miles, might take fifteen to twenty days, weather permitting. It took weeks longer if one became stormbound on the way. The roadhouses charged several dollars a night for lodging, and meals were a dollar apiece. The food was often poorly prepared by a slovenly cook. Sleeping quarters were usually unheated, and the bed only a hard mattress laid on board slats in a bunk, and you furnished your own sleeping bag. Travelers in the Alaskan bush, understandably, were quick to take to the air.

Alaska, with its vast distances, swamps and mountains and forests, great lakes and swift rivers, frozen muskegs and springtime runoffs, was a difficult country through which to build and maintain highways and railroads. Any wealth found in the North was dependent upon some form of transportation to bring it out. Dogs and snowshoes in winter and river steamers in the summer were not the answer. Aviation was. The airplane might well have been invented for the sole benefit of Alaska. It was love at first sight and a happy marriage for all concerned.

In the beginning the flimsy old crates of wood and fabric, with their short range and undependable engines, made flying over unmapped, un-settled country extremely hazardous. There were no aids to aerial navigation other than natural landmarks—river bends and towering mountains—by which the pilot found his way from point to point. Magnetic compasses were erratic and almost useless in a region so heavily mineralized as many parts of Alaska are. There were few instruments available for blind flying, and fewer men who knew how to use them. The prudent rule was that when the weather was bad, you stayed on the ground. If caught aloft by fog, blowing snow, or bad weather, you got back down as quickly as possible and made yourself comfortable until it was safe to fly again. Bush pilots always carried emergency rations of food and warm clothing in case they had to wait out a storm.

In no place else in the world has air transportation meant so much as it does in Alaska. Over the last fifty years every other person in the state of Alaska has traveled by air, especially so in the northern half where there are no roads or trains. Alaskan bush pilots are known for their ingenuity. In the wilds or primitive areas almost any place where a pilot has twice made a safe landing is regarded as a landing field. Alaskan flyers are among the world's best, being in a land where fog, whiteouts, and blizzards can wipe out landmarks on which many bush pilots have had to depend. In the early days of flying in Alaska, the U.S. Weather Bureau and the U.S. Signal Corps cooperated closely in giving reports to their stations scattered widely over the territory. It was not until 1929 that the U.S. Weather Bureau inaugu-rated weather reports for planes. So there was no guessing, and a pioneering bush pilot had to have more than an ordinary amount of resourcefulness, courage, and instinctive good judgment.

A private pilot for a mining company operating on the slopes of the Endicott Mountains on the Koyukuk River northwest of Fairbanks and a handful of Native boys and men cleared the rocks from a space just wide enough for a runway on a mountainside so that he might land uphill at about a forty-five degree angle. When the wind conditions in the canyon were right, he could land and takeoff. Once, when coming in for a landing, he saw what looked like a large boulder in the middle of his two-by-four field. Seeing that, the pilot thought, "Now where do I land?" Taking a once-over for a closer look, he discovered it was a big black bear, which he frightened away by buzzing low over the field.

My brother Tony flew commercially in Alaska for over eighteen years. Tony and his compatriots in the flying business in Alaska, were literally flying bird-men—they flew instinctively half the time. They landed and took off from seemingly impossible places in an emergency or as circumstances permitted—on mountainsides, river bars, mud flats, gravel beaches, or glaciers—and considered this all in a day's work. They knew they had to do this if they were to fly. Good landing fields or aids to commercial aviation were (and still are in most of northern Alaska) few and far between. When Tony was flying supplies in from Kotzebue or Nome to the Kennicott Mining Company at Ambler, he used skis in winter, wheels in summer, and pontoons to land on rivers and sloughs. He had his air taxi service for many years, doing business as Bernhardt Air Service out of Kobuk, Alaska. He had much competition from other bush pilots and Wein Air Service. In the mid-seventies the small outfits crowded each other out, and Tony sold his Cessna 180 and his Heliocourier and, later on, his Piper Super Cub. In 1987 he retired, and he lived in Hilo, Hawaii, for many years.

Tony, besides operating his own air taxi service, was appointed by Governor Egan to the Fish and Wildlife Commission and held that post for several years. On top of that, he was a licensed big game guide for his part of Alaska, which took in all of the northern Seward Peninsula, the Brooks Range, the western part of the North Slope, Kotzebue, and Barrow. He took many famous people from the south forty-eight as far east as New York, Florida, and Chicago on the hunt of their lives. Whatever game they chose to hunt, whether it be wolf, bear, polar bear, Dahl sheep, mountain goat, or walrus, he knew where to go to get their prize trophy.

Steamboat travel on the Yukon, Tanana, Koyukuk, and Kuskokwim in the summer was much safer and more comfortable than winter travel, but still slow compared to flying. For instance, going from Teller the one hundred miles to Nome as the crow flies, we were three days on the trail when Papa took me there by dogsled that time to have my amputations.

Returning on the *Bessie B* took a day and a half. But in 1932 the first time I flew from home to Nome, we were in the air only an hour. So the convenience of flying was obvious.

All things considered, the benefits of air travel far outweighed the dangers and lack of comfort connected with those flimsy three-seater airplanes. What made the difference was the very special breed of pilot that developed air travel. They were the survivors of the early years of Alaskan flying, men who profited by their own mistakes and of others not so lucky. Even today, with the latest and best of equipment, the North will kill the reckless and incompetent. The bush pilots who continued to live were the cautious, methodical men who kept their aircraft in top condition, filtered their gasoline several times, respected the weather and the country over which they flew, and took to the sky only when the odds were in their favor. Eventually, though, most of the early day flyers died at their profession. It was just that some lasted a bit longer than others. Usually the "killer factor" was the unpredictable weather, something over which the pilot had no control—fog, whiteouts, wing and propeller icing, and blowing snow.

Carl Ben Eielson was such a pilot. We got to know him well at Teller. In fact, we watched him take off from there on his last flight. Born of Norwegian parents in North Dakota in 1897, Ben Eielson learned to fly as a cadet in the U.S. Army in the closing months of the First World War. After barnstorming around the country for a time with a flying circus, he returned to college to complete an education interrupted by the war. While at Georgetown University in Washington, D.C., Ben met Alaska's congressional delegate, Dan Sutherland. His interest in the North was kindled by stories told by the former sourdough, and when Sutherland offered him a job teaching science at the Fairbanks High School, he took it. Ben got there in September of 1922.

In the North people soon learned that he was a pilot. A group of Fairbanks businessmen, impressed by a flight of four army planes from Washington, D.C. to Nome in the summer of 1920, believed that the future of Alaska would be best served by air transportation. They put up the money to buy a war surplus JN-4 training plane, powered by an OX-5 engine. The crated *Jenny* arrived in Fairbanks on an Alaska Railroad flatcar in late June of 1923. Assembled by Eielson and his backers, it was soon taking passengers aloft for $15 a ride. The cost of the *Jenny* and its shipping charges were paid for in the first ten days. It was the first airplane to fly in the interior of Alaska.

When a mine owner asked Ben if he could fly some machinery parts to his mine, six days away by trail, Ben said, "I can give it a try." He flew there in an hour, landed on a sand bar in a river, unloaded the machinery, and returned to Fairbanks. This was the birth of commercial aviation in Alaska.

That fall Ben returned to Washington. With the aid of Delegate Sutherland, he arranged for a mail contract with the Post Office Department to fly an experimental mail route from Fairbanks to McGrath, nearly 300 miles to the southwest. The contract called for ten round trip flights, twice each month, to start in January of 1924. An army airplane would be used, a DeHavilland. The pay would be two dollars a mile, half the cost to move the mail by dog team.

The DeHavilland, an open cockpit biplane, arrived by sea from the States and went by rail to Fairbanks during the winter. It was powered by a Liberty engine with four times the power of the OX-5 in the *Jenny*. Ben equipped the new airplane with skis made by a local carpenter. On the morning of February 21, 1924, with the temperature at twenty-five degrees below zero, he took off from the Fairbanks ballpark with 500 pounds of mail. Flying down the Tanana River to Nenana, then up the Kantishna to Lake Minchumina, he followed the north fork of the Kuskokwim to McGrath. He landed there on the frozen Takotna three hours after leaving Fairbanks. The same trip by dog team normally took twenty days.

Getting a late start for the return trip, Ben reached Fairbanks after dark. The ballpark landing field was outlined by bonfires that had been lighted when his engine was heard coming in the distance. He hit a tree while landing, and the first scheduled air mail flight in Alaska ended with the DeHavilland wrecked. The damage was not serious, and the airplane was flyable in time for the next scheduled flight to McGrath. The following six trips were made without incident, but when coming in for a landing after the eighth flight Ben struck a soft spot on the field and the DeHavilland was badly wrecked. He believed it could be repaired, but the post office department canceled the remaining two flights of the contract and the army plane was shipped back to the States.

Soon other airplanes were brought North to be flown by other pioneering pilots. In 1926 Ben Eielson was hired by the Australian explorer Sir George Hubert Wilkins to be one of the pilots in an Arctic expedition he was organizing. In a single-engine Fokker the two made several flights from Fairbanks to Point Barrow far out over the Arctic Ocean ice pack and were the first to do so. They had no navigational instruments other than a magnetic compass, an air speed indicator, and a watch. They proved that airplanes could be flown in the Arctic and that landings and takeoffs could be made on the ice pack.

In April of 1928 Wilkins and Eielson took off from Point Barrow in a Lockheed Vega monoplane. Their destination was Spitsbergen by way of the Arctic Islands and northern Greenland. After a stormy flight of 1,100 miles, with Ben at the controls for a solid twenty hours and twenty minutes, they landed at Spitsbergen. For their accomplishment Wilkins was knighted Sir Hubert by King George V of England, and Eielson was awarded the Distinguished Flying Cross and the Harmon Trophy by President Herbert Hoover.

Two months later Eielson and Wilkins were on their way to Antarctica by ship. With them was the Vega they'd flown from Alaska to Spitsbergen and another airplane. They traveled on a Norwegian whaler to Deception Island, 700 miles south of Cape Horn, and when the two Vegas were put ashore, they were the first airplanes in the Antarctic. In late November 1928 Ben made history's first Antarctic flight. A few days before Christmas he and Sir Hubert flew 1,200 miles over the Antarctic Ocean, discovering six previously unknown islands.

Back in Alaska in 1929 Eielson bought out the Fairbanks Airplane Corporation that his friend Noel Wien had organized several years earlier. His plans were to pick up freight and passengers and to service every town that offered a place to land. Business was good and the company did well.

In late October 1929 word was received that an American trading schooner, the *Nanuk*, commanded by Olaf Swenson of Seattle, Washington, had been caught in the ice off North Cape, Siberia. She was carrying a crew and several passengers, among them Swenson's eighteen-year-old daughter, Marion, and a cargo of a million dollars worth of furs. The market was falling and each day the value of the skins declined. The owners offered Eielson's company $50,000 to pick up the cargo and passengers and fly them back to Alaska. Ben's intent had been to stick to the management end of the business, but the offer was a challenge that was too much for his adventuresome nature, so he decided to participate personally. With a mechanic, Earl Borland, he left Fairbanks for Teller in a Hamilton cabin monoplane that had good carrying capacity. We met them as they came in and landed on the Grantley Harbor ice. They set up headquarters at one of the roadhouses. The frozen-in *Nanuk* was 400 miles away on the north coast of Siberia. The day after arriving in Teller the weather was good and Eielson and Borland took off for Siberia. Landing on the ice beside the three-masted schooner, they loaded on six of the passengers, including Captain Swenson and his daughter, and $100,000 worth of furs and started back. Bad weather forced them down at a Chukchi village, but four days later they were able to make it back to Teller.

Then a wild northwesterly blew in. Day after day Ben and the other pilot, Frank Dorbandt, who was helping move the furs and the crew of the *Nanuk* back from Siberia, sat on the ice at Teller awaiting a break in the weather. It was the first week in November with only a few hours of daylight, and each day that passed, there was less. In another week there would be no daylight at all at North Cape—just a very few hours of dusk—and in an hour or so after takeoff it would be dark again. Impatience gnawed at Eielson. After six years of Arctic flying, in which he'd helped make most of the rules, he violated the most important, caution.

On the morning of November 9, we watched Eielson and Borland take off and vanish into the gray sky over Port Clarence Bay, not realizing that we would never see Carl Ben Eielson and Earl Borland alive again. About fifteen minutes later Frank Dorbandt took off on the same mission. He returned three hours later as he said visibility became nil, and weather conditions became worse as the day progressed. By evening there was a blizzard blowing, the wind gusting to sixty miles per hour. Frank Dorbandt and his mechanic, Clark Bassitt, put their plane in a makeshift hangar (we called it a garage) built on the harbor ice. It was a framework of two-by-fours with a tarpaulin stretched over the top and sides. It had burned down one afternoon, and they had to rebuild it. No one was hurt, and the plane was pulled out in time to save it. The rest of the month of November and all of December and January passed with no word of the missing flyers, other than wireless reports from the *Nanuk* that they had never arrived.

Teller was the headquarters for the searching aircraft. On some days there were as many as six aircraft on the ice of different types and models. There was one Canadian pilot, Pat Reid, aiding in the search. Also there were two Russian Junker planes with grizzly Russian pilots and mechanics who were real friendly and jovial. They liked to talk to us young people who would stand around and watch the activity and the planes coming and going. They would only speak a word or two of English but used sign language along with Russian words. Our American mechanics always had a pot of coffee brewing on their Coleman stoves in the hangar, and the Russian pilots seemed to crave our American coffee. They would give us kids a taste of their dark bread and hardtack (a sort of large round soda cracker).

I kept a personal diary of the drama after the *Nanuk* froze in the ice in Arctic Siberia and as its crew and the million dollars in furs were rescued by daring Alaskan pilots. These entries attest to the terrible weather conditions over the winter months and also what dedicated individuals those American, Canadian, and Russian pilots were in their rescue efforts:

Diary of Eielson and Borland Rescue, Winter 1929–1930

October 29, 1929, Tuesday—Pilot Frank Dorbandt took off for North Cape, Siberia at 8:30 AM. He arrived at the ship at 4:30 PM.

October 30, Wednesday—Ben Eielson took off for North Cape with fair weather in the offing.

October 31—Both planes left North Cape with one ton furs and six passengers from ship. Stopped at Chukchi village four days. Too stormy to continue journey to Teller.

November 4—Both Eielson and Dorbandt took off from Chukchi village, Eielson going straight to Nome with crew off the *Nanuk* and furs. Dorbandt stopped here (Teller) for 15 minutes then went on to Nome with four of the crew from ship. Both pilots returned to Teller same day.

November 5—Airplane garage caught on fire about 9 PM. Mechanics Earl Borland and Clark Bassitt put it out. Nearly all the canvas was burned.

November 9—Pilot Dorbandt hopped off for North Cape for more furs and the rest of the crew of *Nanuk* at 8:30 AM. Ben Eielson and mechanic Earl Borland had left 15 minutes earlier. It started to storm after Dorbandt left. He returned at 11:30 AM on account of poor visibility.

November 16—Pilot Frank Dorbandt and Clark Bassitt were going to hop off for Siberia in search of Ben and Earl as nothing has been heard of their whereabouts yet. Just as they were taking off, one of the skis got loose and the plane fell on the ice. It didn't get damaged any.

November 27—Pilot Dorbandt took off for Siberia to try to locate Ben and Earl but had to return on account of stormy weather.

November 28—Pilot Joe Crosson arrived here from Fairbanks and Nome to help search for Ben and Earl.

November 30—Pilot Crosson left for North Cape in search of Ben Eielson and Earl Borland. Returned 15 after 2 PM on account of stormy weather and fog.

December 3—Pilot Joe Crosson and Frank Dorbandt hopped off for North Cape to locate lost flyers. Were forced to return again.

December 6—Pilots Dorbandt and Crosson took off again for the rescue. They got as far as Little Diomede Island but were forced to return again at 1:30 PM.

December 8—Pilots Dorbandt and Crosson tried to go to Siberia but just as Dorbandt was lifting off, he dropped a ski and was forced to the ground.

December 10—Pilot Barnhill and Fred Moller in a Standard plane from Fairbanks arrived here at 25 to 11 AM.

December 11—Pilot Gillam and Pilot Ed Young, a Canadian, the former in a Stinson and latter in a Steerman, arrived here 15 after 2 PM. They came from Fairbanks and Nome.

December 13—All the planes went up for a spin, Dorbandt, Crosson, Barnhill, Gillam, and Young. Too cloudy to go anywhere. The ice field at Teller became a busy airfield.

December 18, Wednesday—All four planes took off for North Cape in search of Eielson at 10:15 AM. Pilot Joe Crosson was first, then Barnhill, Ed Young with Gus Masik, and Gillam was last. They all were forced to return on account of poor visibility. Pilot Mat Neminen and mechanic Alonzo Cope arrived here not long after those four planes took off. He left Cope here and Mat left 15 to 11 AM.

December 19—Pilots Crosson and Gillam in their Stinsons took off for North Cape at 9:30 AM. They both made it to a small Chukchi village along the Siberian coast where they last heard the hum of the ill-fated Hamilton. Stayed overnight, next morning Gillam made it to the ship 2:30 PM.

December 20—No news of the whereabouts of Crosson.

December 21—Crosson reached the ship, *Nanuk*, the next day.

December 22—Pilot Ed Young and Mr. Masik hopped off for North Cape at 25 after 10 AM. Forced to return, storms encountered.

January 25—Reported that the ill-fated Hamilton was sighted by Joe Crosson and Harold Gillam while flying around 50 miles east of *Nanuk*. The plane was badly wrecked. Motor was torn completely from cabin and lay 100 feet away. Parts of tail lay 300 feet from cabin.

Russian search plane looking for Eielson, Teller, 1929.

Gasoline tins and other stuff scattered in all directions. Scene of crash seven miles from a Native village.

January 26—Pilot Joe Crosson flew over the wreck. Pilot Vic Ross arrived here in Standard plane with load of gas from Nome at 4 PM.

January 27—Both Fairchilds took off for North Cape at 15 to 10 AM. Pilot Young and mechanic Macauley, Pilot Reid with mechanic Hughes, two Canadian pilots.

January 27—Pilots Ed Young and Pat Reid in Fairchilds arrived ship at 2:30 PM.

January 28—Two Russian planes arrived *Nanuk*. Six planes there altogether.

January 28—Have nine Native men digging for bodies. Found Earl's helmet and mitt.

January 29—No flying to ship as visibility is poor. Foggy up there, fine here.

February 7—Captain Pat Reid arrived here at 2 PM from Siberia with Captain Milovsov of the S.S. *Stavapol* (Russian ship).

February 10—Captain Pat Reid, alone, made attempt to fly to Cape Serdge with gas at 9 AM. Got as far as Lost River (on our mainland), too foggy across the straits, so was forced back.

February 10—After unloading gas from plane, pilot Pat Reid took off for
Nome at 10:30 AM.

February 12—Captain Pat Reid and his mechanic Hughes arrived here
from Nome at 9:30 AM. Didn't even stop engine, just loaded on gas,
and Reid alone took off for Cape Serdge at 10 AM.

February 12—Pilot Reid was forced back again at 11 AM accounting to
poor visibility over straits.

February 16—Earl Borland's body found, dug up by Russians. Body was
four feet under snow and lying fifty feet from motor. Had instanta-
neous death.

February 18—Colonel Ben Eielson's body found, or rather dug up. Body
lying six feet under snow and 200 feet from Earl Borland. Also was
killed instantaneously.

February 20—Pilot Reid with 16 cases of gas left for Cape Serdge at 15
after 10 AM. Returned at 3 PM.

February 21—Pilot Reid took off for North Cape at 9:30 AM. Planes out
of gas up there so can't do much. Have to wait till Pat brings some.

March 3—Pilots Ed Young and Joe Crosson and mechanic Macauley arrived here from North Cape with corpse of dead aviators at 25 to 4 PM.
Soviet Junker arrived here 10 after 4 PM. All flags at half mast, everyone
down at hangar on the ice. Too stunned to even speak. All was quiet.

March 6—Fairchild and Soviet Junker took off for Fairbanks at 5 to 8 AM.
Got as far as Ruby (on the Yukon River).

March 8—Planes got to Fairbanks with bodies of dead aviators.

March 12—Funeral procession at Fairbanks for Ben and Earl.

March 22—Bodies arrived Seattle on S.S. *Alaska*, also Reid, Macauley,
and Hughes.

The old timers had a down-to-earth reason for the crash of Ben
Eielson's plane in Siberia. Considering the time of year, knowing how harsh
weather conditions can get, Carl Ben Eielson and Earl Borland probably decided to set the plane down and wait out the storm and in so doing plowed
into a hummock of ice. They found one wing a couple of hundred feet from
the fuselage and parts of the tail another hundred feet or more away. The
thought was that they died instantly. When the bodies were brought to Teller, there was a guard stationed at the plane during the time that it sat on
the wind-swept Grantley Harbor ice awaiting favorable weather to go on to

Airplane bringing back to Teller bodies of Ben Eielson and Earl Borland from Siberia, 1930.

Fairbanks. We all felt so sad to see the drifting snow slowly covering up the skis of the plane with the much-loved pair inside, flier and mechanic, their lives silenced by the rigors of this harsh cold land. I was seventeen years old, and little did I realize that twenty-five years later, I would have a brother flying in the same weather conditions and terrain as these two brave men of the North. The only difference was that in that day so much improvement had been made in the airplane, the equipment in them, and the techniques of flying. But Mother Nature has not changed, in that she can be unpredictable.

* * *

With Sarah and David gone, there were still chores to be handed down to the next in line. Anne and Gussie, who were fifteen and thirteen when David went away, took over the care of the dogs and hauled ice for winter water, with the help of Albert, who was ten. At seventeen, I was quite an adept seamstress and was making most of the family's clothing. While the rest did all the outdoor chores, I helped my mother tan the skins, saw that they dried properly, and then made them into mukluks, parkas, mittens, and pants. Whatever was on the priority list was made first. If Papa needed a pair of sealskin pants or a new parka to replace an old worn-out one, he got them before anyone else got anything new for he was the organizer and main supplier of all our needs. Ten-year-old Albert had David's outdoor bent. Already an expert hunter, he brought in lots of rabbits and squirrels, ducks and ptarmigan. Now the oldest boy at home, he became my father's right-hand man, as Tommy and David had been before him.

When the runs of fish were heavy and there was too much work for Papa and Albert to handle by themselves, the rest of us pitched in. The freshly caught salmon were brought from the nets to a butchering table on the beach where they were cleaned and split, filleted and sliced, and either salted in the barrels or canned or smoked. The work was hard, and the hours were long, and we never stopped until the last fish caught in a day was taken care of. But we had incentive for everything we did. The harder we worked, the more prosperous was our season. If one of us began to slack off or get lazy, we were prodded back to action by the others. We could be considered capitalists, but we never had more than met our actual needs.

After we three older girls were mature enough to do most of the housework and care for the little ones, Mama would spend a lot of time outdoors, fishing with the other Eskimo women and snaring ptarmigan and rabbits. She also prepared the skins of the animals that Papa and Albert trapped or shot and with my help tanned the hides to make our cold-weather reindeer parkas and mukluks and sealskin pants. She was at her happiest when doing such tasks and fulfilling the life purpose of the Eskimo wife and mother—to help feed and clothe her family and make things easier for her husband. Childbearing and the extreme and constant struggle to make a living aged our mother prematurely and eventually resulted in her early death. But she would have wanted it no other way. To have not done her utmost in caring for her family would have been unthinkable in those days of either survive or starve. There were few lazy Eskimos. In her young days, the nonproducers starved and died, and the others worked themselves to death trying to survive. There was always the primeval battle for survival.

When you have to live off the land and sea, especially with six or seven months of winter conditions as in northern Alaska, just finding enough food to eat is a constant struggle. That is the way it was when my mother was growing up. If you want creature comforts, for instance, even to have warmth in your abode, it literally entails a 24-hour a day struggle. If the weather looks threatening and you must go to the beach to get driftwood, you must go! For if the storm sets in tomorrow, it may last four or five days, so you must gather the wood while and when you can and not wait until tomorrow.

The next stage in the plan for survival is having clothes to wear, and that means the acquisition of the animal from which you get your furs and hides to make the article of clothing. For this you need to have physical strength, good health, and the will to brave the elements, harsh as they may be. In comparison, the people who live in the temperate zones of this good earth have it so much easier, if you call living off the land easy.

It was in 1930 that my life changed abruptly. All the years that I had been corresponding with my Uncle Ed and Aunt Matilda in Pittsburgh, Uncle Ed had encouraged me to "observe" and "absorb," and "know what's going on around you." He often commented in his letters about things I had written to them. "I think you could be a fine writer, Elizabeth. You have a knack for writing things in a way that is interesting to others." In my letters I was always asking them about things I'd heard or suspected. Of this he wrote, "You have a thirst for knowledge. Take advantage of it while you are young." I have always been interested in writing, and that I suppose is what prompted the diaries that I kept for many years. In my high school years I wrote short stories, and some were published in our school papers. Two of my high school efforts won prizes in our high school writing contests: one a short story and one a poem, both first prizes.

In 1930 I was eighteen years old and had finished the eighth grade several years before. Since we had no high school, anyone who wanted further education had to leave Teller. Few ever did. I was the first half Alaska Native to graduate from high school in my part of Alaska. Most parents believed that reading and writing and a little arithmetic was sufficient. The girls usually married early, and the boys became fishermen or left the country to become seamen on ships that would take them around the world. There was a public high school at Nome, and a government boarding school for Natives at White Mountain, southeast of Nome at the head of Golovin Bay. I was eligible to go to either. But way back there in Pennsylvania, Uncle Ed had heard all about the Alaskan educational system and wrote, "Even if you graduate from one of those schools you won't be qualified to enter college." A devout Methodist, he also knew about the Jesse Lee Home at Seward, Alaska, a boarding school for Alaska Native children operated by the Women's Home Missionary Society of his church. The standards there were as high as in most Stateside schools, and the high school was accredited. I could have gone to Chemawa Indian School, near Salem, Oregon, as my sister Margaret had, but Uncle Ed wanted me to stay in my own native

Alaska, so the decision was for me to attend Jesse Lee with Uncle Ed paying all the expenses.

There were several ways I could have traveled to get to Seward. The quickest and most direct would have been to fly from Teller to Nome, thence to McGrath, and across the valley of the Kuskokwim and through the Alaska Range by way of Rainy Pass to Anchorage, then to my destination of Seward on the southeast side of the Kenai Peninsula by Alaska Railroad. The flying distance was about 800 miles, and weather permitting, would have taken two days. Flying was in its infancy and costly in those days in Alaska. The second choice was from McGrath I could have flown up the Kantishna Plains to Fairbanks by way of Ben Eielson's first mail route, and then taken the railroad from there to Seward. This would have been a four-day trip of 1,200 miles. The third alternative was to go by sea to St. Michael on Norton Sound, then by riverboat up the Yukon and Tanana Rivers to Nenana where I could have caught the train to Seward. The 1,700 miles by this route would have taken about two weeks.

But all these ways would have been expensive. We couldn't afford it, and Papa, frugal with other people's money as well as his own, didn't want to burden Uncle Ed with the cost of my transportation when I could travel free on a government ship. So that's the way I went, by the longest and slowest and by far the most adventurous method available. But I'm glad now that I went by sea for it gave me the opportunity to see places I never would have otherwise, and besides, being the daughter of an old salt, I also happened to like the sea.

So on October 26, 1930, I departed family and friends for the second time not of my own volition, with my mother and father again sad of heart but happy for me that I would prepare for a useful future life. I boarded the USMS *Boxer*, not by way of a Jacob's ladder as anyone else would have, but a bosun's chair, which Captain Whitlam had the crew rig up for me. I could never have made it aboard any other way for the seas were rough, and it was already freezing outside.

It was a cold wintry afternoon. Mama and Papa and all six of the brothers and sisters were on the beach bidding me farewell. Mama and Papa hung on to me until the bosun said, "All right, Elizabeth, it's your turn to get in the launch and don't be afraid, we will help you." Papa's last words of advice to me were "Study hard, behave yourself, and always do the best you can." He was always very protective of us, and I felt that he was a little reluctant to let me go for he always thought that I needed someone to protect

Elizabeth, age 18, Teller, 1930.

me. Papa and Captain Whitlam had quite a long talk just before we pulled away from the shore. The last thing I heard him say to Captain Whitlam was, "Take good care of her, Captain." Captain Whitlam said, "That goes without saying, Albert, for you know how I feel about Elizabeth." Captain Whitlam always had called me by my formal name, Elizabeth, and I was to be called by that name during my years at the boarding school. The wind was blowing cold, and it was beginning to snow.

Everyone from the ABs (able-bodied seamen) to the captain was considerate of me. I learned a lot on this trip about people in general, and I garnered every bit of knowledge and information I could by listening and keeping my eyes open.

The United States ship the *Boxer* was a historical old ship, operated by the U.S. Bureau of Indian Affairs, an agency of the department of the interior. The little ship was commanded by Captain S. T. L. Whitlam, a very good friend of my father's whom we had known for many years. He had sailed these waters since the late 1890s. The duty of the *Boxer* was to look out for the welfare of the Native village inhabitants north of the Aleutian Islands. Only 125 feet in length, she was a little larger than the *St. Roch*, which successfully traversed the Northwest Passage in the 1940s.

The *Boxer* had been late returning south from Point Barrow and arrived in Port Clarence with the ice pack in sight a few miles north. As long as the wind blew from the southerly directions, we would get ahead of the ice after we left Diomede Island and King Island, thence into the Bering Strait. After loading water and reindeer meat at Teller Mission, we sailed for King Island, which had been bypassed on the way down from Barrow because the surf was too high to land supplies on that piece of rock in the middle of the Bering Strait. En route there we dropped off at Little Diomede Island the public health nurse, Mildred Keaton, who was contracted by the Bureau of Indian Affairs to remain and look after the health of the Natives there. Mildred Keaton was well known throughout northern Alaska for her stamina in traveling by dog team with a driver to isolated villages, where she administered shots and medication to many Natives and thereby saved many lives.

When the *Boxer* returned in the spring, the nurse would tour the villages to administer shots or tend to the ill. The USS *Northland* (the U.S. Coast Guard cutter) carried on its tour of duty in the Arctic a public health doctor and dentist who administered to the ones who needed tonsils or

Early 1900s King Island, Alaska.

adenoids taken out or a vaccination for some communicable disease that had begun in the Lower 48 and spread to the Native territorial population. The dentists onboard inspected teeth, filled the ones that needed it, and pulled the bad ones. The dentists many times remarked how the Eskimos' teeth condition had changed through the early 1900s to the 1930s, saying there was a great increase of tooth decay in that span of thirty years according to the records they kept. This was because of the simple reason that gum and candy were more available in the latter part of that span of thirty years.

When I returned home from Nome after my hospital stay, Mama said that I had developed a white man's appetite for meat and potatoes. As she said, "I turned up my nose at seal meat, seal oil, and fish," but I did acquire a taste for beef, potatoes, and a variety of fresh vegetables in salad form and aspics, which I never had before. She said they made a "white man out of me," but she seemed proud of it. So of course the food on the *Boxer* was even more strange to me, especially with the addition of fresh fruits and vegetables at every meal. Also I couldn't get over the idea of a dessert after every dinner. For the first time in my life I ate cantaloupe, fresh frozen strawberries on ice cream, and fresh (cold storage) peaches with cream (cow's cream, not canned cream). I was impressed with all the new foods being prepared by the cook, Sig Sundt, who loved to tease me because I blushed like a shy little violet.

I had seen the *Boxer* many times in my life as it anchored in the bay, but I never realized that I would one day be a passenger aboard her. The course to Little Diomede Island was north by northwest, and we had to quarter into the wind and seas and the old *Boxer* wallowed and rolled. Up to this time this was the largest ship I had traveled on. Of course we were in open water by this time, and I thought to myself, "If this is what we go through to get to Seward, I'd rather go by dogsled," not realizing that this was just the beginning of the journey on rough seas. With the pitch and heel of this proud little vessel, I began to feel lightheaded and so went down to my cabin, which I shared with another girl who was going to the island of Kodiak. But I felt even worse as the ceiling and walls of the cabin began to whirl around me. Then I went up to the pilothouse and talked to the chief officer, and of course they teased me into not feeling sorry for myself. I learned a lot on this trip, not academically but psychologically and philosophically, for it was the first time I was around adults other than my parents or older sisters and brothers. New places and new faces. I might have to watch what I said, I thought, but Papa always said, "Be yourself, and don't put on any airs, and always tell the truth, then you don't have anything to remember." My father often quoted Mark Twain. So after I remembered all the things that our father told me as we were growing up, I became at ease and wasn't so shy anymore.

I learned to play backgammon, parcheesi, and cribbage, which was taught to me by the chief engineer, Herman Sanwick. One of the oilers taught me how to play the guitar in his off-duty hours, so by the end of the month-long trip I could play pretty well. He said I picked it up very fast, and I took to it like a duck takes to water for my first love was music. Then the wireless operator took me to the radio shack and showed me how they send and receive messages. It was all very interesting. Onboard ship I learned to balance myself to where I could get around almost as well as anyone. Most people take movement for granted, but I think out my moves beforehand. It comes to me in a flash and to my complete advantage so that I save myself energy and time. By this time, I was walking on my third pair of prosthetics.

Approaching the Diomedes, we encountered drifting ice cakes, the forerunners of the ice pack, but the nearness of the approaching floes made for calmer seas. As we sailed away from the Diomede Islands, we crossed the International Date Line, and we were in tomorrow for a short while.

USS *Northland*, 1940.

Little Diomede and Big Diomede Island lie in the Bering Strait, with Big Diomede being the possession of Russia. The distance between the United States owned Little Diomede and the Russian Big Diomede is only three miles. The two Diomede Islands and tiny King Island are probably remnants of a land bridge from Siberia to North America.

We then sailed 150 miles southward for St. Lawrence Island in the Bering Sea, and with the wind and seas coming from astern, the *Boxer* misbehaved worse than ever. I thought that the wrenching and groaning meant that she was being pulled apart. I told Captain Whitlam of my fears, but he tried to reassure me. "Don't you worry, Elizabeth, if she wasn't flexible she wouldn't have lasted as long as she has." The northeast gale whipped the sea into a raging, foaming, wild mass of blackish gray water, reflecting the dark gray of the sky, dense with whirling snow. We were only fifty miles from the east coast of Siberia. I wondered which was worse, to be frightened to death or drowned in a sinking ship. And did anyone ever die of seasickness? There was a porthole beside my bunk, and as the ship rolled one way, through the two-inch thick glass, I could see the dark sky, then green water would rush by with some water squirting in around the porthole. There was the smell of diesel oil fumes coming up the companionway leading from the engine room. I prayed that Captain Whitlam would change course and take me back to Teller. If this was the price for an education, I could do without it.

It took our little ship a day and a half to reach Gambell, the northwest point of St. Lawrence Island. There was a regular blizzard blowing, the sky was a very dark gray and large flakes of snow were whirling down. We were only there a few hours, and I think even Captain Whitlam was more than happy to get out of there. I went up to the pilothouse and talked to the bosun while he steered a course directly east to Savoonga, the eastern point of St. Lawrence, which was only a half day's journey. We anchored during the night, and early the next day the St. Lawrence Island Eskimos scrambled aboard the ship from their *oomiaks* and kayaks with their furs and ivory and ivory carvings. They were a tough-looking people who spoke only a few words of English and lived in the old ways in the manner of their ancestors. They dressed much like their Siberian counterparts, the Chukchis, who used to come to Nook each summer.

The St. Lawrence Island men were quite tall, straight, and the nicest looking of the Natives in the Bering Strait region. They were energetic, and even the older men were spry and quick of movement. They all gave me the eye, and began jabbering in their Native tongue, of which I did not understand a word. They said something like the word *kabloona*, which is sort of a pidgin Eskimo word for white man. They asked Captain Whitlam if I was the new school marm for Savoonga. Wife-purchase was still practiced in some regions, and the chief asked Captain Whitlam if he could buy me. "Sure, I'll let you have her for twenty-five white fox skins." The old chief began to count out his white skins and would give me a glance to see what expression I had on my face. I was getting pretty worried that this was not a joke the captain and the chief were conjuring up. I knew that Captain Whitlam had quite a sense of humor and would carry a joke quite a ways. But I was really scared until I saw the twinkle in his eye and he said, "Don't worry, Elizabeth, I wouldn't sell you for all the white fox skins in the world, and besides, I will protect you with my life if they should want to kidnap you." Having Captain Whitlam around I felt safe, like he was my own father. Still, I wasn't completely convinced he wasn't teasing until the last of the St. Lawrence traders was away in his *oomiak*, the anchor was weighed, and we were on our way again.

Captain Whitlam was famous around Alaska not only for his wry sense of humor, but for the preposterous yarns he told, especially to cheechakos, the first trippers to the North, about what they might expect to find when they got to where they were going. He had practical reasons for it. The young missionaries and school teacher couples, traveling to far-off villages where they were expected to do all things for the Natives in their charge—doctor the sick, sew up their wounds, deliver babies, and bury the dead—usually were quite apprehensive about the future that they faced. It all sounded so romantic when they applied for the job months before leaving the States. After seeing a few of the settlements and the people who lived in them, they would begin seriously to wonder why they had applied for the job to begin with. After a few rounds of Captain Whitlam's exaggerations, though, the things they actually found were seldom what their imaginations, whetted by the stories of the captain of the *Boxer*, had them believing. Then, when it came time to face up to the really unpleasant aspects of life in an Arctic outpost, they were prepared for the worst. Many of them would be transferred from one outpost to another.

Captain Whitlam was one of the calmest men I have ever seen. He was well liked by everyone, crew members and passengers alike. He invited me to sit with him in the dining room at the officers table at every meal. Having not been away from home since the long-ago dog team trip to Nome, I had never eaten out, so I watched everything he did, which fork he used, how he held his knife, and his other table manners. He knew I was watching him, so when the waiter set a plate of ham and eggs before him, Captain Whitlam put pepper on his eggs, then salt. I peppered mine too then salted them. I took a glance at Herman Sanwick, the chief engineer, who sat across the table, and he did his the usual way. The Captain said, "Elizabeth, nearly everybody puts salt on their eggs first, then pepper. Do you know why I put the pepper on first?"

"No," I said, hesitantly.

"Well, the salt is heavier and it holds the pepper on the eggs so it won't fall off when the ship is rolling."

At breakfast we were served a half grapefruit first. I had never tasted grapefruit before and was waiting for Captain Whitlam to start on his as I was not sure how I was to eat it. I thought to myself, "Here I am eighteen years old and tasting my first grapefruit!"

Departing St. Lawrence Island we had to go to the mainland at Hooper Bay, almost 200 miles to the southeast, then on to Nunivak Island, where the inhabitants live as close to their original Native culture as do the St. Lawrence Islanders. They still lived in sod and driftwood huts such as my grandparents had, but the old culture has disappeared.

The ship loaded reindeer carcasses at Nunivak Island for the Seattle markets. The best reindeer meat is raised on this island—it is as close to the taste of veal as you could get, for the simple reason that they have a large range of lichen to graze on without having to range for long distances to find it. We left the mainland of Alaska for the Pribilof Islands, 300 miles off the coast near the middle of the Bering Sea. These islands, in the spring and summer, are the home of the Steller sea lions, the largest in the world. The males can weigh as much as a ton or more, and they comprise the largest congregation of sea animals in the world. We made a stop first at St. Mathews Island to pick up a government worker, then on to the largest of the island group, St. Paul. After leaving St. Paul Island, we headed for Dutch Harbor in the Aleutian chain, 300 miles to the southwest.

The temperature outside was freezing and with each wave that broke aboard, wind-blown spray froze to the rigging. The wind began to rage to gale force. Every so often seamen had to bundle up and go on deck and chop off the ice from the rigging otherwise too much could accumulate and make the ship too heavy, and she could roll over and sink. The sky was dark with swirling snow, large white wet flakes came down, then froze as they hit the deck and caused more concern for the captain. The men who worked to keep the deck clear of too much accumulation that would freeze quickly surely had a job on their hands. They tried hosing the thick soggy flakes, but the temperature was against the operation, causing more ice to form.

Everyone was getting seasick, even some of the crew. The ship rolled so that the cook was not able to do his chores in the galley. About halfway to Dutch Harbor the wind now reached ninety miles per hour, and the waves were forty to fifty feet high. The forward hatch cover was washed away, and water washed down the companionway and into the engine room. What more could happen? The crew hastily put down a large tarpaulin over the hatch and battened it down. If the wind didn't blow it off, we could make it into Dutch Harbor without flooding the companionway and the engine room. Water began washing into my stateroom floor by this time. The old *Boxer* rode the waves like a water-logged duck, and as the stern of the ship came up the propeller broke out of the water and the engine had to be slowed so it would not cause too much vibration. Every time the little ship took a nosedive, she shook and shivered until we all thought she would come apart. At one time Captain Whitlam ordered fuel oil drums to be put over the side. He said that would pacify the wild combers. Inevitably no meals had been prepared for two days for it would have been an impossible task. No one had a real desire to eat anyway, but they drank a lot of coffee, and everyone hardly closed their eyes to sleep for you couldn't stay in your bunk without bracing yourself with pillows or an extra mattress.

Captain Whitlam told me afterwards, and so did the chief engineer, Herman Sanwick, that it was the worst storm they had seen in the thirty-five years Captain Whitlam had plied those waters. At one point in the journey, reefed sails were set on the fore and main mast to help steady the ship and aid the laboring engine. We limped into Dutch Harbor on the third day after leaving St. Paul Island. We lay for several days at the dock while the ice was knocked off as it began to thaw from the ten-degree milder weather than what we had been through. The population of Dutch Harbor said we looked like a ghost ship coming in, with ice-crusted rigging and gear on deck coated white with an inch or so of ice. While at the dock we had the necessary repairs made, including the hatch cover. The ship was cleaned, and most of all we got our appetites back to normal.

Not long after leaving Unalaska and Dutch Harbor, on our way to Sand Point, we passed smoking Mount Shishaldin, a 9,500 foot active volcano in the Shumagin Islands. After departing the wild Bering Sea for the tamer waters of the north Pacific, along the rim of the Aleutian Chain, bad weather dogged us for the reminder of the voyage though it was nothing at all like crossing the Bering Sea had been. We made several stops along the

Aleutian rim, and we could always see the smoking volcanoes of the Valley of Ten Thousand Smokes, which comprise the lower southwest portion of the Alaska Peninsula.

Soon we reached Kodiak Island, which was the seat of government when Russia owned Alaska, until they moved their headquarters to Sitka in 1848. It is quite a picturesque harbor with inlets all around. We all took a trip uptown on the shank's mare. We especially wanted to see the Russian Orthodox church, St. Michael Cathedral, which was dedicated in 1840. The exterior of the cathedral belied the interior of the edifice for there were priceless religious paintings of Christ and his apostles and also of the Mother Mary in solid gold frames, icons of gold set with precious stones, altar cloths and vestments embroidered in gold thread, and crucifixes, large and small, of pure gold. It was all quite unbelievable. I had never seen so much gold even when my father would bring home pokes of gold nuggets after a season of sluice mining. These furnishings of the cathedral were all brought from St. Petersburg, Russia, as early as the beginning of the seventeenth century, and as I gazed at all the gold and precious stones, I said to myself, "Just think of it, these priceless furnishings have been in this country over 200 years now." In a glass case near the altar was a crown of gold, studded with priceless gems, which our guide said had been worn by the archbishop of the church 200 years before. The original church and these priceless furnishings were nearly all destroyed in a fire in 1978.

As we pulled out of Kodiak Harbor, bound for the mainland, we encountered high seas so then we put into Woman's Bay on Spruce Island awaiting favorable weather conditions in crossing the stormy unpredictable Shelikof Strait. The next day we left the foul weather on the open sea as we came into the shelter of the Kenai Mountains at the entrance to Resurrection Bay on which Seward is located. It seemed so relaxing to stand out on the deck in fairly smooth waters and look at such breathtaking scenery. The porpoises ran us a race, as they playfully dipped in and out of the surface of the blue-green waters which took on the reflections of the tree-lined mountainsides. Everybody was saying, "You'll soon be home, Elizabeth," reminding me that my journey would soon be over. I felt a little strange when I realized that these fellow shipmates would soon be on their merry way to their destinations, and I would be dropped off in Seward where I knew not a soul. I felt a reluctance as my journey was coming to an end.

8

The air was crisp and clear, not a cloud in the sky, and the gentle wind blowing from the shoreline seemed to caress my face. From astern a low bright sun cast a long shadow of the vessel and her rigging as the ship slowly cruised a straight course through the choppy green water. Besides the familiar scent of salt sea and kelp, there was an aroma in the breeze that I could not identify. I asked, "What's that sweet smell?"

"That's the woods, the spruce trees."

This was my first look at real, live trees. The ones I had seen before were in pictures and books. I thought to myself, "Just wouldn't the kids at home, and Mama, like to cast eyes on these lovely, stately, nice-smelling overgrown willows!" On the mainland to the left and on the islands to the right, there grew more trees than I would have believed grew in all the world. Except for the stunted alders and willows that struggled to thrive along the streams back home, these were the first trees of any size I'd seen and the first evergreens. I have loved trees ever since.

Before the day was over, I would experience many more firsts. It was not just Resurrection Bay that we were entering, but a completely new world

155

for me. This being the last day of November just a few minutes in the brisk wind was enough, and I was glad to reach the warmth inside the pilothouse. A seaman was at the wheel, and the mate on watch was peering through a partly opened window. Off to the left a string of snowy peaks rose abruptly from the water. "That's the Aialik Peninsula," the mate said. "Up there over the port bow is Bear Glacier." A great tongue of ice—reaching almost to the bay ahead, white on its surface, blue in the shadows, and a dirty gray at its front—filled the two-mile width of the valley. It was the largest of many such tongues thrust impudently out of the mouths of other valleys and canyons from an ice field overflowing from the highlands between two mountain ranges. Here and there small islands of barren rock pierced the calm sea.

To our right were other islands, steep and wooded, snow-crowned sentinels guarding the fiord-like harbor we were entering. In the distance smoke was rising from the base of a peak where the water ended and the land began. "There's Seward," someone yelled. The view ahead was gorgeous, a range of jagged, snow-covered mountains on either side of a blue-green harbor. A whale rolled and spouted steamy spray half a mile away. For a time we were escorted by playful porpoises with black backs and white underbodies. They plunged and jumped and raced along the side of the ship. They were the welcoming committee.

The throbbing diesel engine, aided by a flood tide, carried us quickly through Resurrection Bay. Soon signs of human endeavor began to rise from below the tree line. First, a radio tower, then large buildings, some oil tanks, and the masts of two steamers lying at dock. Soon individual houses took form. To the right, beyond the town, a fair-sized river flowed into the bay. One of the steamers was just leaving, and as it pulled away, I saw a black locomotive sending jets of steam and puffs of smoke into the air and pushing railroad cars out onto the pier. It was the first train I'd ever seen! "What an iron horse," I said to myself.

Captain Whitlam pointed out to me on a hillside in a snowy clearing in a forest a couple of miles from Seward the Jesse Lee Home. "There's your new home, Elizabeth." A black sedan drove onto the dock. "And there's the car come to get you. I'll bet you'll be glad to get off this tub." I told Captain Whitlam I enjoyed the trip except for the crossing of the Bering Sea. I think Captain Whitlam sensed that I was a little reluctant to leave the *Boxer* and the shipmates who had become my good friends on this thirty-five-day voyage.

He said that on the way back north come spring, he would check up on me. "You'll make out all right. The Hattens, and everybody out there, are fine people. You won't be a stranger long."

Almost as soon as we were moored to the dock and the gangplank was rigged from ship to shore, the driver of the sedan came aboard. He was introduced by Captain Whitlam as Mr. Hatten, superintendent of the Jesse Lee Home. He was a tall pleasant man with a stern demeanor. He helped me across the gangplank to the dock and into the car. Mr. Hatten, who was a minister, was friendly, but I wasn't sure whether we would be compatible or not. To some of the boys at Jesse Lee he was the nearest to a real father that they ever knew. As we drove along the icy streets, past the business district, and up the winding road to the school, Mr. Hatten told me all about the Jesse Lee Home.

The mission boarding school had its start at Unalaska in the Aleutians in 1890. It was named for Jesse Lee, a traveling preacher who brought the Methodist religion to New England in the early days of our country, and the school was founded by a young New Englander named Agnes Soule. The school was moved to Seward in 1924. The Jesse Lee Home was a school for homeless children and also a school for children who lived in villages where there were no schools.

The sun still shone on the upper crags on the far side of the bay, but it was dusk already on our side in the shadow of Mount Marathon, which rose abruptly from the back edge of town. The street lamps were on, and lights were shining through the steamed-up windows of the establishments on either side of the street. As we drove cautiously through the few blocks of the business district, I saw a movie theater, steamship office, hotel, pool hall and cardrooms, a couple of cafes, a bakery, photo shop, hardware store, grocery, laundry, and bank. For the first time in my life, I saw many shops and places of service. I realized that it takes all kinds of businesses to make a town a "town."

That was my first automobile ride, and I didn't enjoy it nearly as much as I expected I would. The ice-glazed road was so slick that in spite of Mr. Hatten's careful driving, the car slithered and bumped so from the chuck-holes in the road that I was scared half to death and glad when we reached the school. Out of the car and on solid ground again, I had the feeling that there was still a rolling deck beneath me. I grabbed for Mr. Hatten's arm to keep from falling. "What's the matter, Elizabeth?" he asked.

The Jesse Lee Home boarding school, Seward, Alaska, 1932.

"It just felt like I was on the ship again," I explained.

He laughed. "You've still got your sea legs," he said, then, hurriedly, "You'll be all right in a little while," as though the mention of "legs" in my presence might be insensitive. It wasn't of course. It was just part of being me to have strangers be curious as to why I walked as I did. Everyone at the school knew about my condition before I arrived so there was a lot of natural curiosity and staring at the underpinnings of the "new girl with wooden legs." Some of the staff and older girls were inclined to be over solicitous about my welfare. But I was perfectly capable of caring for myself as I had always done.

The Jesse Lee Home was open to any child with Native blood, whether Indian, Aleut, or Eskimo. Only a very few were Eskimos, most being of Indian descent from the Kenai Peninsula and Cook Inlet and Aleuts from Kodiak, the Shumagin Islands, and the Aleutians. A few of the children at the school were the illegitimate offspring of Native mothers and unknown fathers, usually seasonal cannery workers or fishermen or passing seamen on a spree ashore. These were not necessarily white men because many of the children had the facial characteristics of Filipinos and other Asians. There were others whose white fathers had been legally married to their mothers, but who'd abandoned their families leaving the mother with several youngsters she could not support and with no choice but to send them to the orphanage. Alcohol, more often than not, was responsible for such liaisons and subsequent desertions.

There were also true orphans at the Jesse Lee Home whose parents were both dead. The life expectancy of the Alaska Native was short then, especially to the westward where the rates of accidental deaths were high, principally from drownings at sea or in swiftly flowing rivers as the Natives pursued their way of subsistence. Many died of gunshot wounds while hunting miles from assistance of any kind. Nearly every year on Kodiak Island and the Alaska Peninsula, unwary hunters, hikers, and campers were killed or mauled by the great brown bear, the grizzly, whose domain they invaded. Those who survived the hazards of merely existing, could expect to die at an early age of tuberculosis, malnourishment, and other diseases. If they were spared from accident or disease, then poisonous alcoholic concoctions, such as *mokoola*, brewed in any sort of receptacle, finished them off or blinded them. Communicable diseases brought by the white travelers took their toll. Few Natives lived to reach their fifties then.

A few of the residents at the Jesse Lee Home were of full blood with the ivory skin, dark hair, and eyes of their aboriginal forebears. There were some though whose fair hair and skin and blue eyes indicated Scandinavian ancestry, yet they still qualified as Natives. One girl was as blonde a person as I had ever known. She had a Russian name and considered herself to be an Aleut. Most of the girls were good-looking and the boys handsome, and ninety-nine percent Russian, Norwegian, or Swedish on their paternal side. There was no age limit. I was in A Group, which was for girls sixteen and older. B Group represented the twelve to fifteen year olds, C represented the eight to eleven year olds, and D was the small children and babies. Each group was supervised by a deaconess or matron who had a private room adjacent to the dorm she governed. In the boys' dormitory they had deacons or male teachers in charge. The men in charge all were married, and their wives were often teachers or matrons. The dining room was in the basement of the girls' dormitory, as was the extensive kitchen with modern furnishings. We ate at long tables assigned according to age group, but boys and girls could dine together if they chose.

The Jesse Lee Home was not a resort for idlers. The rules were strict but fair. In addition to our classwork, everyone had to take two-week turns at different tasks. For the boys it was caring for the cows, pigs, and chickens; sawing and splitting wood; shoveling coal into the furnaces; and working in the laundry. In the summer months, they worked in the hay fields and vegetable gardens or fished for salmon in the little gill-net boat owned by the school. Some of the older boys owned rifles, and during hunting season they would shoot moose, mountain sheep, or goats, which added to the larder. I experienced many firsts at the Jesse Lee Home. For instance, new kinds of food such as fresh vegetables grown from acres of tilled soil: spinach, celery, potatoes, cabbage, carrots, and beets (mostly root vegetables). Though I had to acquire a taste for certain fresh vegetables, I actually grew to like them. I had also my first taste of fresh milk, which I must say was foreign to my taste buds. Also for the first time in my life, I enjoyed a diet of such protein as beef, in the form of hamburger for meat loaf or meatballs. We had no such thing as beef steaks for that was reserved for the teachers and school supervisors to be savored on their weekends at their own retreats. I also had my first taste of pork through the efforts of the older boys in raising porkers, which were butchered in the fall. I would refuse to drink a glass of milk at times until the teachers would say, "All growing youngsters need milk." I did not like the taste of fresh milk.

    Another plus I found at the Jesse Lee was readily available health care; there was an infirmary on the upper floor of the boys' building and a registered nurse in charge. She administered to the sick, whether it be for the flu, an outbreak of an infectious disease, a broken finger, or any non-medical condition. She would do whatever was deemed necessary to help us, whereas when I was growing up at Teller, we had no professional health care person available. The injured or ill person would be treated according to a "wait and see" approach. In any case, as I have noted we at home were treated by our father, who was very knowledgeable in which course of treatment a sick person required. He had a closet shelf supplied with all first aid requirements, such as aspirin, salves, rubbing alcohol, emollients for sore muscles, and such.

    The girls worked in the kitchen and dining room, the laundry, and the ironing and sewing rooms and tended the small children. They even worked as aides to the RN in the infirmary. We learned to make jams and jellies from the wild berries that were picked by the groups who went on berry-picking jaunts when the high- and low-bush currants were in season. Also every fall just before Thanksgiving, there would come a large shipment of apples from the eastern Washington fruit growers who were kind enough to donate this much needed commodity to the school. We would make applesauce and apple butter to spice up our tables during the cold dark days of winter. This was the first time in my life that I could eat apples to my heart's content, and I did just that. The availability of fresh fruit in the Far North was almost nil. I thought many times how fortunate a family was who could just go to the grocery store or fruit stand and buy any variety of fruit they desired (fresh and not canned or dried as we had). If someone at Nome had a yearning for any kind of fresh fruit during the long winter months, they had to mail order it from a store in Fairbanks and have it flown by plane to Nome, wrapped well in newspaper, then double boxed in cardboard boxes so the cold air couldn't penetrate and cause frostbite. If someone in Teller had a craving for fresh apples or oranges in the middle of winter, they had to order it from the Nome source, double wrap it again, and put it into a reindeer skin bag to insure it wouldn't be frozen by the time the mailman, who depended on his dog team, got it to Teller.

To help my generation hold our own in the competitive culture brought to our land by the white man, the staff at Jesse Lee prepared us with education, hard work, and large doses of Christian doctrine as laid down by the Methodists. Grace was said before each meal and a good share of every Sunday was devoted to religious activities—Sunday School, church services, and evening vespers. On Wednesday evenings, there were prayer meetings and also weekly gatherings of the Epworth League. As a paying student, it was not mandatory that I participate, but the deaconesses and the superintendent and his wife were always encouraging me to take a more active part in the religious part of the program. One day Mr. Hatten admonishingly said, "Why don't you like to go to prayer meeting and Epworth League, Elizabeth?"

I responded, "I was born a Catholic, and I want to keep on being one. I will celebrate my inherited religion in my own way." The subject was not brought up again, and I know the matter must have been brought to the attention of my Uncle Ed, probably in a letter to him from Mr. Hatten.

At the beginning of my residence at Jesse Lee, I was exempt from being assigned most of the usual chores, as I was a paying student. Having arrived three months after the school term commenced, I had more than enough to do to catch up with the freshman class, but I was eager to tackle the challenging subjects at school. By the beginning of the second semester I was up with the rest of the class and sailing smoothly along. When summer vacation time rolled around, the matrons would take their charges on picnics and outings in the beautiful countryside. Soon the second school term rolled around, and we were quite content to keep busy with our studies and chores during the long dark, rainy, and cold days.

Holidays were always exciting, starting with Halloween, when the eighth to twelfth grades would have a big party in the gym. Then, of course, there were Thanksgiving and Christmas, which were great days, with everything from the religious aspect of the celebrations to great feasts.

In my second year, I was encouraged by Mrs. Hatten to take journalism along with the other requirements. It was a fascinating subject, and one that I seemed to fit into. I found that I could write a story on the least hint of a subject. And as my uncle said, I had a way of using descriptive words most effectively. Besides my regular studies, I took piano lessons and practiced at every opportunity, but only after I did my stint at sewing and ironing, folding and sorting clothes, and using the mangle machine in the laundry room. I spent a lot of time with my English teacher, Mrs. Bernice Groth, a niece of the famous author Samuel Clemens, better known as Mark Twain. She believed that my future was in writing. She told me, "You've had a remarkable background, Elizabeth. You've known some famous people and seen history being made. Why your parents' and grandparents' lives are stories in themselves. You have a natural bent for telling things in a way that makes others feel that they were with you when it happened. You must learn to put things on paper as well as you can." With encouragement from her and Mrs. Hatten, I began to write little short stories and poems and to win prizes for them at school.

My curriculum included all the necessary subjects: math, English, world and ancient history, Latin, typing, home economics, and so on. Because of my disability, I did not go out much in the winter months. Compared with northern Alaska where the winters were much colder, but very dry and usually clear, the Seward weather was damp and foggy most of the winter. Moist winds warmed by the Japan Current flowing through the Gulf of Alaska a few miles offshore blew across the Kenai Peninsula ice fields and generated violent williwaws that could at times easily knock even a person with normal walking ability off his feet. Overnight a south wind off the ocean converging with cold air from the glaciers could dump two feet of snow on Seward. This could be immediately followed by a frigid norther that blew most of the snow back into the sea, leaving walks and roads and stairways slick and dangerous. I was aware of all those hazards.

Adjacent to the railroad yards, built out over the bay on pilings, was a long low building which was the San Juan Salmon Cannery. Behind a breakwater near the cannery and hauled up on the shore were fishing boats, pleasure craft, and small barges. During the summer when this cannery and a smaller one on the other side of town were in operation, a few of the older boys from the home worked there. In those days there was a saying that the steamship companies owned Alaska. Most Alaskans said that a dollar never changed hands without the steamship lines taking a bite out of it. For instance, a person living in Seward could not go to one of the local canneries, even if he worked there, and buy a case of salmon for his own use, nor could a store owner buy it there for resale. In order to have a steamship company carry its product to the States, a cannery had to agree that its entire pack, every last can, would be shipped to Seattle. Anything to be consumed locally then had to be shipped back north again, virtually doubling the freight charges. Before a can of salmon produced at the San Juan Cannery could be used by a householder a block away, it had to travel a 3000-mile round trip, not to mention loading at Seward, unloading at Seattle, transferring to a warehouse and back to the dock, reloading to another ship, and unloading from storage again upon returning to the point of origin in Alaska.

It was no wonder that most Alaskans begrudged the steamship companies. There was no competition. There was not, and still is not, any railroad from the contiguous United States to Alaska, and in those days there was no highway and no long distance air freight. Air freight was out of the question, as it was too expensive. You either used the steamships on the companies' own terms, or you did without. Seward, being a seaport town and the south terminus of the Alaska Railroad, was also a busy port for freight and passengers going west to Dutch Harbor and Unalaska and points along the way to the Aleutian Chain or to Fairbanks and points in between.

Once a group of men at Seward, thoroughly disgusted and angered by a newly-contrived money-making scheme of a major steamship line, took things into their own hands. In those days there was little work in the North during the winter months except for trapping for furs and chopping wood. But in the countryside along the government-owned and operated Alaska Railroad were hundreds of men and women who lived near the rail route and who cut railroad ties to supplement their earnings after a few months of fishing or working in the canneries or mines. Officials of the steamship companies did not like the tie-cutting business at all. Anything that was produced and used locally put no money into corporate treasuries, and 470.8 miles of mainline plus sidetracks and yards used a lot of ties each year.

So company lobbyists in Washington were alerted and soon an order was issued by the Department of the Interior, which ran the Alaska Railroad, that henceforth ties would not be bought locally unless they met certain specifications: they must be sawed, not hewn; steam-creosoted; and competitive in price with ties produced in high-speed sawmills on Puget Sound. Men working with crosscut saws and axes could by no means produce ties for what they could be purchased stateside. And as for creosoting them under steam pressure, that was an utter impossibility.

The Alaska residents, whites and Natives, were often hired only as menial beach gang laborers or cannery workers at an hourly wage which gave no incentive to work any harder than they had to. Labor unions had not yet gotten a strong foothold in the North, and a workman could be fired at the whim of his foreman. Another sore point that caused bitterness in the Alaskan labor force was that imported fishermen and cannery men were paid a base wage that commenced the day they boarded a ship in Seattle for the ten-day or two-week trip by steamer to the cannery and continued until they returned to the port of departure. This usually meant three to four weeks' pay each season for doing nothing but riding a steamship. Thus an outsider could expect to receive four months' pay for a three-month season, plus his "lay" or percentage of the pack, and could return home with a fair-sized nest egg.

But what could anyone do about it? Who could buck anything as big as Uncle Sam working in connivance with the greedy directors and stockholders of the monopolistic steamship companies? The tie-cutters of the Kenai Peninsula section of the Alaska Railroad did something about it though. Taking a tip from an earlier group of American citizens outraged by the policies of a far away government, they pulled their own version of the Boston Tea Party and dumped hundreds of manufactured and creosoted ties off the Alaska Railroad dock at Seward into Resurrection Bay, with the threat that other cargo would be given the deep six, too, if the stateside ties continued to be imported.

The action didn't change the Department of the Interior's mind at all, but the publicity generated by the "Seward Tie Party" focused nationwide attention on the workers' plight, and in the early years of President

Roosevelt's New Deal, many federal projects were ordered for Alaska that more than offset the tie-cutters' losses and also generated even larger profits for the steamship companies in transporting building supplies and construction equipment. They made more fortunes, too, carrying Depression-hurt people who came North in droves on steamships, attracted by newspaper stories of lots of work and big wages in Alaska. Such information was often traceable to press releases put out by public relations agencies for the same companies whose false advertising had lured the throngs to Nome over thirty years before. Few steamers docked at Seward during the hard times of the thirties without bringing destitute workmen and families in their steerage who'd spent all they had for tickets to the "Land of Promise." Many were returned to the States on the same ship on which they had come at public expense or with contributions. Wages were higher in Alaska, and those with jobs wanted no competition from men with hungry families who might work for less than the going rates. And it was cheaper to pay someone's passage back to Seattle than support him. Some came North believing they could live off the land with only a rifle and a fishline. Then there were the farmers who had moved to Alaska to live life anew in the Matanuska Valley, sometimes called the grub box of Alaska. They were refugees from the Dust Bowl of Oklahoma, Kansas, and neighboring states. The younger generation of this influx of people are still there, some on the same farms.

Seldom did one of the older girls who lived at the school as a worker go to town that she did not return with the story of being offered money or drinks to go aboard a ship with some sailor, or to a hotel room, or to somebody's shack. We were trusted but were chaperoned whenever we went to town, so we had no opportunity to get into trouble. Occasionally one of the boys would get caught smoking out behind the barn or in town and be hauled up before Mr. Hatten for a lecture. The biggest problem that faced the residents of the Jesse Lee Home and other boarding schools for Alaska Native children was what we would do when we finished high school and had to leave. The boys could go to sea, become cannery workers, fishermen, miners, or section hands on the railroad. The girls, though, except for summer cannery work, had little to look forward to but returning to their home villages or marrying some local fellow. Finding a mate was no big problem if a girl was not too particular for there were plenty lonely trappers, prospectors, homesteaders, and fishermen. These men were generally much older than the girls they wanted and always on the lookout for girls from

Jesse Lee as they were usually good homemakers by training. The staff tried to make sure that the prospective husband was a good risk before giving their blessing for a marriage. Too often, after a few years of hard work and several babies, a pretty girl would get fat and sloppy, lose the good looks that had attracted the man, and he would wander off, leaving more children to be raised in a government school or church-run orphanage. This is the general situation, not only in Alaska, but nearly anywhere you go. After the girls were eighteen years old, the Jesse Lee Home had no legal authority to prevent them from marrying, but everything was done to see that they got a decent man, especially one with a sense of Christian responsibility and sober habits. In general, the matches seemed to work out fairly successfully and many of the girls returned to their hometowns and married and had families. I heard from a few in later years and found they were leading normal family-oriented lives. After finishing school, many of the girls went to town to work as live-in housekeepers for the people who owned businesses, some doctors and lawyers, and the wealthy of Seward. Some of the scholastically superior girls were sent "outside" to the Lower 48 for higher education in such schools as Chemawa in Oregon.

As for me, I intended to honor my Uncle Ed's and my father's trust in me by finishing my education and becoming a useful citizen. I studied hard and concentrated on getting as much out of my lessons as I possibly could cram into my head. I absorbed all my curricula like a sponge. I never knew there was so much to getting an education. Math and history were my favorite subjects, and although Latin was a drain on my brain, I still made good grades and even took several years of it.

Often I had to work late into the night and many hours on the weekends. I was so busy studying that I hardly had time to dwell on homesickness. There were weekends though when my thoughts would take me back to home and family. Through letters from my Uncle Ed and my father, encouragement was given to me in large doses. I kept telling myself, "I must put every effort into learning for the sake of them and for myself." The more and harder that I applied myself, the easier it became for I had the backing of two important men in my life, namely the one to whom I owed my life and the one who was involving his life to make something of me.

There were all kinds of school activities to engage everyone. There were competitive high school sports, such as basketball, volleyball, and baseball, for the boys. Mr. and Mrs. Hatten allowed us to attend while they chaperoned. There were quilting bees for the girls and music recitals. Then there were get-togethers in the parlor, which was a large sitting room with a huge fireplace at one end. We were allowed to entertain one visitor a month in the parlor. Many of the students had relatives who would come to visit and lived within a few days' traveling distance from the home. My visitors would come when the USMS *Boxer* arrived on her annual trip to the Bering Sea. Then I would have such distinguished callers as Captain Whitlam, the chief engineer, or the chef, Sig Sundt, come and spend a few hours with me. In that way they would have a firsthand account to give my father and mother when they reached Teller that summer.

I have always loved music and dreamed of the day when I would be able to play some kind of musical instrument. Every one of my five brothers played one or more musical instruments. Robert, the youngest, played professionally in a band in his spare time as an army soldier at Fort Richardson. By summer I began to take piano lessons, and my teacher said I advanced surprisingly well, reaching the second-year class by the time school started again. There were so many piano students that we could only practice once or twice a week, and then it would have to be by appointment for even though there were three pianos in the two buildings, they were always in use. The Jesse Lee Home had a harmoniously pleasing glee club and a cappella choir. They were much in demand for special occasions in Seward as well as in other larger towns, such as Anchorage and Fairbanks, to which they would travel by train. They were deemed the best in all of Alaska. The majority of the students played some musical instrument even without instruction.

One of the most worldly wise and popular people I knew was a classmate of mine at the Jesse Lee Home. His name was Benny Benson. He was the boy who designed the Alaska state flag. He was an intelligent, good-looking lad from Chignik, a village out on the Alaska Peninsula west of Kodiak Island. His father was a Scandinavian fisherman who'd had to put Benny and his younger brother in the school after his Aleut mother died. He was an ingenious fellow, who could do anything from overhauling an engine to smoking salmon and playing the guitar and piano. Benny Benson was an outdoorsman and in the winter had a trap line out in the woods where he trapped for fox, mink, and marten. He was the headman in tending the milk cows for the school and maintaining the school's small dog team, which consisted of only five dogs of undetermined breed. He hunted moose, coyote, bear, and ducks. In the summer he was in charge of the salmon fishing for the institution. And when we took day-long trips to Tonsina Creek, Bear Glacier, and Rugged Island, it was usually Benny who ran the boat. He was sixteen when I came to the Jesse Lee Home. In 1926, when he was twelve, the American Legion in Alaska sponsored a contest for schoolchildren to design a territorial flag. Benny Benson's entry, a blue banner with eight stars of gold depicting the Big Dipper and the North Star, won first prize. He was awarded a gold watch engraved with the flag he designed and a trip to Washington, D.C., to present the first Alaska flag to President Coolidge. Before he could make the trip, his father became ill, and they were not able to go. He was given $1,000 for winning the first prize. This came fourteen years after Alaska became a territory. This same flag now is the official flag for the state of Alaska. I am very proud of the fact that I was a schoolmate of Benny Benson.

Things began to buzz in my head. What a new kind of world I was now living in: automobiles which I had never seen before going to and fro on the road near the school, trains traveling on tracks just below the hillside from the school, and stores with newfangled products I'd only seen in Sears or Montgomery Ward catalogs. All this seemed so strange in my fast-changing world. New friends, new sights, new sounds, and new experiences. Everything was so different from back home. The winters were milder and shorter. In the spring my thoughts went back to the breakup of the harbor ice back home. It was something to witness the coming of spring at Teller—the sound of the harbor ice breaking up was like a continuous roar of thunder. At Teller spring came upon us instantly when it did arrive. The lengthening days and brilliant sunlight that rotted the sea ice caused leads to open up. Patches of bare ground appeared here and there, showing the dead brown grass of the previous season. Trash and lost articles covered during the winter by succeeding snowfalls, came into view. One day in June an offshore wind would blow strong enough to spread the ice floes apart and move them out to the Bering Sea. Once Grantley Harbor and Port Clarence Bay were free of ice, ships of all descriptions would begin moving in and out. That was summer in northern Alaska where I grew up.

In Seward it was entirely different. There was a slow transition from spring to summer. The sea never froze, which was the reason Resurrection Bay had been chosen as the terminus of the Alaska Railroad because ships bringing freight, mail, and passengers could be handled all year round. The thaw came many weeks earlier than it did at Teller, where long after spring was on the calendar in Seward, winter was still upon the land up north. But on the Kenai Peninsula late in April, a warm wind would blow in from the Pacific Ocean and the Japan Current just offshore, bringing banks of low clouds that carried the warm rains in across the mountains to the west. Within a day or so, the waterfall on Mount Marathon began to flow full force again after months of frozen silence. Iron Mountain, the sheer 4,000 foot peak directly behind the school and just one mile away, commenced to shed its winter mantle in thundering avalanches that caused heavy reverberations that shook our buildings, rattled the windows, and terrified me the first time they happened. I thought the whole mountain would tumble down upon us. It was not unlike an earthquake when the ground would shake beneath. We felt earth tremors also at Seward every now and then, usually when there had been a quake in the Aleutian Chain or on the Kenai Peninsula.

After a few days, except in the gullies and deeper shadows of the forest, the ground was nearly bare of snow, as were the steeper faces of the mountains. Roads and pathways became mucky, and cars and trucks were always getting stuck as there were no paved roads. Finally the heavy clouds blew over, the sun came out bright and hot; soon green grass was shooting up from brown fields and pastures and meadows on the upper slopes. The gaunt trunks and branches of winter-naked willows, cottonwoods, birch, and alder were quickly clothed in soft foliage that rustled in the wind. Wildflowers popped up everywhere. Roadside thickets were pink with blossoms of the wild roses and fireweed and white with the salmonberry bushes and three-petaled trillium poking out everywhere. The warming atmosphere was permeating the air with a hundred new fragrances.

New life was everywhere. In the chicken yard I saw for the first time hens with baby chicks, and the gallant rooster scratched up tidbits then called his flock to come and eat while he stood by self-satisfied. Sows with winter-born piglets were turned out to root, and calves kicked up their heels and frolicked about, tails held high, exuberant with the joy of discovering the world of freedom beyond the confines of dark stalls inside the barn. We saw wild young creatures, too. Black bears with cubs born during winter hibernation would come out of the woods at evening to raid the garbage cans. Great ugly moose cows, gaunt and bony from long months on short rations, brought long-legged ungainly calves to browse on the tender leaves and new growth of the willows and alders that grew along the edge of the cemetery adjoining the property of the school.

Summer vacation did not mean rest and leisure for the residents of Jesse Lee, either staff or students. When classes ended for the term, everyone who was old enough to work did his share. The buildings were given a top-to-bottom spring cleaning, repaired, and painted. Bedding and mattresses were taken out for sunning and airing. Heavy winter garments were laundered, repaired, and stored away until needed again. When the ground had partially dried out enough for tilling, the old Fordson tractor that had been donated by a Seward businessman was cranked up, and the garden tract plowed, harrowed, and planted. Lots of potatoes were put in, as well as cabbage, kale, spinach, and Brussels sprouts—all sturdy, iron-filled leaf plants—and carrots, turnips, and other root crops that would keep well after harvesting. The vegetables flourished well in the short but fast growing season practically astride the sixtieth parallel of latitude, two-thirds of the way between the Equator and the North Pole.

A few days after planting, what had been naked ground one evening would the next morning have rows of seedlings that had sprung up in the daylight of night. When the weather was clear, the sun, reflecting from the surrounding glaciers and ice fields, was in the sky from half past two in the morning until nearly ten PM. The temperature sometimes would go up to over eighty. If there was no wind, it cooled off only a little during the few hours that the sun was below the mountains to the north. Being from a region where gardening was neither practical nor practiced to any great extent, I was fascinated by the growing crops and how fast they grew during the long hours of daylight.

Summer was also a time of increased earthquake activity. Though we'd had small tremors now and then throughout the winter, with the coming of warm weather there was hardly a month when we would not feel the trembling of the ground beneath the buildings, see the electric lights swing overhead, and hear the rattle of chinaware in the cupboards. It was said the increase was caused by the movement of the glaciers as they were lightened by millions of tons of melting ice. The rock beneath the ice was being forced upward by pressures deep within the earth. Whatever the reason, apparently it was an omen or forewarning of violent things to come. On March 27, 1964, Anchorage, Seward, Valdez, Kodiak, and many other towns and villages in this part of Alaska were partially or totally destroyed by the Good

Friday earthquake and the seismic waves that followed. During the temblor, the bottom of Resurrection Bay dropped hundreds of feet, the water vanished, and for a few moments the bay was as dry as a drained bathtub. Then a wall of water came rushing in from the ocean to fill the void. Sloshing back and forth from end to end of the bay, it washed hundred-foot boats, diesel locomotives and boxcars, bulldozers, and vehicles high up on the hillsides. The docks, oil tanks, canneries, buildings, and houses near the shore were wrecked and deposited in the trees on the lower slopes of Mount Marathon, along with the bodies of the victims. Being on high ground beyond the head of the bay the Jesse Lee Home was spared.

The big event of the summer season was the Fourth of July celebration. The canneries closed, fishermen tied up their boats, stevedore and railroad operations stopped. The highlight of Seward's Independence Day celebration was the annual race up to the top of Marathon Mountain. There was a flagpole at the summit, and the first person to reach it and raise the flag got a hundred dollars. One of the fastest times ever made was by one of the Jesse Lee boys, Ephriam Kalmakoff, fifty-five minutes from starting line to flagpole. He later died of tuberculosis brought on, some believed, by overstraining his lungs during trial runs up the mountain. He won the marathon race three years in a row. During the Second World War, when over 3,000 soldiers and sailors were stationed at Seward to defend the port facilities and the railhead from an expected Japanese attack, the Fourth of July race was discontinued.

The salmonberries ripened in July. Sweet and juicy, they did not keep and had to be eaten fresh. The blueberries weren't ready until late August. There were thousands of acres of them on the lower slopes of Mount Alice, Bear Mountain, and other peaks on the east side of the bay and valley. Mama would have loved it here, I used to think, as I picked a gallon of the fat, sweet berries without moving from my tracks. We shared the blueberry thickets with black bears. It was not uncommon to be filling our buckets within a hundred feet of several bears, sleek and fat and stinking from the spawned-out salmon they'd gorged on along the streams. We had an agreement with the bears that if they would stay on their side of the thicket, we'd stay on ours. If we came on one unexpectedly it usually ran. If it stood its ground and growled, we retreated.

We never heard of anyone being harmed by a black bear. Brownies were something else again. Weighing as much as 1,600 pounds, the great

Alaska brown bear, or grizzly, is one of the largest carnivores in the world, second only to the polar bear. When surprised or wounded, or if their young are threatened, they are the most dangerous and vindictive of wild creatures. Almost yearly in brown bear country, someone is killed or maimed. It only happens to people who invade the bears' home territory because, unlike the smaller blacks, the big fellows avoid human habitations. We were warned that when we were in the woods, we should make lots of noise to alert any brownies that might be in the vicinity. They would then slip away deeper into the forest, and you'd never know they had ever been there except for their tracks and the fishy stink they left behind. Experienced travelers of Alaskan trails often carried bear alarms—empty tobacco tins with pebbles in them that rattled as they walked and gave notice of their presence to the brown bears. At home in northern Alaska, whenever we went berry-picking, Mama always carried a tin dishpan, and every now and then she would take a stick and beat on the tin pan to let the bears know that we were picking berries also and to let us be. If, however, you came on one unexpectedly, and he reared up on hind legs to his full nine feet a few yards away, woodsmen said the wisest thing was to stand your ground and talk to the bear in a normal voice, and he'd usually drop down on all fours and amble off. If startled though, he'd charge the thing that frightened him and attack with fangs and claws. If there was time and a tree was handy, you could scoot up to safety because a grown brownie is too heavy to climb. You dared not stop until you were at least twelve feet up into the branches because the erect brown bear could reach that high and drag you down. No such incidents happened to us though. Moose, too, that could bowl you over with their antlers and chop you to bits with their sharp hooves, were best dealt with by standing still and calling to them to be on their way. The animals, standing six feet tall at the shoulder, not wanting an encounter, usually faded away into the underbrush. If it happened to be a cow with a calf, a bull in rutting season, or a rogue of the moose world, it was good to have a tree at hand. It is said that men have climbed trees with snowshoes when being chased by a moose. Now, this may be one of the entertaining tales invented by Alaskans for the benefit of cheechakos, but I wouldn't swear it is.

9

It wasn't all work and no play in the summer of 1931 for the kids at Jesse Lee. When the crops were planted and the cleanup and maintenance work was done, we had some free time. It was often spent going camping or picnicking, taking boat rides on the bay or motor trips out the Hope Road. We all loved those carefree times. We felt happy walking the clean, sandy beaches.

A bunch of us would pile onto the school's old truck after breakfast and ride out to see the old mining camps at Sunrise and Hope, sixty miles away on Turnagain Arm, the north side of the peninsula. Hope, a few miles west of Sunrise, was famous for being the only place in Alaska where apple trees would grow and produce. The town consisted of a few buildings and cabins remaining from the gold rush days when, like in Teller and Nome, hundreds had come, hopeful of getting rich quick, and then gone away disappointed. Side roads led up several gulches to small mines that were still operating back in the hills.

The gravel road, a single lane on the straight stretches but wide enough to pass another car at the corners, was muddy and bumpy in many places.

But who cared! The scenery was spectacular, winding through dense spruce forests, up narrow valleys with snow-topped crags hanging over, past rushing streams and placid lakes, with blue glaciers in almost any direction we went. We'd see dozens of snowshoe rabbits, wearing summer brown, and spruce hens, or grouse, in coveys or flying up into the branches where they teetered, unafraid. We called them "fool hens" because they were so fearless. Ducks and geese fed in the sloughs and ponds and marshes. Bald eagles, hawks, and other predatory birds soared and dove to kill and carry off rabbits, grouse, and spruce hens.

We saw great beaver ponds backed up by dams as long as a mile from end to end. If we wanted to see the builders, someone would open a gap in a dam. As the water poured out, the beaver would come swimming from their lodges, dragging branches, and bringing mud up from the bottom of the pond to plug the opening. Sometimes, while stopped to watch the beavers working, we'd hear a tree come crashing down, usually a silver birch or aspen, and could see the spiked stump and tree trunk where one of the big, flat-tailed rodents had chewed it through. Occasionally a beaver would be found under a fallen tree, dead of a broken back. We saw muskrats, too, and mink that took up residence along the edges of the beaver ponds. My brother David would have liked it there with so many things to hunt and trap.

This was big game country, and we often saw cow moose with their calves browsing in the thickets along the road or belly deep in ponds, heads under water as they dredged up the roots of lily pads. The bulls were more wary, and we only saw them at a distance, black backs and racks of yellow antlers glistening in the sunlight. Around almost every bend in the crooked road, we'd come upon black bear that would go scooting off into the bushes. They say there were brownies in these areas also, but we never saw one. The noisy engine of the truck and our yelling, singing voices might have deterred them. Once while stopped beside the road to look down into a narrow gorge, we saw a bear moseying up a rocky streambed, pausing now and then to scoop a fish out onto the bank where he'd gobble it down in a bite or two, then wade out and catch another.

Besides the placer operations at the mining camps, where men with high-pressure water nozzles washed the gold-bearing sand and gravel down for sluicing, a big attraction was watching the bore come up Turnagain Arm. The difference between high and low tide was over thirty-three feet. At low ebb the three-mile-wide flats went virtually dry, across which the returning tide came in as a wall of muddy water as much as six feet high, traveling at twenty miles an hour up the shallow, ever-narrowing inlet. This wall of water was the bore, one of very few in the world. We heard of people stranded in dories on the flats by the receding waters who were drowned by the bore when the tide came in again. There was no escape by getting out and wading to the safety of the shore. The flats were covered by a slick sticky mud into which a person could sink out of sight or be trapped waist deep and overwhelmed by the incoming flood. Next to the Bay of Fundy on the eastern coast of Canada, Turnagain Arm of Cook Inlet has the second highest tide in the world.

One trip that we all liked was out to Alaska Nellie's hunting lodge at Lawing on Kenai Lake, about twenty-five miles from Seward. Nellie Neal had sought adventure, found it in Alaska, and liked to talk about it. There were Alaskans who were a bit skeptical of some of the experiences she claimed to have had, but we never doubted a word this remarkable woman used to tell us.

Born Nellie Trosper at St. Joseph, Missouri, in 1885, she went to Cripple Creek, Colorado, when she was eighteen to work as a waitress in the gold camps. Shortly after her arrival a lot of miners were killed by a bomb explosion during labor strife. The morgue was next door to where she worked, and she saw the shattered bodies being carried there. She later married an assayer named Wesley Neal. Once, when home alone, she was robbed and badly beaten. The next time a robbery attempt was made, she shot it out with the holdup man, wounded him, and he was sent to prison. Her husband turned out to be a heavy drinker, and she left and divorced him.

She arrived in Seward in December of 1915 and was off the steamer only a few hours when she was offered a job as cook at a gold mine. The camp was at the end of a steep, five-mile road leading from the railroad at Mile 26 back into the Kenai Mountains. Part of the job was to shoot wild game to feed the hungry miners. Nellie's accounts of face-to-face encounters with brownies and bull moose while out after spruce hens or rabbits for dinner were hair-raising, and with each telling seemed to become more so, a common trait of many avid storytellers.

Though the minor details might become a bit embellished over the years, the attacking bear get larger and fall dead from her rifle shots a bit closer to her, the basic facts of Alaska Nellie's stories always remained

Gold dredge, Fairbanks, Alaska, 1959.

intact. No one doubted that she'd had her share of wilderness excitement, but some of her contemporaries, perhaps a bit envious of her fame, felt that she was not as woods-wise as she claimed, but, rather, "a fool who went where angels feared to tread," being ignorant of danger and downright lucky. But to the Alaska born and to the foolish, the element of luck can be said to not exist. The law of averages does, though, and that is evidence enough that Nellie Neal was a superb woodswoman and an expert shot. She lived a long life and died quietly in bed long after some of her detractors had been killed or crippled by big game.

When she first came to Seward, the railroad was privately owned. Known as the Alaska Central it went only as far as Kern Creek, seventy miles away on the north side of Turnagain Arm, having been built to serve the gold mines of the region. Forty-five miles further on, where Anchorage now stands, there was nothing but a few log cabins at the mouth of Ship Creek, not worth extending the railroad to. A few years after Nellie's arrival, the government bought out the Alaska Central, and the railroad was built the rest of the way to Fairbanks. My son's great grandfather, Mike Callahan, helped build the railroad.

After several years of working at different mining and railroad construction camps, Nellie became engaged to marry a railroad man. He was killed in an accident a few days before the wedding day. She wrote to the man's cousin in Tennessee, a Billie Lawing. He answered, wanting to know more about the country and about her, and soon they were corresponding regularly. He proposed by mail, she accepted, and he came to Seward. He turned out to be an extremely handsome and charming man. The day he arrived, they were married on the stage of the Seward Theater after the show.

They bought a spacious log cabin close to the Alaska Railroad tracks at Roosevelt at Mile 25 on Kenai Lake. The name of the station was later changed to Lawing. After twelve years of happiness together, during which they operated a roadhouse for travelers and hunters and a commercial boat on the lake, Billie died one winter of a heart attack while shoveling snow. She buried him at Seward. She lived on alone at Lawing, operating her roadhouse. The crews of freight trains usually stopped there for meals, and conductors would stop their trains at Lawing for ten minutes so Nellie could show travelers her hunting trophies and tell the story of her life. A small box beside the door invited cash donations. For many years this was her only livelihood, and many times the pickings were slim indeed, except for the game she shot and the fish she caught. She wrote her autobiography, *Alaska Nellie*, and in 1940 it was published.

The big front room of Lawing Lodge had wide windows that faced out upon blue-green Kenai Lake and the green wooded mountains beyond. The walls were covered with the mounted heads of every kind of game that inhabited the Kenai Peninsula, and some that did not. Moose, brown and black bears, goats and sheep were local. The polar bears, caribou, and cougars were not. There were stuffed eagles, swans, owls, grouse, ptarmigan, marmots, lynx, rabbits, beaver, and muskrat. The rugs were made of the skins of bears and wolverine with heads intact, mouths agape to show the fangs, and glass eyes that stared at you.

Next to Nellie's love affair with her husband, whom she called "my sweetheart" to the day she died, the highlight of her life was the day in 1923 when President Harding arrived in Alaska to officially open the recently completed railroad. He got off his special train at Lawing to visit the lodge, sign the guest book, and be photographed with her. She was one of the real Alaskan characters, and I'm glad that I had a chance to know her.

Another trip we used to take was to Cooper Landing at the west end of Kenai Lake, where the Kenai River begins its sprawling, crooked journey to Cook Inlet, seventy-five miles away. Not far from Cooper Landing was the Russian River. Here, back in the days before 1867 when the Czars still owned Alaska, the Russians had a penal colony where criminals and political prisoners were exiled for a life of hard labor. There were no ruins left to see, but it was said that upstream at Lower and Upper Russian Lake were the remains of crude mines where the convicts had dug for gold. It was said, too, that in years past, skeletons had been found there with rusty chains still shackled to the leg bones.

Except for the minor human frictions that occur even in well-adjusted groups and happy families, if we had any problems at the Jesse Lee Home as that first summer of 1931 came to an end, it was finding time to do all that had to be done in preparation for the new school term and the coming winter. Late running silvers and humpies had to be caught and prepared and canned or smoked for human consumption, and the chums, or dog salmon, split and dried for dog feed. Railroad cars of coal from the Matanuska Valley and Healy Mines were spotted on the siding near the school for the boys to unload and haul to fill our coalbins. Other boys spent their days out in the woods with saws and axes, cutting down trees for kindling and fireplace fuel. It always seemed like such a waste of precious trees to me, being from a land that had no trees. The hay had to be mowed and piled on pointed stakes to cure, then hauled to the barn and stored in the loft. We didn't grow enough to see our cows through the winter so tons more of baled hay came down from Fairbanks on the railroad or from farmers in the Matanuska Valley. Another donor, to whom we were all grateful, was the eastern Washington orchardists who each year sent a hundred or so boxes of C grade apples that could be used for pies, applesauce, and other cooking.

While the boys were doing their heavy outdoor work, there was plenty to do inside to keep us girls busy. We girls made jams from the wild berries and altered clothes to fit young bodies that had grown inches and gained many pounds during the summer months. A big shipment of garments came from the Women's Home Missionary Society, and everything had to be sorted and distributed.

Harvesting the big garden was in full swing by mid-August. How we loved those fresh things, especially those of us who grew up in the Arctic and the Aleutians and who'd only had fruit and vegetables from cans. We could never seem to get our fill of spinach, cauliflower, and all the other wonderful tasting things that were grown. Cabbages, carrots, rutabagas, beets, turnips, and potatoes could be stored in the cool cellar for later use, but almost everything else had to be used soon after it was gathered or canned for winter use.

One thing at Jesse Lee in particular that I was continually thankful for and that everyone seemed to take for granted was the bathroom facilities. It was there whenever you had to use it, a nice warm comfortable place to sit as you answered nature's call. And to cleanse your whole body, all that you had to do was fill the tub from an unending supply of warm water from a faucet and not even have to go out to get the ice to melt it into water on the kitchen stove. What a luxury the bathroom was compared to the inconvenience of taking a once-a-week bath in the same water, in the same galvanized tub, for four of us in succession as we had to do at home. Then the next week the other four would go through the same ordeal, always the smallest ones first. If someone happened to open the front door while you were in the tub, the cloud of cold air would seek out the hot steam from the bath water, and when the two opposing temperatures met, it would cool the room down twenty degrees, it seemed, even though the room used as a "bathroom" was two rooms away from the front door.

Sometimes looking out an upstairs dormitory window, I could see a pod of killer whales (orcas), or blackfish as we called them, rolling and blowing as they fed on salmon and smaller fish in Resurrection Bay. That put me in mind of Teller in the summer during berry-picking time. From the high hillsides on each side of the Tuksuk River, we saw beluga whales under the surface of the clear waters, making a return trip from the Tuksuk going out into Grantley Harbor and eventually out to sea. Before the end of the berry-picking day Mama would look at her traps, which she had set earlier in the day, and bring home two or three squirrels. We would have squirrel stew for our supper, to which she would put onions, potatoes, and a handful of rice. It would be a change from the fresh fish we had as a usual meal in the summer. We also witnessed otters playing hide-and-seek among the rocks near the shore of the Tuksuk, oblivious of us in their carefree, playful mood. In the spring, at home, we would see the gray whales, the females with their young getting a free ride on their backs, coming up the channel following the runs of salmon coming in from open water.

The Eskimo now are in a state of cultural transition. They are combining the old way of life with the new. Schools and pubic health facilities have been established for them. With the advent of the oil money that came with the settlement of the Alaska Native Land Claims Settlement Act, the older Eskimos are realizing better housing, oil for heating and cooking, and, in some areas, the latest bathroom facilities; all this in contrast to the harsh life of their parents and those previous to them. Education and training have made it possible for Eskimos to obtain jobs in the new industries, and wages enable them to replace fur clothes with cotton and wool garments, homemade equipment of bone and ivory and the harpoon with rifles and manufactured hand tools, and a diet from the land with canned, packaged, and fresh food.

*   *   *

At the age of eighteen, I began to have quite a bit of discomfort with my left leg. The two bones below the knee, the tibia and fibula, were growing out of the stump and causing discomfort in the prosthetics of the left leg. I had mentioned this in a letter to Uncle Ed in Pittsburgh, and he suggested that I have a doctor look at it. Mr. Hatten took me to see Dr. Haverstock at the Seward General Hospital. The operation was scheduled for January in the Seward General, and in a few weeks, I was able to walk out of there and back to school.

While in the hospital in Seward, I had the honor of meeting Anthony J. Dimond, the prominent Alaska congressman, who through many years of political service became a popular figure in the fight for Alaska statehood. He also urged the building of the Alaska Highway during the Second World War. While the Japanese harried us in the Aleutian Islands, Mr. Dimond was telling us that we could end the isolation of our great land by building a link to the United States via Canada. So in 1942 the U.S. Army Corps of Engineers began to tackle the huge project. Winding through narrow river valleys, along the sides of solid rock mountains, and over seemingly endless muskeg flats, the route presented problems that engineers had not encountered since the Burma Road in Southeast Asia was finished in 1938. During the summer months of 1942, the army engineers found their way blocked time and time again by bogs which consumed rock and gravel as fast as it could be poured in. The bane of the North, mosquitoes, added much more to the discomfort and frustration of the workers. With the onset of winter the road builders were confronted with temperatures ranging down to sixty and seventy degrees below zero in the Yukon Territory of Canada. It took some 10,000 American troops from seven Army Corps of Engineers regiments and approximately 6,000 civilian workers through the summer and early winter of 1942 to finish the road. This road had been cut through an untracked wilderness at the incredible rate of eight miles a day and was completed in eight months and eleven days. The total cost for the 1,422 miles of road was $138,312,166. Ownership of the road reverted to Canada after the war, with a provision that travel would be open to one and all. Now known as the Alaska Highway, the route was first known as the Alcan Highway. It is a scenic drive traveled by many, and the trucking business was a boon to Alaskans and Canadians.

I had no sooner returned to the classroom when I became aware that the left leg was ill-fitting after the surgery. And besides the brace and straps on both limbs needed replacing. Having informed Uncle Ed of this new development, I realized that the nearest place I could have these things done was in Seattle, which could be reached only by a six- or seven-day trip by steamer. After receiving a round trip steamer ticket, I left Seward for Seattle on February 10, arriving Seattle on the seventeenth. The trip south on the Alaska steamship line's *McKinley* was one I will never forget. Traveling the Inside Passage of southeastern Alaska, we stopped at Skagway, the city with the history of Alaska's gold rush days and Soapy Smith. We also stopped at the capitol city of Juneau, nestled on a plateau just large enough to set the city on, with towering mountains on three sides and the Gastuneau Channel on the west and the Mendenhall Glacier around the corner to the east. From there and keeping a southern course, we made Wrangel and Petersburg, two smaller towns with fishing and lumbering as their main stock in trade. Finally we reached the First City, Ketchikan; as the name implies, it is the first city you come to after leaving the lower United States. The weather all the way could not have been better considering the time of year. Low clouds hugged the mountainsides which were heavily forested to the waterline with the greenery of spruce, hemlock, and pine. The ship moved its way through narrow passages and around and between hundreds of thickly wooded islands, some I am sure a human being had never set foot on. Every now and then as we came around one small island to the next, we could see a waterfall spraying fine mist as it meandered down the shear cliffs.

The passengers seemed to have a merry time all the way. There were dances in the social hall every evening as the dancers swayed to the piano music by Johnny Chitwood, the famous Seattle nightclub music-maker. Every day the stewards set out the deck chairs and lounges for those, such as I, who found enjoyment and enchantment in the panoramic scenery unfolding as one sat comfortably wrapped in a thick wool blanket. Many walked the promenade decks in pairs, walking briskly in the fresh, cool, unpolluted air, invigorating one to the very core. It is no wonder that the cruise ships on this run were always booked up in advance. The food they served on the S.S. *McKinley* was excellent and almost made one forget about watching the waistline. Contrasted with the old *Boxer*, the steamship *McKinley* was a floating palace, which ten years later would be destroyed near the Aleutian Islands by Japanese bombs during World War II. The one person on the ship whom I will remember perhaps the rest of my days was the stewardess, Mrs. Elizabeth Rogers. She kept an eye on me and saw to it that I was guarded from the overzealous male passengers, some of whom had not seen a young woman for months or years, and from old-time miners and fishermen making their first trip "outside" in many moons. She also noticed that the wireless operator, Sparks as he was called, was seeking my company on deck and spending hours talking to me. But she needn't have worried for I knew my bounds. Mama had warned us of strangers even before we became teenagers, especially men who would try to come too close before we innocents could have a chance to analyze the what, where, when, and how's of a situation. She used to say, "Watch out for the ones who want to work fast."

Anyway I had a real guardian angel in Mrs. Rogers. About the third day out from Seward, she inquired of me as to whether I had anyone to meet me in Seattle. I told her I did not know a soul in the big city, but that I had a letter from my oldest brother Tommy just a few days before I left Seward in which he said that his ship was expected to be in Seattle for awhile. So she suggested, "Why not send him a telegram in care of the Sailor's Union of the Pacific." I did this, and Sparks, the radioman, was happy to send the message.

For the last two days before our arrival in the port of Seattle, it had been spread around the ship that this was my very first trip "outside" and first also to a metropolitan city. They all wanted to see what expressions I would have at the sight of the city skyline and all the wonders of big city life—neon lights, trolley cars loaded with people going up and down the steep hills, bustling crowds on city streets and in the stores, automobile traffic coming and going from all directions, and the Smith Tower, which was the tallest building in Seattle. As our ship approached Pier 48 and slid along the slip ready for the gangplank to be let down in place, everyone was scanning the welcoming crowd on the deck. I stood as close to the railing as I could, working my way through the crowd on the ship, and who should take hold of my arm and share the excitement with me but Mrs. Rogers. "If you can find your brother in that crowd then we know that you will be all right."

I had not seen Tommy in eleven years, since he left home way up at Teller, Alaska, in 1921 on the MS *Herman*, Captain Pederson's ship bound for San Francisco. Finally, I spotted a resemblance of my brother, so I waved, and Mrs. Rogers took both of my hands in hers and made me wave with both hands. Soon people were rushing down the gangway and shaking hands with others on the dock, and some were embracing, tears running down their faces, reuniting with families after, perhaps, many years of separation. Mrs. Rogers told the purser that it would be better if I waited until the mad rush down the gangway to the dock dwindled so that I could take my time going down, and just as she was saying that here comes my brother Tommy, taking long strides up the gangway. He gathered me in his arms and gave me a big bear hug, then put me away from him at arms length and said, "Is this the little sister who could so easily have not been here when Papa and I saved her life." The last time he saw me, I was nine years old and was just learning to walk on my first pair of artificial limbs. He complimented me on how well I looked and that I was getting along so famously on the prosthesis. He then asked me where I had hotel reservations, and I replied, "The YWCA." I think he thought to himself, "Well, that's the safest place for a young woman these days."

From the first time that I entered the doors of my hotel, I hardly had time to myself. First the two Seattle major newspapers sent newsmen and photographers to the hotel to interview "the native Alaskan on her first trip to the great outside." This was on a Saturday so, of course, the news and pictures were splashed on the front pages of the Sunday issues through the AP wire services, from New York to San Francisco. They emphasized the fact that I had come through such a shocking experience in Alaska at such a tender age. The newspapers dubbed me "Queen of Arctic Alaska" and judging from the many telephone calls and messages in my hotel mailbox, many in the city and surrounding area wanted to take the "queen" out to dinner or to show off the big city. I made some lasting friends, and even after I returned to school at Seward, I got letters from people who did not get the opportunity to meet me after reading accounts in the papers.

The people who benefitted the most from meeting and talking with me because I was from Teller, Alaska, were Mr. and Mrs. Borland, parents of

Earl Borland, who crashed in the plane with Ben Eielson during the winter of 1929. They wanted most of all to talk to someone who had seen him for the last time, and I and some of my sisters and brothers were standing on the Grantley Harbor ice when the two flew into the gray sky westward towards Siberia on their last flight that cold November morning.

I was invited to many homes for dinner but could not begin to accept all the invitations. I saw my first movie, and being that I was a student member of a church organization, the Jesse Lee School, I was flooded with requests to attend "a special" at such and such church, and I was asked to speak "firsthand about Alaska" to assemblies at a large high school in the city. Of course, the work that had to be done on my prosthesis was of first priority.

The day after the newspapers came out with all the publicity, I had a phone call from Captain Whitlam of the USMS *Boxer*. After chatting for awhile he said, "Elizabeth, there is a new ship being built here for the service of the Bureau of Indian Affairs to replace the *Boxer*, and I'm to be her master. She's being built at Berg shipyard in Ballard. She's nearly ready to be launched and the Bureau of Indian Affairs has been looking for a Native Alaskan girl to christen her. I think you would be a perfect choice to do the honors." Thrilled by the thought that I should be chosen for the opportunity that many girls would envy, I said I would accept and arrangements were made for me to christen the *North Star*, a 225-foot wooden hulled vessel, valued at $389,000. The launching date was still several days away, and Charles Hawkesworth, then an agent from Washington, D.C., in the Department of the Interior, was to be present at the christening. After his arrival Captain Whitlam brought him up to the hotel lobby to meet me, and over lunch in the "Y" dining room, our conversation never left the subject of Alaska. Upon leaving, both men said they would see me at the christening ceremony.

I spent many hours nearly every day at the prosthetic plant, where they were making the new limb. The right one, they thought, would not need anything but new straps, but the pulley in the knee might need overhauling. The prosthetics I had were already four years old, but they still fit me all right, except for the left leg that needed to be remade. Before I could go out on my own, so to speak, I had to practice with one of the fitters present to see that every aspect of them fit. Finally, when they were all done and ready for my debut, I walked down Third Avenue just like anybody else. I stopped in a department store to buy some city-type clothes. People in the store said, "Aren't you the Miss Arctic Alaska whose picture was in the paper?" Or while standing in a crowd waiting for a light to change or for a taxi, I would hear someone say, "There's Miss Alaska right there."

The day was nearing when I would have to christen the *North Star*, but I thought, "I'm not ready to walk up that flight of stairs and then on a scaffolding to the bow of the ship, let alone walk on a straightaway." And I knew I would be even more nervous with hundreds (perhaps thousands) of people watching. I conjured up all kinds of negative thoughts until I finally convinced myself that I couldn't do it. I was afraid to call Captain Whitlam to tell him that I didn't think I could do the honors, but I did. He was very disappointed that I had changed my mind and pleaded with me to go ahead and do it. I explained to him that I would be self-conscious going up those steps to the scaffolding and that I was afraid I would stumble and fall down. He said, "All right, Elizabeth, I think I see your point, but you don't have to feel that way, for I know you can do it. Remember, I have known you since you were a little girl, and as far as I can see, you have more of what it takes than a lot of people I know."

On the appointed day the *North Star* was christened, and the girl who did the honors was one of the Pullen girls from Juneau, Alaska, who was a student at the University of Washington. Although not an Alaska Native, as the Department of the Interior had preferred, she was from an Alaskan pioneer family.

I didn't think that I could ever adjust to city living; it was so very alien to the life from whence I had come. There were crowds of people everywhere. I used to think, "Where do they all come from?" and "Where are they all going?" I almost got claustrophobia from being surrounded by so many people. The S.S. *Victoria* took me on the return trip to Seward, after about three weeks of fantastic new happenings on each day spent a couple of thousand miles away from school. I thought I had seen everything after traveling on a large steamship, experiencing all the sights and sounds of a busy seaport city, seeing my first moving picture, riding in an elevator in a skyscraper, and using the telephone. But this was only the beginning of my life in a big world, and I found life in it could be exciting and broadening.

After the first week in March, it was back to the old grind, and I must admit it was a little difficult to concentrate and dig in where I had left off

1932, Elizabeth on board USS *North Star*.

Elizabeth, chief engineer, and Marble Ivanoff on board USS *North Star.*.

at school. But I worked hard and studied evenings and made up the three weeks in short order. By the time spring arrived and school had recessed, I was ready to go home to Teller for summer vacation. I received my uncle's permission and when the S.S. *North Star*, the same ship I was first chosen to christen in Seattle just a few months previously, called into Seward on her way to Bering Sea duty, I was ready to go.

After leaving Seward and the comparative protection of the mainland waterways, we crossed the stormy Shelikof Strait to Kodiak Island, and from there the *North Star* made her usual ports of call to villages large and small. Taking a westward course, we skimmed along the southern shore of the Alaska Peninsula, past the Valley of Ten Thousand Smokes, and on to Dutch Harbor. Leaving the North Pacific and the Aleutians, we entered the Bering Sea through False Pass, the Panama Canal of the North. After that, the course was nearly due north, up through the Bering Sea. Having made this trip in the reverse, that is, north to south, just a few months short of

Elizabeth with Captain Whitlam and crew on board USS *North Star*

two years previously, I began to feel like an old salt. But what a contrast in weather and traveling conditions. Compared to the old *Boxer*, this ship was a regular cruise ship, with spacious cabins and a large dining salon, and I had the privilege of traveling with the same crew who made that miserable stormy voyage in the fall of 1930, crossing the Bering Sea when we all thought we would "go down to Davey Jones's locker."

After about three weeks of traveling, we arrived at Nome, which was practically next door to my home at Teller. To my great surprise, I found that airplanes were getting to be the regular form of travel. Another surprise—it only took sixty minutes to go from Nome to Teller, the same distance that it took my father and Tommy three days by dogsled to get me over to the hospital. I wasted no time in getting to Teller via airplane and a trusted bush pilot, Frank Dorbandt.

It goes without saying that I was happy to see my mother and father and five younger brothers and sisters. We had much to talk about. I was asked such questions as, "Are cities like Seattle really big? So big that you have to take a street car to get from one end to the other, instead of walking to wherever you have to go?" and "Are the buildings really so tall that you have to take an elevator?"

Also, something new was going on around my hometown. The MS *Nanuk* was anchored on the north side of Nook, where ships don't usually anchor. Papa said the MGM movie company was shooting a picture about the Eskimos. It wasn't long before we met the whole company, from the director W. S. Van Dyke to the cameramen and the actors and actresses playing the parts in the movie. Never in our wildest dreams did we ever imagine that a moving picture would be made, for all the world to see, in our own front yard. The ship *Nanuk* was frozen in the ice and the entire crew of the MGM movie company were stuck at Teller during the making of *Eskimo*, from October 1932 to July 1933. The walrus hunting shots were made off the coast of Siberia, and the polar bear scenes were made at Herald Island due west of Point Barrow in the Arctic Ocean.

My father rented our house at Teller to the movie company, which they used for the Royal Canadian Mounted Police headquarters and interior scenes. The British flag flew over our house. A sign over the doorway of our house read, "Headquarters of the Royal Canadian Mounted Police." We made lasting friendships with the movie crew, some of whom we saw later in films made back in their home studios in Los Angeles. The leading lady was Lotus Long (her filmmaking name), and she and I corresponded for many years. She gave me an autographed photo of herself. She had parts in movies that Dorothy Lamour made. The leading man was "Mala" (Ray Wise), born in northern Alaska. The story was taken from the book, *Eskimo*, by Peter Freuchen, the six foot, four inch tall Danish author, explorer, and geologist. We became good friends, being that we had one thing in common: we both had the experience of freezing our feet in the cold northern climate. After studying geology at the University of Denmark, he mapped the southwest coastline of Greenland for the Danish government when he was quite young. He and his dog team were caught in a blizzard for days, and, with no protection from the elements, they waited out the storm only to find that he had frozen his right leg which had to be amputated above the knee. He used to set me on his lap and tell me about his ordeal and then he'd ask me about mine. I have a large autographed photo of him in my livingroom, which reads, "Thanks for winter 1933, yours truly, Peter Freuchen."

My younger sister Augusta had a part in the making of the picture as they used the local population as extras, and a year or so later when the picture was released, it was great seeing my little sister on the screen, along with other familiar faces. Papa was hired as a technical advisor in the building of snow houses and the making of snow glasses that they used in some of the scenes.

Nome, Alaska at midnight, 1936.

I spent an interesting summer at home. When school opened its doors in the fall, I found myself attending the Nome High School, after making arrangements to board with the principal and his wife. At one of the social functions attended by the greater population of Nome that winter, I met one of the Coast Guard boys stationed there at the time. It was the closet thing in my young years to being in love. He was a German boy, and he said he had met my father the previous summer while on routine patrol in the Coast Guard launch to Teller. I was never allowed by Mr. and Mrs. Dunbar (the family I boarded with) to be in his company alone, only at large social functions, but we carried on our love affair by writing letters, even though we were in the same community. By the time the next fall rolled around, I had made plans, with my Uncle Ed's permission, to attend school in Washington state as I found the winters in my home area were too severe, and it was difficult for me to get to classes in the snow and icy conditions.

In the fall, sailing on the S.S. *Victoria* from Nome, I and a few hundred people from the surrounding area—mining men, seasonal workers, captains, and pursers of the Yukon River boats—headed south, away from the oncoming winter that would last seven to eight more months. "It will be good to see Seattle again," I thought. I applied myself in school with a lot of hard work. I found myself enjoying my classes. I was the first Eskimo to attend Roosevelt High School and the girls' advisor, Miss Rose Glass, thought

I should be honored. She was about to make arrangements with the portrait painting class for a sitting for me when I came down with appendicitis and had to spend weeks in a hospital with complications from that attack. Miss Glass thought it would be nice to have my portrait hang next to the Queen of Romania, who had gifted the school with her portrait a year or so before. But it was not to come out that way as the timetable for my classes overlapped the appointment with the art class.

Being a Native of Alaska and having firsthand knowledge of the life in that cold clime, I was asked to speak at a school assembly about Alaska. I thought they asked me some outlandish questions when they asked, "Did you live in a snow house?" or "Did you have a seal oil lamp to keep you warm or to cook your food?" I told them those were the conditions of a generation or two before mine. They couldn't believe that a certain amount of civilization had come to remote Alaska by the time I was growing up. They had read too many outdated books! They said since I knew so much about Alaska, the old and the new, why didn't I write a book about it. I told them someday I would do that. The fact of the matter was that the Last Will and Testament of my graduating class, stated that I, Betty Bernhardt, would be a writer of children's stories for radio broadcast.

The previous year, I had met some friends who lived in Edmonds, Washington. I liked the little town, and the families I met were like people back home. I paid board and room at a home near the high school where I attended my senior year. I graduated as of one of the ten highest students for scholarship that year. As the registrars of universities and colleges usually do after getting the list of honor students, such institutions as Washington State University, Whitman College, and Western Washington University at Bellingham sent me letters, encouraging me to register for classes in the coming fall term.

It was time again to get a new pair of prostheses, I having worn out the present pair to a point beyond repair. I had been going steady with the handsome young Irishman whom I met on the S.S. *Victoria* the last trip south from Nome. Being normal young people and thinking we knew each other well enough to spend the rest of our lives together, we decided to get married. So Elizabeth Bernhardt became Mrs. G. Michael Little. The first few years of our married life we lived in Wenatchee, Washington, where my son was born. When he was two years of age, I miscarried my second child when I slipped and fell on the icy front porch. I was not responding to the hospital care I was receiving at this time, and tests showed that I had tuberculosis. For almost a year then, I received treatment at the famous West Coast Center for Tuberculosis at the Laurel Beach Sanitarium in West Seattle. During this period, I could only see my small son through glass doors or through my open window as he played and romped on the lawn while in the care of his paternal grandmother.

In the spring of 1940, my father wrote to each of us girls that our mother was very ill and getting weaker all the time. In the spring the year before this, my nineteen-year-old brother Albert, Jr., while hunting seal in the open leads with a friend that he had grown up with, drowned when his small boat capsized among the ice bergs. For days, weeks, and months my father and mother searched the beaches for his body, thinking it would finally surface somewhere. But upon reasoning this matter out, we surmised that since the boy who was with him said his body did not surface, it was carried under the ice by the swift current, never to be recovered. For the rest of the spring, summer, and into the fall, my mother and father spent every spare moment looking for some sign of him—clothing, boots, or even physical parts of him that may have drifted on the beaches that they walked. Most of us older girls who were away from home at the time made it home by the end of August. Mama passed away the ninth of September, 1940, at the fairly young age of about fifty-six. The nearest hospital was ninety miles away. My father said she had been slipping silently for the past five or six months, and when she lost her "Albut" (Albert), she didn't seem to have enough reserve strength to overcome the great sorrow and grief both Papa and she had to bear. It was tuberculosis that killed her, but grief and sorrow hurried it along. I don't care who you are or your station in life, it seems easier to bear the loss of a loved one, such as my brother Albert, when you have a resting place for the remains.

Papa bore the task of making Mama's casket, which he made out of raw lumber that he had on hand; the only material he had. We had a family friend by the name of Jenny Thompson, about my mother's age, whom my father enlisted to help him in preparing my mother's body for burial. Papa brought out a woolen army blanket, lined her casket with it, tenderly laid her body on it, and combed her hair. He laid another blanket on top as we children looked on sobbing and hugging each other in our deep sorrow. Mrs. Brock, the minister's wife from Teller Mission, was present, and she led us in singing "Rock of Ages." With a heavy heart, my father was

Elizabeth in front with son Michael, sister Wilma, 1940.

the last to walk away from my mother's graveside. Not only did my father make my mother's casket, he, with the help of a youth from Teller and my sixteen-year-old brother Tony, dug the grave where my mother's remains were laid.

✳   ✳   ✳

My son's father had gotten a job with the army engineers at Nome, so we wintered there. As for myself, not yet having had the opportunity to put my education to use, I received an office position with the Reindeer Service, an agency of the Bureau of Indian Affairs. After spending a year in Alaska, we again took the last steamer out of Nome heading for Seattle. On

November 7, 1941, we docked at Dutch Harbor where more passengers embarked for the trip south. Word got around as we were leaving the Aleutians that we were to travel "blacked out," and all the passengers were in the dark as to the reason for the order. We arrived in Seattle on the twelfth of November. One month to the day after we were in the Aleutians, the Japanese struck Pearl Harbor.

We settled in Edmonds for a few years. My son began his first years in elementary school there, and for a change, I felt settled down. Every able-bodied man and boy was being drafted into the armed services. The little town of Edmonds was getting bare of young men. My husband, however, had asthma nearly all his life, therefore was not able to serve his country. His brother Bill was taken by the draft and served in the European theater in the Battle of the Bulge and was one of the lucky ones who came home in one piece.

Mike again hearkened to the call of Alaska, and he left my son and me in our comfortable little place in Edmonds to take a job with the Civil

Michael, Elizabeth, and Wilma, Teller, 1941.

Aeronautics Administration in Juneau. He was to find a house or apartment and then send for the two of us, and we left in the middle of Mickey's third year of school. For the next two years, it was one move after another trying to keep with, and be near, his father. In one year, my son attended three schools. In the winter of 1944 my son's father notified us by mail that we were to return to the state of Washington because he would be moving around in Alaska even more often as time went by, so he shipped us back to Edmonds where he expected us to stay with his folks until he got good and ready to come back and settle down with his little family. I wrote him in a letter that I was not about to live off his folks since he was irregular about sending money to help pay some of our living expenses. Although his kindly father and loving mother were thoughtful of us and said we could stay as long as we wished, I was not the mooching type.

In the next few months, having exhausted every avenue of prospective employment in the little town of Edmonds, I decided to go to the big city of Seattle to see what promises it held. I began at the YWCA as an elevator operator at about twenty-five cents an hour. That barely paid my room and board. I felt that I wanted to go into communications (telephone and telegraph), so I went to the representative of the International Brotherhood of the Electrical Workers Union. Finding out that I had no experience in that line, the business representatives referred me to a private school for training telephone switchboard operators. I worked at the YWCA on weekends and evenings to keep myself solvent, but barely. When I finished the course, I reported to Miss Vanderbeck at Local 77 IBEW, and she had a position ready and waiting for me at the Elks' Lodge #92 in Seattle. I held that position for several years, where I met people from all walks of professional life, including George Meany of the AFL-CIO, the original Harlem Globetrotters team, and the leading lady who played Mother Barber of the famous radio series. Also, one time a young man came in and, as I was at the receptionist's desk, asked me if he could see the night manager. I called upstairs to the seventh floor lounge and told the manager that a Mr. Charles was at my desk and wanted to see him. This was Ray Charles's first Seattle engagement in the field of entertainment, and he later became famous singing in Seattle clubs, which led to making records.

About the time that my son was ready for high school, I began to think seriously of moving to Edmonds and raising him myself for his sake since it seemed out of the question that his father and I would ever get back together in a home life. I thought, "If he could just have even a one-parent home atmosphere" as he surely deserved, I would be willing to try it. It was pretty difficult to find a job for a woman at that time because of all the men flooding the job market soon after the war ended. I, however, did get on at the West Coast Telephone Company as an operator in "traffic" (they used that word in those days). I did everything I could to be both parents for the boy. I did my best. I took him to league baseball games in Seattle and to the circus whenever it was in town. I also took him to the first hydroplane race held on Lake Washington. While he was in the Boy Scouts and Explorers, I attended as many doings as I could while still working. I went to his high school basketball games to cheer him on and also to the school football and baseball activities. Interestingly, my son had some of the same teachers at the Edmonds High School that I had had when I attended there.

My wages barely covered our expenses—at $69.50 a week, it took everything I made to pay rent, utilities, the milkman, food, union dues, and his Boy Scout dues and insurance, let alone buy much in the way of clothing. Mike paid no mind to our struggling, though his mother let him know. He paid me no child support at any time. My place of work was five long blocks from where we lived, and having no motorized transportation, I walked the ten blocks each work day. That is if I worked a straight shift, which was seldom. As most telephone operators work split shifts (that is, four hours now and four hours later), I had to walk twenty blocks on many days. There were days when my sore stumps could hardly carry my body five blocks let alone fifteen more to get to the end of my working day. Many times I walked to work when I really should have doctored my sore legs. When the weather was rainy, which is 85 percent of the time in winter, I walked for I could not afford a taxi ride. Once in a while the Edmonds police would pass me as I trudged in the rain, and they would give me a ride home. I worked night duty for almost two years, which meant that I had to do "information," "rate and route" department, "T&C" (time and charges), and whatever else the public demanded of me, being the sole operator on duty.

Things began to happen in Korea, and the men were going to war again. In fact, my son's cousin fought on Pork Chop Hill, Korea, and was wounded and sent home. He later was to receive the Purple Heart. Most of my son's high school buddies who graduated the year before were joining up with the armed forces. I think that influenced him into doing the same.

My son Michael, "Mick" off duty, in Seoul, Korea, 1954.

Mick in Seoul, Korea, with his guard dog, 1955.

I was not reluctant to let him go for I figured he had to face the big, wide world sooner or later. He took basic training at Lackland Air Force Base in Texas and Parks Air Force Base in California. He was trained as an Air Force policemen. Fighting in Korea had barely ended when he was assigned to the Demarcation Zone near Seoul. We wrote letters frequently. He wrote of TDY to Tokyo's Tachikawa air base in Japan. Thirteen long months later he was back, like he said, "in the good old U.S.A." In the meantime, having been a divorcee for ten years by this time, I had written him at his outpost in Seoul, that I thought I had found "a nice man whom I might decide to marry." By this time Mick had arrived home on the USS *O'Hara*, a more grown up man than when he left.

My new husband, Sherman Pinson from Pikeville, Kentucky, was a WWII veteran and had not been back home in the U.S. long when we met. He had served in the South Pacific Islands, hopping from Tinian to Saipan to Guam with the U.S. Army Signal Corps, as the army retook island after island with the help of the U.S. Navy. Soon after our marriage he talked me into moving to San Francisco. I worked in a prominent hotel as PBX operator/receptionist and met many famous people in the sports, television, and movie world, including Joe DiMaggio, Don Drysdale, Ella Fitzgerald, Ted Williams, and Dizzy Dean. I once was hugged by Cheeta, the chimpanzee who had parts in many films and was the main character in the Tarzan movies.

In the latter fifties and early sixties, having moved again to Alaska, I went to work for the federal government in telecommunications. At the time, the Alaska Communication System was operated by the Department of Defense with headquarters at Anchorage. By the mid-1960s, the condition of my stumps was such that I was not able to get around without a lot of misery. The formation of cysts on both stumps was persistent. There was nothing else to do but apply for Social Security disability. We were now settled in the Seattle area where most of my family lives, including my son and his little family. Also last but not least, it was handy to be near my prostheses manufacturers, should I need repairs or get new ones. I knew them all in the Seattle area, having dealt with them nigh onto fifty years.

By 1949 my father saw the last of his offspring leave the nest at Teller. Robert, the youngest, enlisted in the U.S. Army, serving at Fort Richardson in Anchorage. My father, now alone at the old homestead, having reached the age of seventy-four and having spent fifty-two consecutive years in the

1957, my father's four oldest daughters, left to right, Mary, Sarah, me (Betty), and Anne.

Arctic, after much wheedling on the part of us girls, finally decided to leave there. He first lived with my oldest sister Mary in Fairbanks, and in the year of 1950, he was inducted into the Pioneers of Alaska. In about 1952 he moved to Anchorage and lived next to his daughter and family. After mulling over the idea of making one more trip to the U.S. to San Francisco and San Pedro, his ports of call during his sailing days, and perhaps visiting some old-time friends who were still living, my father, accompanied by our youngest sister Pauline, made the trip he had dreamed of. He visited old friends, including some of note like Rear Admiral F. A. Zuesler in Seattle, Dr. Bates in San Francisco (whom he hadn't seen for over fifty years), and more old salts, including Captain Louis Lane and friends in San Francisco. Then finally he continued on down to San Pedro.

When they came back to the Seattle area, he stayed awhile with Pauline and also with me in Edmonds. But he was once again longing for the peace and quiet life in Alaska. In his seventy-ninth year, Papa was beginning to become unstable and forgetful. With the insistence of Admiral Zuesler, we decided that he needed special care, and he entered the Alaska Pioneer Home at Sitka, where he would get constant care in the hands of those experienced. Robert, the youngest brother, was then living and working in Haines and would pay visits to our father whenever and as often as he could. I wrote often and would have liked very much to have visited him personally. The calendar reminded me that Father's Day was on June 16. I picked out a nice Father's Day card and called up the local florist shop in time so that they would deliver to my father an appropriate flower arrangement for his room. Early on the morning of June 16, 1954, the phone rang. It was Western Union from Seattle. As the Western Union operator read the telegram from Sitka, "Sorry to advise you that your father passed away very early this morning . . . ," I realized that I was beginning to feel sort of numb. After I composed myself, I called my sister Pauline in Seattle. Neither one of us was able to go to his funeral, but the three other sisters (Sarah, Wilma, and Mary) living in Alaska at the time and my two brothers (Tony and Robert) paid final tribute to our dear father. He spent eighty years on this earth, nearly three-fourths of them fighting for survival for himself and his family in cold and barren northern Alaska. For him it was a life of freedom; freedom from religious and political strife, such as he had experienced in his early life in Germany until he left at the age of fourteen. He was not only our father; he gave us inspiration.

Epilogue

The four youngest in the family never knew the two eldest in the family. Tommy, the eldest of the clan, left home at the age of twenty-one. He was experienced in handling boats with our father; consequently, when he made up his mind to become a seaman, Captain Pederson of the old MS *Herman* took him aboard as a member of his crew on his way south from the Arctic to San Francisco, his home port. Tommy never came back north, but he spent thirty-seven years sailing the seven seas. Through all those years, he sent me post cards from just about every sea port on the six continents. During WWII as Tommy sailed the seven seas, he witnessed the destruction of other ships by bombings, submarine torpedoes, and strafing by destroyers. In one of his letters, he wrote the following; "My Lord was watching over me, for any ship I was on during the war was a safe harbor, for I always reached port safely."

Margaret, the oldest girl, passed on in 1942 in Galveston, Texas, where she had married and lived since 1929. I also lost two of my sisters, Mary and Wilma, within five years of each other in the 1970s. Pauline died in the late 1990s, and Sarah passed away in 1997. Robert, the youngest brother, died an accidental death at Haines, Alaska, at the tender age of twenty-nine.

Our brother David, the next oldest after me, has lived in the Canadian Arctic (Northwest Territories) all his life and is, at this writing, ninety-three years old. When he left home on the MS *Patterson* in 1929, little did any of us realize that that was the last time any of us would see him again. After trading with his schooner all along the Arctic rim of Canada for many years, he settled in Coppermine, Northwest Territory, Canada, and now lives in Kugluktuk. On one of his dogsled trips on the Arctic ice, he came upon a polar bear cub about six weeks old. He could see no sign of the mother, so he thought to himself that he was not about to let the little cub starve out there by itself. He took the cub back home with him. It became quite a pet until it was four months old and started to bat him around. He took it out on the ice floes and let the beautiful white bear go free. We have corresponded regularly throughout all these many years.

My younger brother Tony made his living as a bush pilot and big game guide in Kobuk, Alaska, and flew passengers and freight to and from villages and mines in the region. He served on the Alaska Fish and Game Commission for some years. He is now retired and living in Anchorage, Alaska. Wilma, who was eight years younger than I, had a brief career in Hollywood for Universal Studios. She was in the picture *Arctic Manhunt* with a Canadian actor named Michael Conrad. She also posed for promotional pictures and postcards displaying the Alaska flag when it joined the forty-eight states as the forty-ninth state.

All through my high school years, which were the depression years, the girls would remark, "You sure do travel a lot," which I did do to get my high school education. They asked how I did it. I would reply that I had a rich uncle in Pittsburgh, Pennsylvannia, who paid for all my expenses. The saying about a rich uncle was, in truth, very real in my case. Not that he was rich monetarily, but rich in the giving and sharing of what he had to others, including me. Although I never met him in person, I felt that I knew him personally. Without him all these good things could not have happened to me. In 1928 before I went away to school, he sent me a picture of himself and my Aunt Matilda, and that was the nearest I ever got to them. They were very devoted to one another for he so stated in his many letters to me. In 1943 I received word that Aunt Matilda had passed on. She had been

Sister Wilma, Teller, 1938.

suffering from the shingles for many years. About six months later, my Uncle Ed joined her in the hereafter, where I believe they will always be together. I regretted not meeting them personally, but it seemed that it was meant to be that way. They were in their eighties when they passed away. I mourned Uncle Ed in his passing as I would mourn my own father. He was, however, more of a father-figure to me, and according to his letters, he thought of me as a daughter for they never had children.

Since my retirement years ago, I have been active in volunteer work. I have put in a few hours a month at the March of Dimes in the main office in Seattle or helping in church organizations making quilts and crocheting afghans for nursing homes and for the poor. I also enjoyed answering the telephone at the Democratic campaign headquarters. As of this writing, I still crochet baby afghans and send them to the Children's Hospital and Harbor Medical Center in Seattle.

All in all I have had a good life. The years have taken their toll and of the large Bernhardt family of thirteen children there are four of us left on this earth—one sister, Anne; two brothers, Tony and David; and me.

Wilma making movie *Arctic Manhunt*, Universal Studios, Hollywood, CA, 1950.

As I look back on the many times that my life could have come to an end, beginning at the age of six, I feel very fortunate that I have lived this long. I believe I have had the hand of providence leading me on. I have traveled this highway of life and had my share of tragedies and periods of great physical suffering. Through it all I have also had times of elation and happiness and times when I would "stop and smell the roses." My only heir, my son Michael, gave me four lovely and lively grandchildren who are now grown and on their own. My two granddaughters added three great grandsons to our family. I am fortunate they all live in Washington, and they visit often, especially during the holidays. In 2002 my youngest granddaughter Renee held a four-generations family reunion at her home with me as the matriarch, proud and happy that I had all this to show for my life. I can say truthfully that I have felt the hand of the Almighty on my shoulder, helping me, always giving me comfort and strength. More than twenty years have passed since I first began writing my life story, a story of survival and a colorful history of events that I have witnessed.

References

Bixby, William. Track of the Bear. NY: David McKay, 1965.
———. *My Life with the Eskimo*. NY: Macmillan, 1913.
Freuchen, Peter. *Eskimo*. NY: Horace Liveright, 1931.
Lawing, Nellie Neal. *Alaska Nellie*. Seattle: Seattle Printing and Publishing, 1940.
Stefansson, Vilhjalmur. *The Adventure of Wrangel Island*. NY: Macmillan, 1925.

Index